THE HIDDEN THEME OF THE SONG OF SONGS

THE HIDDEN THEME OF THE SONG OF SONGS

Adavimannath Devadas Jesudas

ISPCK
2009

The Hidden Theme of the Song of Songs – Published by the Rev. Dr. Ashish Amos of the Indian Society for Promoting Christian Knowledge (ISPCK), Post Box 1585, 1654, Madarsa Road, Kashmere Gate, Delhi-110006.

ISBN: 978-81-8465-024-2

Laser typeset by

ISPCK, Post Box 1585, 1654, Madarsa Road, Kashmere Gate, Delhi-110006 • *Tel:* 23866323

e-mail: ashish@ispck.org.in • ella@ispck.org.in
website: www.ispck.org.in

DEDICATED TO

the Everlasting Memory of Our Loving Daughter

LILY GRACE

at present with the Lord

CONTENTS

ACKNOWLEDGEMENTS xi
PREFACE xiii
GENERAL ABBREVIATIONS xix
BIBLICAL ABBREVIATIONS xxi

INTRODUCTION 1
(The Keys to the Mystery of the Song)

I. THE FALLACY OF PURSUING SPECULATIVE METHODS TO INTERPRET THE INSPIRED WORD OF GOD 2

II. A BRIEF SURVEY OF THE SPECULATIVE INTERPRETATIONS OF THE SONG ATTEMPTED HERETOFORE BY SCHOLARS OF THE VARIOUS SCHOOLS OF BIBLICAL INTERPRETATIONS 2

III. THE CLUES LEADING TO THE INTERPRETATION OF THE SONG ADVANCED THROUGH THIS BOOK 6

IV. THE IMPORTANCE OF THE STUDY OF THE SONG OF SONGS TO REINFORCE AND REJUVENATE OUR CHRISTIAN FAITH 9

V. THE SONG, A BOOK "WRITTEN WITHIN AND ON THE BACKSIDE" 11

VI. THE SONG AS A SEALED BOOK 11

VII. THE TITLE AND AUTHORSHIP OF THE SONG 12

VIII. THE IDENTITY OF THE LOVERS 13

1. The Identity of the Beloved 14
2. The Identity of the Lover 17

IX. THE THEME OF THE SONG IN DETAIL. 18

1. Why does God and matters pertaining to the Spiritual realm appear mysterious to us? 18

2. In fact, God had made known to Abraham that the Gentiles were to be Partakers of the Promised Blessing 19

3. The action-plans to bring the blessing of Abraham upon all the families of the earth that were in the Lord's mind when He used the prepositional phrase, "in thee" 19

   a. "*In*" the Seed of Abraham 19

      i. In Christ, the Seed Par Excellence of Abraham, in the Covenant 19

      ii. In the Church that was to comprise of the Spiritual Seed that the Lord promised to Abraham, in Gen 22:17, saying, "in multiplying I will multiply thy Seed as the Stars of the Heaven" 20

   b. In the Abrahamic Covenant of Promise 22

4. Reasons for believing that, in the Song's reckoning, Israel that was born of God at Peniel was not an Individual, but a corporeal entity, to wit, the Church of the regenerated 23

5. The six major epochs across which Israel, the beloved church that was born at Peniel, continued to exist 24

6. Why does Christ, the Spirit, require a body (the Church) to carry out His redemptive work? 25

   a. The Visible and the Invisible Churches in the Song 27

   b. The Mode of Appearances of the Lovers 28

      i. The mode of appearances of Christ, the Lover 28

      ii. The mode of appearances of the beloved (church) 29

7. The Salient Points of the Father's Redemptive Scheme that the Lord made known to the Holy Apostles and Prophets, by the Spirit 29

X. THE PLOT OF THE SONG. 30

XI. THE METHODOLOGY. 31

1. The Disclosure is made in the form of the Story of the Birth, Growth and Development unto Maturity of a Female, namely, of Israel, the Church of the Regenerated 31

2. The Disclosure is made after the Pattern of the narrative of Jacob's Nightlong wrestle with the Lord until the Breaking of the Day 32
3. Certain Episodes coming within the Disclosure of Israel's Redemptive Story in the Song are Patterned after Parallel Events that took place in Jacob's life-story 36
4. Typology is used to Disclose certain Old Testament types that find fulfillment in Antitypes in the Risen Christ and the Primitive Jewish Christian Church 36
5. The Emphasis throughout the Disclosure is on Faith as the Sole Criterion for Salvation 37

XII. THE CONSTANT SHIFT OF MOTIFS IN THE SONG 37

XIII. THE SONG AS A PROPHETIC MONODRAMA IN COMPOSITION 38

XIV. THE HOUSEHOLD OF GOD 39

1. The Choice from the Household of Jacob and his Seed exclusively to be the Covenantee gave rise to Jealousy and Strife 40
2. The Election of only a few from the Multitude of Jacob's Seed to be made Faithful by Regeneration and become the Heirs of Promise gave Occasion to the rest of Israel to Hate and Spite His Church that comprised of the Elected and Regenerated Ones 41
3. The Contrariety of Natures between the Natural and the Spiritual Seeds of the Covenant gave rise to further Jealousy and Strife 42
4. The Addition of the Sinai Covenant to the existing Abrahamic Covenant of Promise gave room for the Natural Seed to gain an upper hand over the Spiritual 42
5. After the Advent of the Holy Spirit on the day of Pentecost, the bone of contention between the Natural and the Spiritual Seeds turned out to be whether the means of Salvation is receiving Jesus of Nazareth by faith as Christ the Lord or observing the stipulations of the Mosaic Law 44

6. The Constituent Members of the household of God appearing in the Song 45
   a. The Father/Lover 45
   b. The Mother 46
   c. The Beloved 46
   d. "My Mother's House(hold)" 46
   e. The Watchmen and Keepers of the Walls 47
   f. The Daughters of Jerusalem 48
   g. The Virgins and Daughters 49
   h. The Companions and Friends 50

XV. THE ARTFUL USE OF FIGURES OF SPEECH IN THE SONG 50
1. The Similes in the Song 50
2. The Metaphors in the Song 54
3. The Symbolism in the Song 55
   a. The Symbolic word "Lily" 55
   b. The Symbolic word "breasts" 56

XVI. THE IDENTITY OF THE LOVER 58
1. Is "King Solomon" an Actual or a Received Name? 59
2. To What Purpose did the Lord make the Appiryon for Himself? 63
3. A List of the People who are described in the song as parts of the body of Christ 64
4. Why did the Lord pave the midst of the Appiryon with love for the daughters of Jerusalem, rather than with love for all the families of the earth? 65

XVII. OUTLINE OF CONTENTS 68

XVIII. COMMENTARY 75

BIBLIOGRAPHY 263

APPENDIX 265

ACKNOWLEDGEMENTS

All praises go to the Lord Jesus Christ who had been preparing me beginning from the time my life began, through various providential dealings, to bring out this Conservative Evangelical Exegetical Commentary on the Song of Solomon.

I am greatly indebted to the late Dr. Renthy Keitzer, former principal of Eastern Theological College, Jorhat, Assam, India, for the words of encouragement and valuable assistance given towards the preparation of this work. In addition to furnishing clarifications to various doubtful Hebrew words, he went to the extent of taking extra pains to make available to me a copy of the book, 'Poets, Prophets, and Sages' authored by Robert Gordis, Indiana University Press, London.

The valuable guidelines given by my one-time teacher and well wisher Rev. Ernest W. Arloff of Baltimore, Maryland, USA, for the preparation of this work cannot go unacknowledged. On my trip to the United States of America, in the fall of 1987, the Arloffs gladly accommodated me in their residence for over two weeks, and treated me with unbounded hospitality. I was surprised to find that Rev. Arloff himself was busily engaged at that time to bring out an independent translation of the Song of Solomon. Putting in months of labour to the task, he translated the former half of the Song, (1:1-5:1), and sent to me a copy of the same for my use.

I had the blessing of the late Dr. John E. Douglas Sr., Founder President of the World Missionary Evangelism Inc., Dallas, Texas USA, and his philanthropic family, in the production of this work. On my request, Dr. Douglas gladly cleared the way for my visa to visit the United States of America to seek for additional help and guidance from possible sources.

I am greatly indebted to Rev. Arun Kumar Wesley, a veteran pastor, and a professional editor, who had painstakingly gone through each and every page of the MSS and corrected it. I am deeply grateful to Mr. Praveen Paul, a close friend of mine, and a doctoral candidate of United Theological College, Bangalore, India, who had checked the MSS to verify the correctness of the meanings and applicability of the Hebrew words used herein.

The last but not the least, I am grateful to my daughters Sharon Rose and Annie, and my son Joel for correcting the MSS and taking print outs of the same over and over again whenever required.

- A.D. Jesudas

PREFACE

That the Holy Bible comprising of the sixty-six canonical books is the verbally inspired word of God has been one of the fundamental doctrines of all Christian churches that have originated in a sound Conservative Evangelical faith. Ironically, the founding fathers of these churches, in spite of their pious intentions, had formulated the doctrines of their respective churches without knowing what one of these sixty-six books, the Song of Solomon, is all about.

I was neither interested in the Song of Solomon, nor had I ever dreamt of writing a Commentary on it. But, when I look back now to the turn of events that have taken place in my life beginning from my childhood days, I come to realize that the Lord has been preparing me to write this Conservative Exegetical Commentary on the Song.

My father was a village pastor. He died of tuberculosis in his mid-thirties, leaving orphaned four of us, all below ten years old. After a couple of years our mother left us under the care of the maternal grandmother and went to live with another man. The grandmother happened to be a gem of a woman, a truly devoted, committed and meticulously honest Christian, who had retired from a life-long active service for the Lord, in full-time ministry. Like Timothy's grandmother, Lois, she brought us up in the true fear of the Lord and trained us up from childhood to be honest and truthful to the Lord in every sphere of our life. This made us proud of our grandmother, particularly of her honesty, piety, and Christian convictions. She taught us to be punctual in reading the Bible, praying and attending church services.

On a Sunday, however, I skipped devotional service and was waiting anxiously for the grandmother's return from service to be provided with something to eat. But, when I noticed her from a distance, as she was coming down from the church, a serious doubt crept into my mind, as to whether she blindly believed what the Bible says about God and eternal life, because she was not educated other than knowing to read and write. As for me, blindly following the traditional religious beliefs of one's ancestors or parents, without verifying the authenticity thereof, amounted to self- deception. At the same time, I had the conviction deep down in my heart that, in case what the Bible declares about God and eternal life happen to be true, they must be believed whole-heartedly and adhered to at any cost.

With the foregoing in mind, I resolved, then and there, to profess and practice Christianity only after ascertaining the trustworthiness thereof. .

The process of reasoning and reading that began from that time, sometime in the year 1931, increased with added intensity throughout the years 1943-46 when I was in the thick of the battles, in the Second World War, in the Burma Front, and during the years 1947-48, when I was serving in a contingent of the British Commonwealth Occupation Forces (BCOF), in Japan. All throughout those years I found myself deeply engrossed and struggling restlessly within to find out answers to the questions pertaining to the ultimate reality that were cropping up in my mind day and night. After the War, I was released from the Army, and I set up a Chemist and Druggist shop of my own, first at Madras city, and later in Thiruvananthapuram city, the capital of the Kerala State.

By that time, I had already arrived at the firm conviction that, as a part cannot contain the whole, human beings who are comparatively but a tiny speck of this apparently infinite universe, with their limited God-given senses and puny brain cannot comprehend the ultimate realities pertaining to the universe, and far less can they comprehend the matters of fact pertaining to the Creator and Sustainer of everything. The perplexing thoughts, particularly about the riddles pertaining to the topic of time and space, and of seeming and being, made me crazy to the extent that I began to spend sleepless nights with difficulty to breathe, leading to palpitation of the heart. Scores of doctors whom I consulted failed to find out any systemic disorder in me. Only after I was healed did I realize that the physical disorders that I had been suffering from were the outcome of absence of faith in anything, inclusive of in my own existence.

It was the testimony of a brother whom the Lord healed of a medically incurable disease, while he was fasting and praying, that finally opened my eyes of understanding to see that the numerous similar stories of miraculous healings found in the Bible, particularly in the gospels and Acts of the Apostles, are true. And when faith set in, the physical afflictions by which I had been tormented vanished. However my mind continued to rise doubtful questions one after the other. But the Lord graciously provided answers to each of them, one by one.

Paradoxically, what prompted me to begin the intense prayerful study of the Song of Solomon was a feeling of spiritual lethargy that I felt on that unforgettable day sometime in mid-1983, and the consequent search for a title that could inspire. The title that appealed at first sight from among those on the nearby book-shelf happened to be 'The Song of Songs' by Watchman Nee (trance. By Elizabeth K. Moi and Daniel Smith: Christian Literature Crusade, London, 1967). The book appeared to be just that which was anticipated; a boon direct from the hand of God to get my soul stirred up and awakened. While studying the book, genuine questions did arise on the permissibility of arbitrarily allegorizing and attributing meanings of one's own imaginative ingenuity to words and expressions without any rhyme or reason. However, the rising questions were deliberately overlooked in preference to the edifying lessons, which were being given on Christ's love for the church, and vice versa.

The unacceptability of the allegorical method came home only while trying to scribble notes on the request of a handful of those who were fascinated over a series of lectures delivered on the Song, on the lines of Nee's interpretation. However, on further contemplation, it became clear to me that the Song could not have found the place that it does among the canonical books of the Old Testament under the name, "The Song of Songs," unless it was based, like the rest of the Old Testament books, on the redemptive history of the chosen people of God. Eagerness to ascertain the truth of the matter gripped my mind so much so that things of everyday life seemed to be of less consequence. No book or commentary within reach came up with any sort of convincing answer. Waiting on the Lord for days and nights over the years that followed turned out to be the only option left.

Spiritual lessons are learned in the school of hard and painful experiences. At about the wee hour of 2:00, on March 28, 1987, while waiting as usual, this time, for enlightenment on the significance of the portrayal of vv. 3:6-8 of the song, the Lord made it clear that the unit occurs as a satirical expose of the six hundred thousand footmen of Israel, so-called as "the valiant of Israel" (3:7), who perished in the wilderness, on account of the debacle of Kadesh-barnea, and the resultant curse. This disclosure brought home to me the awful consequence of unbelief and fear.

At daybreak, while praising the Lord after sharing with my wife, the enlightenment received on the devastating effect of unbelief and fear, an unmistakable voice came from within: "Jesudas, consecrate your children." It was Lily Grace, my second daughter, undergoing her studies at Madras, whose safety was among my prime concerns that flashed before my mind's eye. "Yes, Lord, yes, Lord," I shouted repeatedly, consecrating and placing Lily Grace upon the altar, little knowing that an appalling letter, followed by an urgent telegraphic message were awaiting us later in the day, hastening us to arrive at Madras posthaste as Lily Grace was precariously ill in one of the hospitals in the city.

Determined not to give room to the waves of natural fears that were up-surging within, I arrived at Madras, along with my wife, by the first available flight. As I had my trust wholly on the Lord, I hoped to be greeted by an all's well glad tiding on arrival. But what greeted us, contrariwise, was a lady doctor anxious to confide the despairing medical report that the sickness is incurable. "But nothing is impossible with God, doctor," I retorted almost involuntarily. "I am conveying the finding of medical science, not of religion," replied the doctor, annoyed.

Lily was emaciated and pale beyond recognition. With tears streaming down and panic-stricken, I rang up the prayer warriors of "The Jesus Calls Prayer Tower" to intercede for Lily's deliverance. Prayer was offered. But deliverance did not come as was anticipated.

In just a couple of days' time, Lily's pulse rate shot up to 200. Knowing that the end was not too far off, the doctor wished to know if we wanted to try other hospitals. The doctor was, in fact, speaking her mind; that medical science had given up hope. With none to turn to, I entered one of the vacant rooms of the hospital, and, as Jacob did at Peniel, wrestled with the Lord until the breaking of the day.

With Lily's condition gradually improving from the next morning onwards, the attending lady doctor, surprised, kept whispering to the streams of visitors who were coming to see Lily Grace, "miracle, miracle, this is not the outcome of medicines, but of prayer."

The horrible ordeal was far from over. Certain symptoms persisted, and tests conducted proved that the sickness, systemic lupus erythematosus, was incurable. Struggling between faith and fear, we remained in the hospital for about four months. While the mother's part was to attend to the suffering daughter's needs, mine was to rush to different parts of the city to fetch the prescribed medicines and provisions. While on the move, I found myself almost always in tears, questioning audibly, "Lord, how can you fail to keep your promise?"

A dull pain started on my right arm, in the meanwhile, by reason of a tumor growing somewhere on my cervical spine. As the tumor kept its pace of growth, numbness spread all over the body, and by and by, my lower and upper limbs became distorted, leaving me altogether crippled. I could not so much as hold a pen to put a signature, or walk without assistance.

We were back home by this time. Lily in one room, and I in another, the following three years were times of untold pain and sufferings for Lily, for me, as well as for the whole family. Forty days of fasting, with an additional twenty-three, that I underwent for my daughter's healing did little to improve her condition. At last, when it became clear that Lily's days on earth was numbered, I pleaded with the Lord at least to appear personally and console her with words of assurance concerning her salvation. This the Lord did. A few weeks later, Lily, who was ignorant of what was going on between me and the Lord, confided to her mother, saying, 'mummy, I do not know whether I was seeing with my naked eye or it was a vision. Last night, one like the Lord Jesus Christ appeared to me. Pointing his fingers at me, and calling me by name, He spoke to me endearingly, "Lily, because of my unbounded love for you, I have forgiven all your sins, and now the pearly gates are open for you." '

Eventually, both Lily Grace and I were rushed to the hospitals in critical conditions. Lily to a hospital in the neighbouring State of Assam, and myself to the Christian Medical College, at far away Vellore, near Madras. The conditions of both of us worsened simultaneously. I was in the intensive care unit with post-operative complication of a severe type of septicemia, in an almost given up state (this was after the third major surgery which I underwent for the removal of the tumor). Lily, with huge swollen legs in buckets and coughing incessantly, was unable to lie down and rest even for a minute, on account of stiff joints and excruciating pain.

Finally, as I was shifted from the intensive care unit, having miraculously escaped death, Lily Grace silently left us and went to be with the Lord at her destined place within "the pearly gates". My family concealed the shocking news from me until they felt I would be able to withstand the shock. Thus the "Cunning Workman," (SS 7:1) broke both my heart and body and created a "mini Patmos" in the corner of my tiny room to disclose to me the mystery of the Song, in the divine revelations.

- A.D. JESUDAS

MOKOKCHUNG,
NAGALAND, INDIA

GENERAL ABBREVIATIONS

AV	Authorised (King James) Version
cf.	compare
ed.	Editor, edition
et. al.	and others
fem.	Feminine
ff.	and the following (verse(s) etc.)
Gk	Greek
Ibid	in the same place
JB	Jerusalem Bible
lit.	literally
LXX	The Septuagint (Greek version of the Old Testament)
Masc.	Masculine
MS, MSS	Manuscript (s)
NASB	New American Standard Bible
NEB	New English Bible
NIV	New International Version
op. cit	in the work cited
p. pp.	page (s)
RSV	Revised Standard Version
suff.	Suffix
Syr	Syriac
trans.	translated by
v., vv.	Verse (s)
Vol, vols	Volume

BIBLICAL ABBREVIATIONS

Old Testament Books

Gen	Genesis	Eccl	Ecclesiastes
Exod	Exodus	Song	Songs of Songs
Lev	Leviticus	Isa	Isaiah
Num	Numbers	Jer	Jeremiah
Deut	Deuteronomy	Lam	Lamentations
Josh	Joshua	Ezek	Ezekiel
Judg	Judges	Dan	Daniel
Ruth	Ruth	Hos	Hosea
1 Sam	1 Samuel	Joel	Joel
2 Sam	2 Samuel	Amos	Amos
1 Kgs	1 Kings	Obad	Obadiah
2 Kgs	2 Kings	Jon	Jonah
1 Chr	1 Chronicles	Mic	Micah
2 Chr	2 Chronicles	Nah	Nahum
Ezra	Ezra	Hab	Habakkuk
Neh	Nehemiah	Zeph	Zephaniah
Esth	Esther	Hag	Haggai
Job	Job	Zech	Zechariah
Ps	Psalms	Mal	Malachi
Prov	Proverbs		

New Testament Books

Matt	Matthew	1 Tim	1 Timothy
Mark	Mark	2 Tim	2 Timothy
Luke	Luke	Tit	Titus
John	John	Philem	Philemon
Acts	Acts of the Apostles	Heb	Hebrews
Rom	Romans	Jas	James
1 Cor	1 Corinthians	1 Pet	1 Peter
2 Cor	2 Corinthians	2 Pet	2 Peter
Gal	Galatians	1 Jn	1 John
Eph	Ephesians	2 Jn	2 John
Phil	Philippians	3 Jn	3 John
Col	Colossians	Jude	Jude
1 Thess	1 Thessalonians	Rev	Revelation
2 Thess	2 Thessalonians		

Introduction

The Keys to the Mystery of the Song

In thematic perspective, the Song of Solomon is the profoundest of all the prophetic Songs found in the Old Testament, as truly as it claims for itself by its God-given superlative title, "The Song of Songs." (To be noted in this regard, the bulk of the prophetic writings in Hebrew Bible occur in poetic form)[1] The theme of the Song is, in the words of Paul, "the mystery, which from the beginning of the world hath been hid in God, who created all things by Jesus Christ" (Eph 3:9). By the expression, *the mystery, which from the beginning of the world hath been hid in God,* Paul had meant the redemptive scheme conceived by the Father, in Christ, before the foundation of the world for the salvation of His elect out of every nation, Jew and Gentile alike. It was this redemptive scheme which was hid in the Father that the pre-incarnate Christ, appearing as "the God of glory" (Acts 7:2), disclosed to Abraham, saying,

> I will make of thee a great nation, and I will bless thee, and make thy name great; and thou shalt be a blessing: ... and in thee shall all families of the earth be blessed. Gen. 12:2-3.

Israel, the promised seed of Abraham mistook that the blessing promised by God in Abraham was meant exclusively for them. But, in the New Testament dispensation the Lord made known to Paul by the Spirit that, according to the Father's redemptive scheme,

> The Gentiles should be fellowheirs (with the faithful Israel), and of the same body, and partakers of his promise in Christ by the gospel: Eph. 3:6, (paraphrase mine).

---

[1] Robert Gordis, *Poets, Prophets, and Sages,* Bloomington, London: Indiana University Press, 1971, p.62.

The Song, on its part, discloses how the Lord removed the stated myopic misconception of religious bigotry from the entity of the faithful Israel's heart and caused her to make the Gentiles partakers of the promised blessing of Abraham, in Christ, by the gospel[2].

The profundity of the subject matter can be gauged by the words by which the Scripture characterizes it, saying, "Eye hath not seen, nor ear heard, neither have entered into the heart of man, the things which God hath prepared for them that love him" (1 Cor 2:9, with, Isa 64:4). Truly, that the theme of the Song is profound to this extend had not "entered into the heart" of anyone of those who had endeavored to unravel the mystery of the Song heretofore. This has been one of the principal reasons why the Song has remained enigmatic and mysterious thus far. The prodigious methodology pursued by the Spirit for the presentation of this lofty theme makes the Song all the more enigmatic and mysterious.

I. THE FALLACY OF PURSUING SPECULATIVE METHODS TO INTERPRET THE INSPIRED WORD OF GOD.

(See Appendix A).

II. A BRIEF SURVEY OF THE SPECULATIVE INTERPRETATIONS OF THE SONG ATTEMPTED HERETOFORE BY SCHOLARS OF THE VARIOUS SCHOOLS OF BIBLICAL INTERPRETATION.

No other book of the Bible has given rise to as many varieties of interpretations as the Song. Interpretations advanced so far on the book by various schools of thought can be classified under three heads:

a. Jewish Allegorical Interpretations

Rabbinical school of thought regarded the Song to be an allegory of God's faithful dealings with Israel. With this in mind, the rabbis essayed to trace allusions to the history of Israel as well as prophetical elements pointing forward to the Messianic age out

---

[2] In view of the profundity and vastness of the subject matter of the Song, it is treated separately below, under the Head, 'IV, THEME OF THE SONG.'

of the book's imagery. By and large, the rabbis took "Solomon" to be an anthropomorphic representation of Yahweh, and Solomon's bride as depicting Israel, setting forth the Song in terms of the love of Yahweh for Israel. The Targum paraphrases it as a picture of the history of Israel from the Exodus to the coming of the Messiah.

This older Jewish approach, reflected in the Aramaic Targum of the Song, was precise inasmuch as it aspired to discover the history of God's faithful dealings with Israel. However, they failed in the first place, to detect that the bride is the church consisting of the faithful Israel, and in the second place, to decipher the historical and prophetical facts signified by the constantly changing motifs of each imagery. A number of absurdities that the rabbis have contrived out of incoherent contexts demonstrate the extent to which they had missed the mark and floundered in gross errors. For example, some of the rabbis took the statement of 1:4, "Draw me," to refer to Yahweh leading Israel to Sinai; 1:6, "I am black," is said to allude to Israel's confession of the sin in regard to the golden calf incident, and 1:7, "tell me, O thou whom my soul loveth," to Moses' supplication after the golden calf incident. Again, 3:6-10, "who is this that cometh out of the wilderness? ... He made the pillars thereof of silver, the bottom thereof of gold," were taken for the conquest of Canaan and the consequent building of the temple. The expression in 7:12-13, "let us go to the vineyards," is attributed to be Israel's prayer for deliverance from Babylon; and 8:14, "the mountains of spices," is ascribed as speaking of the temple mount in Jerusalem when God brings back a remnant in a so-called final redemption.[3]

Rabbi Ibn Ezra (12th Century A.D.), departing from other rabbis and from the Targum, saw the history of Israel from the days of Abraham, rather than from the Exodus, allegorically and prophetically reflected in the Song. He rightly gauged 2:8-9, the immurement of the beloved behind a wall and latticed windows, as an allusion to the captivity of Israel in Egypt; and the dashing arrival and "peering of the bridegroom through the window, (ii.9)

---

[3] Dr. Otto Zockler, *The Song of Solomon, trans.* W. Henry Green: Charles Scribner & Co., New York, 1871. p.27.

to God's looking down upon His people oppressed in Egypt for their help."[4]

b. Christian Allegorical Interpretations

With the transition from the Old to the New Testament dispensation, the Christian church took up the allegorical method of the rabbis, but read the Song as an expression of the love of Christ for His bride, the Church.

Origan, building on the covenant concept, maintained that the Song of Solomon represents the communion between Christ and His Church. But he also saw it as the communion between Christ and the individual believer, namely, the bride pining for union with Christ, the bridegroom. Origan's views of the 3rd century A.D. became the model for later Christian interpreters.[5]

Augustine, (5th century A.D.), rather than understanding the bride in the Song of Solomon to be the Church of Christ, regarded her as the theocracy in the Old Testament and Luther followed Augustine in considering her to be a description of the theocracy at its apogee, namely, Solomon, as the author of the Song, eulogizing about his own kingdom.[6]

Magn. Father Roos in his book, *Footsteps of the Faith of Abraham* (1773), understood that the bridegroom is Christ, the bride the Church; and that the daughters of Jerusalem and the queens, concubines and virgins mentioned in vi.8 represent the various classes of believers.[7]

E.W. Hengenstenberg in 1853 argued that the Song of Solomon does not describe its earthly author but the "heavenly Solomon," and further, that his beloved is the "daughter of Zion." In other words, the Song is an allegory of the relation between the Messiah and His Church (Israel) in both the Old and New Testament.[8]

---

4 *Ibid.*, p.27.
5 *Ibid.*, p.28.
6 *Ibid.*, p.32.
7 *Ibid.*, p.31.
8 *Ibid.*, p.31.

Thrupp (1862) divided the Song into a six-part drama relating expectation of Christ's coming, His spiritual presence with the Church and the Church's ultimate reunion with Christ.

Somewhat closely following Thrupp in his six divisions of the Song is Franz Delitzsch (1875) who, however, sees in the Song a drama in which King Solomon falls in love with the Shulamite shepherdess and takes her as a bride to Zion. He then related this selfsame drama to the communion and love between Christ and the Church.

We have included in the above those who are said to set forth the Song of Solomon as a type. However, these typical interpretations never wholly depart from the allegorical view.

c. ***Secular or Literal Interpretation***

The proponents of this school of thought maintain that the Song of Songs is a song or collection of Songs expressing worldly love. They claim that earthly love alone is portrayed here, and that nowhere under the figures presented is any indication of a higher love. But there are also some conservative interpreters who take the Song to be a portrayal of earthly love but see in it also the reflection of God's love for man, or the believer's love for God.

In a nutshell, the various secular views are as follows:

i. The Song is a love song, as the Song claims.

ii. The Song is a collection of independent love songs extolling human love (Herder, 1778).

iii. The Song is a marriage song of Solomon's literal marriage, in which the Song sets forth the beauty and holiness of love in marriage relationship, with a hint of double meaning added - that is, it is illustrative of Christ's love for humanity (H.H.Rowely,1952). F. Young (1949) and R. K. Harrison (1969) both conservatives, take this view but consider the Song to be ethical and didactic in purpose and not a mashal (parable) - no double meaning. Young says the Song finds its place in the canon of the Old Testament because it celebrates the dignity and purity that human love should have, and that it is a reminder that God "has placed love in human heart."

iv. The book is a collection of marriage songs based on Syrian custom (J.S. Wetzstein, 1873), in F. Delitzsch's commentary as an appendix.

v. The Song of Songs is a secular drama. H. Ewald (1862) held the view that there were two lovers competing for the love of the maid Shulamuth, one the king and the other a poor shepherd, a rationalist view of the Song as a drama. T.J. Meek (1922) made it a cultic drama or a liturgical work.

III. THE CLUES LEADING TO THE INTERPRETATON OF THE SONG ADVANCED THROUGH THIS BOOK.

i. A careful examination of the structure of the Song is sufficient to see that it is a meticulously devised prophetic song of the Old Testament. For it is divided mainly into two co-equal parts of 111 lines each; i.e. 111 lines (in the 60 verses plus title 1:1), from 1:1 to 4:15, and 111 lines (in the 55 verses) from 5:2 to 8:14. The remaining two verses, 4:16 and 5:1 form a minor third division, coming as it does at the exact middle of the Song.[9]

The very fact that the title, "The Song of Songs, which is Solomon's," is included in the first 111 lines proves beyond doubt that it is an integral part of the inspired text.

Significantly, the divisions are made on the basis of the above cited promise made by God to Abraham.

The former half occurs as a prophetic disclosure, in sophisticated figures of speech, of the ways in which the Lord made the entity of His elect from among Israel, the seed of Abraham, in Jacob, a great nation and blessed her and made her name great during the blessed Solomonic age, in fulfillment of the promise He had made to Abraham, saying, "I will make of thee a great nation, and I will bless thee, and make thy name great" (Gen 12:2-3).

---

[9] G. Lloyd Carr, *The Song of Solomon, An Introduction and Commentary,* London: Inter-varsity Press, 1984, p.169.

The latter half occurs as a prophetic disclosure, in futuristic prophecies, using sophisticated figures of speech, of the ways in which the risen, glorified, Christ called out of the decadent Judaism of the time His slumbering, but faithful, entity of elect, by pouring out His Spirit upon her, and enabled her to bring the blessing of Abraham upon the Gentiles, in fulfillment of the promise He had made to the latter, saying, "in thee shall all the families of the earth be blessed" (Gen 12:3).

Discernibly, the middle section comprising of vv. 4:16 and 5:1 relates to the period between Solomon and Christ. The section occurs as a prophetic disclosure, in sophisticated figures of speech, of the ways in which the Lord commanded the strong winds of enemy onslaught to blow upon Israel, His paradisiacal garden, and scattered His precious elect to the neighboring Gentile nations to spread the sweet savor of His knowledge among them.

ii. One of the principal keys to the mystery of the Song is that the story is set in the household of God. Consequently, all the actors who appear over the scene are members of the household of God. (For details, see below under the head, "The Household of God"). The idea of a household of God arose from that God had made the Abrahamic covenant of promise to generate children unto Him through regeneration. In the process, God who regenerates children in the Abrahamic covenant of promise, through faith, came to be recognized as the Father and the Abrahamic covenant in which God generates children unto Him came to be recognized as the mother. Those who were born of God through regeneration from Israel, under the Abrahamic covenant, by faith, became the genuine children of God. The entity of such is the beloved in the Song. In 6:9, she is stated to be "the only one of her mother, the choice one (i.e. the chosen one, or, the elect) of her that bare her" (paraphrase mine).

The foregoing gives rise to the question of the status of the rest of Israel who were not born of God through regeneration. As they were not the Father's children, the Song distinguishes them from the genuine children of God, by the term, "mother's house" or household; in the words of the beloved, "my mother's house" (3:4; 8:2).

In the Old Testament dispensation, the beloved's mother's household, her brethren according to the flesh, accepted the Lord when the beloved found Him out and brought Him by force, into her mother's household, in the Mosaic (Sinai) covenant (cf. comment on v.3:4). To the contrary, in the New Testament dispensation, her mother's household debarred her from bringing the risen, glorified, Lord into their midst, to teach them, for the simple reason that He was neither a Prophet "like unto" Moses, her brother, nor was His teaching like unto the Law which Moses had taught. (cf. comment on 8:1-3).

iii. The sharp contrast that is shown between the natures of the "watchmen" who appear over the scene in the Old and New Testament dispensations is yet another clear-cut key to the mystery of the Song. The context shows clearly that Moses and Aaron are the watchmen who appear over the scene in the Old Testament dispensation (cf. exegetical comment on 2:17 & 3:3). They appear as helpful guides. To the contrary, the vicious men of the Jewish hierarchy who sat in the seat of Moses and Aaron in the New Testament dispensation are the watchmen who appear over the scene in 5:7. By the manner they beat, wounded and humiliated the beloved, they prove themselves to be wicked monsters.

iv. The fact that the story of the faithful entity of Israel in the Song is patterned after the episode of her progenitor Jacob's nightlong wrestle with the Lord at Peniel, "until the breaking of the day," is another key to the interpretation of the Song. For instance, it is obvious that the threads of the beloved's statement, "I held him, and would not let him go" (3:4), had been taken from the narrative of the Peniel episode and woven into the fabric of the Song. So also is the statement, "until the day break, and the shadows flee away," that occur twice in the Old Testament division of the Song (2:17; 4:6). The threads of this statement also have been taken from the Peniel episode and woven into the fabric of the Song, to indicate that the Old Testament dispensation was one of the night of ignorance and shadows of doubts; that these had ruled the heart of the beloved during the period. The Day Star arises and day dawns in her heart only later in the New Testament dispensation, i.e., in 6:10 ff., where she, in turn, is stated to be looking "forth as the morning, fair as the moon, clear as the sun, and terrible as an army with banners," and rising up over the horizon of the darkened "garden of nuts" (cf. exegetical comment below).

v. Another key to the interpretation of the Song is the fact that allusions are often made to events that took place in the life-story of Jacob, and found to be fitting parallels to portray parts of the redemptive story of Jacob's spiritual seed. For instance, the episode behind the words ascribed to the apostolic church, "Come, my beloved, let us go forth into the field, ... the mandrakes give a smell" (7:11, 13), is that of Leah, the less favored wife of Jacob, waiting for the latter on his way back from the field, to entice him, with part of the mandrakes that her son Reuben brought to her from the field, to spend the night with her in a cottage in the field (Gen 30:14-17).

vi. As for the descriptions occurring of the bodily parts of the beloved, particularly in 4:1-7 and 7:1-9, they are not erotic statements, as commonly viewed, but descriptions of the members of the church, the body of Christ, in operation of the charismatic gifs being imparted to them by the indwelling Christ, exactly as in 1 Cor 12 Paul describes believers possessed with divergent charismatic gifts as corresponding parts of the body of Christ.

vii. Clues are furnished to determine the identity of the lovers. (For detailed expository comment, see below).

IV. THE IMORTANCE OF THE STUDY OF THE SONG OF SONGS TO REINFORCE AND REJUVENATE OUR CHRISTIAN FAITH.

"Whosoever believeth that Jesus is the Christ (Heb. *Messiah)* is born of God" (1 Jn 5:1). The vice versa, 'whosoever does not believe that Jesus is the Messiah (Gk. *Christos*) is not born of God.' Neither is a person who is not born of God a true Christian.

How can we be sure that Jesus is the *Messiah*? There is only one answer, and that is the answer our Lord Himself gave to the Jews, who sought to kill him, "Search the scriptures... and they are they which testify of me" (John 5:39). The only ground on which our faith that Jesus is God incarnate, the Messiah, stands is the fulfillment in Him of all the Messianic types, shadows, and prophecies found scattered here and there in the other Old Testament books of the Bible. The Song of Songs is the one and only book in the Old Testament wherein the entire redemptive work of Christ is revealed beforehand in a continuous story form. The disclosure begins with an indirect hint to the paradoxical turn of events through which the Lord made Jacob, the heir of the promise in the Abrahamic covenant, into an Israel of God,[10] and concludes with the description of the way in which He made Israel, the church of the regenerated,[11] the channel of blessing for all the families of the earth, just as He had promised to Abraham, saying, "in thee shall all the families of the earth be blessed" (Gen 12:3).

The study of the Song, therefore, is a matter of utmost importance to reinforce and rejuvenate our saving faith in the irrefutable fact that Jesus of Nazareth was truly God incarnate, the Messiah.

---

[10] The expression, "the Israel of God" occurs only once in the Bible, i.e. in Gal 6:16, where Paul uses the term to denote believers in Christ. Whether he uses it to denote only Jewish believers in Christ or to denote both Jewish and Gentile believers is unclear. We use the term specifically to distinguish the Jewish believers of the Old and New Testament periods from the rest of the Jews of those periods.

[11] We use the expression, 'Israel, the church of the regenerated,' to distinguish the body of the believers of the Old Testament dispensation from the rest of the Jews of the period. To distinguish the Jewish believers of the primitive Christian church period in the New Testament dispensation from the rest of the Jews of the time, we use the term, 'the primitive Jewish Christian church.'

V. THE SONG, A BOOK "WRITTEN WITHIN AND ON THE BACKSIDE."

In mode of composition, the Song of Songs is similar to the book that John saw in the right hand of Him that sat on the throne, "a book written within and on the backside, sealed with seven seals" (Rev 5:1). That is to say, the words and expressions occurring in the Song are packed with dual senses: an outward deceptive sense, and an inward spiritual sense. The double meanings are generated by the use of an assortment of sophisticated figures of speech, such as, puns, riddles, play on words, double entendre, symbolism, etc. As a result, what appears as an erotic love song is that which is written "on the backside." The actually intended song written "within," is the song of the Lamb that was "slain from the foundation of the world" (Rev 13:8). That Song is, in reality, similar to the song which John heard being sung by "the hundred and forty and four thousand," who stood with the Lamb on mount Zion (Rev 14:1, 3), a song that no man could learn but the redeemed of the Lord.

VI. THE SONG AS A SEALED BOOK

The Song is, in fact, a sealed book analogous to the above-stated prodigious book that John saw in the right hand of Him that sat on the throne. The artful devices used to keep the revealed truths under wraps are esoteric in nature; which is to say, designed especially to conceal its sacred contents from the carnal and casual readers, and to make them known only to the redeemed, as well as to the earnest, prayerful seekers. The use of this kind of esoteric method to disclose the profound spiritual mysteries being revealed in the Song is reminiscent of the way in which the Lord chased out the fallen Adam and Eve from the paradisiacal garden of Eden, and placed "Cherubims, and a flaming sword which turned every way" to ensure that the fallen couple did not stretch forth their hands and take also of the fruit of the tree of life and eat and live for ever. (Gen 3:24).

The measure of disillusionment accrued in the minds of biblical scholars consequent to the non-success met with by them to decode the Song, in spite of incessant endeavors made over the centuries, can be gauged from the following words of Franz

Delitzsch:

> The synagogal and church interpretation, in spite of two thousand years' labour, has yet brought to light no sure results, but only numberless absurdities, especially where the Song describes the lovers according to their members from head to foot and foot to head.[12]

VII. THE TITLE AND AUTHORSHIP OF THE SONG

There are two types of Songs in the Holy Bible: (i), The prophetic songs sung by the prophets as "the Spirit of Christ," who was in them, gave them utterance concerning the things that were to come to pass (1 Pet 1:11), (ii), The devotional songs composed by Spirit-filled men of God, under the inspiration of the Holy Spirit. A careful study of the Song of Songs reveals that it belongs to the former category. It is factually a song sung by Solomon the prophet, son of David, king of Israel, as the "Spirit of Christ," who was in him (1 Pet 1:11) gave utterance.

The unrivalled sublimity of the subject matter of the Song, and the astounding accuracy of its futuristic prophesies, reveal, first, that Solomon sang the Song sometime after the Lord appeared to him at Gibeon and endued him with the charismatic gift of wisdom (1 Kgs 3:5ff.), and, second, that, Solomon personally had no hand whatsoever in the composition of the Song, other than having been the mouth piece of the Spirit of Christ who sang the Song. In all probability, Solomon could have been also the scribe who wrote down the Song.

The opening words of the targum of the Song-the paraphrased, Aramaic translation of the Song-cited below, reflects the belief that was entertained by the ancient rabbinical school of biblical interpretation, with regard to the Song's origin:

> Songs and praises which Solomon, the prophet, the king of Israel spoke by the Holy Spirit before Yahweh, the Lord of the whole world. Ten songs were sung on that day, but this song was more to be praised than they all.[13]

---

[12] Franz Delitzch, *Commentary on the Song of Songs and Ecclesiastes*, Grand Rapids, Michigan: William Erdmans Publishing Company, 1986.

[13] James Hastings, *Dictionary of the Bible*: Edinburg, Moris and Gibbs Ltd., p. 930.

Solomon was indeed an inspired composer of Songs. This is duly attested in 1 Kgs 4:32, where it is stated that "he spoke 3000 proverbs and his songs were 1005" (NASB). Moreover, Solomon was also renowned as a master in the art of contriving and solving hard and unanswerable riddles. Josephus highlights the fact that one of the pleasant royal pastimes of Solomon had been confronting Hiram of Lebanon and other friendly kings of the neighboring countries, with cleverly concocted riddles, and answering with ease, those received from them. It appears that the Spirit of Christ made use of this particular prowess that was inherent in Solomon while giving him utterance to sing the Song.

Contrary to the erroneous notion prevailing among the rationalistic scholars of our day, there is no trace of any addition, emendation, or expurgation anywhere in the Masoretic Text of the Song, excepting for a change in the gender suffixes occurring in vv. 8:5b and 13. (See exegetical comment on these verses).

VIII. THE IDENTITY OF THE LOVERS

The curtain raiser of the Song is the mystifying scene of an unknown woman rapt in praising and adoring the name of her venerable lover, saying, "The king hath brought me into his chambers." The identity of the lovers is deliberately concealed. This is yet another reason why the Song has remained mysterious heretofore. Once the identity of the lovers is ascertained, the main hurdle standing in the way of interpreting the Song is removed.

Over the three millennia since Solomon sang the Song, many a brilliant scholar has spent his/her time and talent in vain to identify the lovers and discover the Song's theme and plot.

Those who write books do so to be read and understood by the readership for which they write. Never does an author write a book to remain an unintelligible mystifying riddle forever. Even the authors who write books of perplexing riddles or puzzles are under obligation to furnish the required keys to solve them, if not directly, at least somewhere on the reverse. The author of the Song could not have been different in this respect.

1. *The Identity of the Beloved*

The hint given to identify the female partner is her own narration of the paradoxical turn of events that took place in her life by way of which the Lord made her the heir of promise in the Abrahamic covenant of promise, to wit, "my mother's sons were angry with me, they made me keeper of the vineyards, but my own vineyard I have not kept" (v.1:6, NRSV).

Discernibly, the person who appears in the guise of the female partner, and narrates the paradoxical events that took place in his life is Jacob, the heir of promise in the Abrahamic covenant of promise, who was born of God into Israel, at Peniel. The paradoxical events to which Jacob, the newborn Israel, refers by saying, "my mother's sons were angry with me, they made me keeper of the vineyards," are those that took place in his life, soon after he obtained his father's blessing of birthright and heir-ship in the Abrahamic covenant of promise, through dupery. Isaac, believing blindly that he was blessing Esau, his elder son, had filled with the Spirit and pronounced the much-reserved paternal blessing upon Jacob, saying, " be lord over thy brethren, and let thy mother's sons bow down to thee" (Gen 27:29).

The crux of the matter is that this paradoxical incident had happened providentially. "For the children being not yet born, neither having done any good or evil, that the purpose of God according to election might stand, not of works, but of him that calleth; it was said unto her (i.e., to Rebecca, the mother), 'The elder shall serve the younger'" (Rom 9:11-12). As Paul makes crystal clear in the cited verse, whatsoever God had purposed before the foundation of the world, concerning a person whom He had elected, had been purposed unconditionally, irrespective of the good or evil that the person would do in everyday life. In case election was conditional, such an election could not have been election at all. Moreover, as human beings are born in sin, none among them is righteous, "no, not one" (Rom 3:12). "For all have sinned and come short of the glory of God" (Rom 3:23). Therefore, God did not elect anyone expecting him/her to be sinless or righteous by him or herself alone. In the case of Jacob, God who foreknew the end from the beginning had chosen him to be the heir of promise in the covenant, foreknowing fully well that he would resort to the most condemnable type of dupery to obtain his father's blessing and birthright, and also as to how He would use the very same perfidious act to lead him to godly-sorrow and genuine contrition.

To understand the rest of the paradoxical turn of events that took place in Jacob's life, one must examine them from the perspective of Isaac's act; whether he was justified in setting his mind to bestow the blessing of birthright and heir-ship of the covenanted blessing of God, upon Esau, the elder.

Isaac foreknew from Rebecca, the mother, concerning the specific prophetic word that came to her from God, before the siblings were born, that "The elder shall serve the younger." But, he was deliberately sidestepping the known purpose of God concerning Jacob, the younger, in preference to follow the established custom of the land, when he called Esau, the elder, and asked him to bring him a savoury dish of venison, such as he loved, so that he would eat it, and his soul would bless him with the reserved paternal blessing of birthright and heir-ship of the covenanted blessing.

Only when Esau arrived with the savoury dish of venison, soon after Jacob left his bedchamber, did Isaac realize the irony of the fact that the paternal blessing that he had bestowed just a little before was upon the imposter. Shuddering at, what he thought, the big blunder he had committed, Isaac told the waiting Esau,

> Who? Where is he that hath taken venison, and brought it to me, and I have eaten of all before thou camest, and have blessed him? Yea, and he shall be blessed. Gen 27:33

> "And when Esau heard the words of his father, he cried with a great and exceeding bitter cry .... And he said, Hast thou not reserved a blessing for me?" (Gen 27:34, 36). To this, Isaac answered

Behold, I have made him thy lord, and all his brethren have I given to him for servants. ... what shall I do now unto thee, my son? Gen27:37).

Burning with anger, Esau said in his heart, "The days of mourning for my father are at hand; then will I slay my brother

Jacob" (Gen 27:41. Then only did Jacob realize that by succumbing to his mother's coercion and resorting to dupery he had been turning the table upon himself. Frightened, he fled for life to Haran, to his maternal uncle Laban, and finding no way to return home for fear of Esau's burning anger, rotted for the next twenty years of his life under harsh servitude to the Labans. It is with these in mind that Jacob, the newborn Israel, in the guise of the beloved, says here, "My mother's sons were angry with me, they made me keeper of the vineyards."

The word, "vineyard," occurs in the Song as a symbol for vocation. Jacob's own vineyard, concerning which he ruefully bemoans, saying, "I have not kept," refers to his vocation as the heir of promise, in the Abrahamic covenant of promise. This is made clear through the parables of the dual types of vineyards that occur towards the end of the Song, i.e., in 8:11-12 (cf. exegetical comment on them in the commentary section of this book).

God does not fail to keep any of His covenanted promises just because of human failure. All that Jacob ought to have kept was his faith in the faithfulness of God to keep His own promises.

But, due to immaturity, and lack of faith, Jacob had presumed that he must do something from his own side for God to fulfill His promise. So when the opportunity came his way, he went ahead and purchased the birthright from Esau for a pottage of red lentils, and made him to bind the transaction with a binding oath (Gen 25:28-34), and later, resorted to the above stated act of dupery.

"All things work together for good ...to them that are called according to his purpose" (Rom 8:28). This is true also of the failures and shortcomings that come about in the lives of the elect of God who are called by Him according to His purpose. As stated, He turns the very failures that come about in their lives to their good. In other words, He uses the failures and shortcomings that come about in the lives of His elect to humble them and lead them to genuine godly-sorrow and contrition.

Accordingly, the Lord turned to Jacob's good the very treacherous act that he had committed. One day Jacob overheard the sons of Laban saying, "Jacob hath taken away all that was our father's; and of that which was our father's hath he gotten all this glory" (Gen 31:1). "Jacob beheld the countenance of Laban, and, behold, it was not toward him as before." (Gen 31:2). Feeling insecure, Jacob fled towards Canaan with all that he possessed; still unsure of whether Esau's burning anger had abated. Peace feelers sent to Esau returned with the frightening news that the latter was on his way to meet him with four hundred of his (armed) men. Terrified and dismayed, Jacob finally landed on his knees, in genuine godly-sorrow and tears before the Lord, who had been designedly waiting for him at Peniel in the form of a man. Holding the Lord tenaciously at His promises, he wrestled with Him "until the breaking of the day." "Let me go, for the day breaketh," said the Lord. "I will not let thee go, except thou bless me," answered Jacob. "What is thy name," asked the Lord. And he answered "Jacob." "Thy name shall be called no more Jacob, but Israel," answered the Lord, "for as a prince hast thou power with God and with men, and hast prevailed. ... And he blessed him there" (Gen 32: 24, 26-29). The Song's storyline commences from this point.

The Song, however, reckons that the one who was born of God into an Israel of God, at Peniel that memorable night was not Jacob, an individual, but a corporeal entity, namely, Israel, the church of the regenerated. Not only this, she, the church, is presented as being the numerically and spiritually growing and maturing body of Christ. At the time of her birth she had possessed only a face which was stated to be 'black but comely' (1:5). Thereafter, commensurate with the addition of new members, she kept growing and developing her bodily members until she finally attained to "the measure of the stature of the fulness of Christ (Eph 4:13), and fulfilled the vocation of her calling of bringing "the blessing of Abraham ... on the Gentiles" (Gal 3:14).

2. *The Identity of the Lover*

The Lover is Christ; the pre-incarnate Christ, in the Old Testament division of the Song (1:2-5:1), and the risen and glorified Christ, in the New Testament division, (5:2-8:14). (For conclusive proof, cf. notes below under the head, 'XV.THE IDENTITY OF THE LOVER).

IX. THE THEME OF THE SONG IN DETAIL

As stated at the outset, the theme of the Song is "the mystery, which from the beginning of the world hath been hid in God, who created all things by Jesus Christ" (Eph 3:9).

The reason why Paul describes the Father's redemptive scheme by the curious term, "the mystery," is that it has been remaining undisclosed "unto the sons of men" in former ages, until it was "made known" unto him and unto the other "apostles and prophets of his time by the Spirit" (Eph 3:5). He describes the Father's redemptive scheme also by a more comprehensive term, "the mystery of Christ" (Eph 3:9), for the reason that Christ, "the only begotten Son" of the Father, was the entirety of the salvation that was envisaged in it.

1. *Why does God and matters pertaining to the Spiritual realm appear mysterious to us?*

The answer to the question is this. As stated, God and the other spirits exist and operate in an alien un-seeming, real world of space and timelessness, which is inconceivable to us who exist and operate under the laws of physicality with its multitudinous limitations. We can think and ratiocinate only in terms of the laws of physicality under which we exist and operate. Immateriality and infinity are incomprehensible to us. Therefore, God, and matters pertaining to His operation, appear strange and mysterious to us.

It must not be forgotten, however, that God has created us in His own image and likeness, unlike the other creatures, with a soul and spirit, to enable us to know Him and to enter into and enjoy constant spirit to Spirit fellowship with Him experientially. But, to know the unknowable things about God and to enter into and enjoy the bliss of constant spirit to Spirit fellowship with Him, one must believe unquestioningly the things that are written down in the canonical books of the Holy Bible, about Him and of the way in which He had been operating in the past. For, faith is to believe God at His word.

2. *In fact, God had made known to Abraham that the Gentiles were to be Partakers of the Promised Blessing*

Though Paul insists in his epistle to the Ephesians, as above, that, in former ages, God did not make known that the Gentiles should be fellow-heirs with the Jews to all the blessings and privileges of the Abrahamic covenant of promise, in his Epistle to the Galatians he not only concedes but also insists that God did make known beforehand that He "would justify the heathen through faith," when He "preached before the gospel unto Abraham, saying, In thee shall all nations be blessed" (Gal 3:8).

3. *The action-plans to bring the blessing of Abraham upon all the families of the earth that were in the Lord's mind when He used the prepositional phrase, "in thee."*

When the Lord used the prepositional phrase "in thee," in promising to Abraham, "In thee shall all the families of the earth be blessed," the prepositional phrase was fraught with the action-plan that He had in mind to make all the families of the earth blessed with the salvation that was envisaged in His Father's Redemptive Scheme. It is true that the Heb. preposition, *"be,"* which is translated "in" in the Authorized Version can also be translated, "by," as JB, or "through" as NIV. However, we the believers, who have been blessed "with the blessing of Abraham" (Gal 3:14), precisely as the Lord had promised, know experientially that we have been blessed "with the blessing of Abraham" not "through" or "by" Abraham, but *"in"* Abraham.

The substances of the action-plan that the Lord had in mind to make all the families of the earth blessed *"in"* Abraham were:

*a. "In"*the Seed of Abraham. b. *"In"* the Abrahamic Covenant of promise.

a. *"In"* the Seed of Abraham

When the Lord made use of the prepositional phrase, "in thee," He had meant that He would bless all the families of the earth in the dual seeds of Abraham, namely,

i. **In Christ, the Seed Par Excellence of Abraham, in the Covenant**. As we have pointed out above, Christ is the

One who appears as the Lover in the Song; the pre-incarnate Christ, in the Old Testament division, and the risen and glorified Christ, in the New Testament division, of the Song.

ii. **In the Church that was to comprise of the spiritual seed that the Lord promised to Abraham, in Gen 22:17, saying, "in multiplying I will multiply thy seed as the stars of the heaven."** The church that had comprised of Jacob, and those of Jacob's seed whom the Lord transformed, through regeneration, to shine "as the stars of the heaven," is the Lord's beloved in the Song.

i. "In" Christ, the Seed Par Excellence of Abraham, in the Covenant.

While using the prepositional phrase, "in thee," the Lord had predominantly in mind His own incarnation as the Seed Par Excellence of Abraham in the covenant, His vicarious death, resurrection, and His indwelling the believers drawn from all the families of the earth; both from Jews and Gentiles alike. His elect out of all the families of the earth were to be blessed with the blessing that He had been promising to Abraham, in Himself. "Now to Abraham and his seed were the promises made. He saith not, And to seeds, as of many; but as of one, And to thy seed, which is Christ" (Gal 3:16).

Christ appears in the Song also in His three-fold offices of King, Priest, and Prophet and as the antitypical Bezaleel, "the cunning workman," who had made jewels of multitudes of Jacob's seed, in the vehement fire of the jealousies of heartless carnal men. (See exegetical comment on 1:4; 3:11; 8:1, 6 and 7:1, respectively, in the Commentary section of this book).

Dr. Wesley L. Duewel, former, Principal of Allahabad Bible Seminary, U.P., India, who was also the President emeritus of Oriental Missionary Society (OMS) International, writes:

> All theophanies recorded in the Old Testament were really Christophanies, for all the revelation of God, in any manifest form, has been through Jesus Christ. God the Father is eternal, immortal, invisible (1 Tim 1:17). Therefore all theophanies have been manifestations of the pre-incarnate Christ (if found in the Old

Testament) or visions of Incarnate Christ (if found in the New Testament).[14]

"In" Christ

Strictly speaking, when the Lord used the prepositional phrase, "in thee," He had meant that He will bless all the families of the earth "in" Christ, rather than merely, 'in the Person of Christ.' The expression, *"in"* Christ, means, in the mystic union of faith with Christ-the "quickening Spirit" (1 Cor 15:45). The salvation envisaged in the Father's redemptive scheme was not merely something, which Christ was to impart; it was Christ Himself. One is saved only when he/she is *"in"* Christ. It is with this mystic union of the believer with Christ in mind that Paul uses the expression, *"in Christ,"* or *"in Him,"* over and over again in all of his Epistles.

To illustrate how Christ, the Head, keeps the members of His body, the church, unified and compacted together with Himself, and with each other, by means of the mystic faith-joint, Paul uses the example of the relationship between the human head and body. The human head keeps every part of the body joined and compacted together to itself and supplies to each part the required life, nourishment and vitality, by way of the joints:

> From whom the whole body fitly joined together and compacted by that which every joint supplieth, according to the effectual working in the measure of every part, maketh increase of the body unto the edifying of itself in love. Eph 4:16.

In Eph 1:23, Paul describes Christ as "him that filleth all in all," and the church as "the fullness of him that filleth all in all." Further, dwelling on the same subject, he writes to the Colossians, "in him dwelleth all the fullness of the Godhead bodily. And ye are complete in him." The church collectively, and her members individually, can be " filled with all the fullness of God," only if the mystic faith-joint that unites them with Christ, the Head, is intact. The only reason why the church collectively, and her

---

[14] Dr. Wesley Duewell, former principal of Allahabad Bible Seminary, unpublished: *'notes on Christology.'*

members individually, are not "filled with the fullness of Christ" lies in the fact that the mystic faith-joint that unifies them with Christ, the Head, is not intact. For it is through the mystic faith-joint that Christ, the Head, who "filleth all in all," fills His body, the church, and its members, with His fullness.

Another equally significant example that our Lord Himself had used to illustrate the effectual working of the mystic faith-joint of each believer with Him was that of the True Vine and its branches (cf. John 15:1-9). For growth and fruition, the branches have nothing more to do than to abide in the stem of the True Vine, which is Christ. Provided the mystic faith-joint that unifies the branches with the True Vine is intact, He, the True Vine, "that filleth all in all," is sure to fill the branches with His entire life and fullness.

Christian life is not, as commonly presumed, imitating Christ, or trying to be like Him, but "Christ in us, " and we "in" Him; an experience realized by way of the mystic union of faith.

ii. In the Church of the regenerated that was to consist of the Seed that the Lord promised to Abraham in Gen. 22:17, saying, "I Will Multiply Thy Seed as the Stars of the Heaven."

The female who appears in the Song as the Lord's beloved is the church that had comprised of the regenerated seed promised by the Lord to Abraham, in the Abrahamic covenant, saying, "in multiplying I will multiply thy seed as the stars of the heaven" (Gen 22: 17). Viewed from the standpoint of election and choice, the beloved is the body of the elect from among the seed of Abraham, whom the Lord made faithful by regeneration, in the Abrahamic covenant of promise. As stated, this is signified by the statement of 6:9, "My dove, my undefiled is but one; she is the only one of her mother, she is the choice one of her that bare her."

b. *In the Abrahamic Covenant of Promise.*

When the Lord used the prepositional phrase, "in thee," in saying "In thee shall all the families of the earth be blessed," He had meant also that He would bring the blessing of Abraham upon all the families of the earth 'in the Abrahamic covenant of promise.' In keeping with this, the Abrahamic covenant of promise had always been in operation throughout all the Biblical dispensations ever since it was made. It is still in operation, in that we, the Gentiles, are being "justified" through faith, by the same "gospel" that the Lord "preached before ... unto Abraham, saying, In thee shall all nations be blessed" (Gal 3:8). It means that the Abrahamic covenant had neither been annulled nor been weakened in any way by the addition of the Sinai covenant. In that "the law (was) not of faith" (cf. Gal 3:12), the Sinai covenant did not possess the efficacy to generate children unto God, through regeneration. All the elect of God who were justified by faith in the Old Testament dispensation were justified, not by keeping the law under the stipulations of the Sinai covenant, but by the faith that they had reposed in God, on the ground of the veracity, trustworthiness, and immutability of the promise that He had made to Abraham, in the covenant.

4. *Reasons for believing that, in the Song's reckoning, Israel that was born of God at Peniel was not an individual, but a corporeal entity, to wit, the church of the regenerated.*

We have stated that the Song regards Israel, the beloved who was born of God, at Peniel, not as an individual, but as a corporeal entity, namely, Israel, the church of the regenerated. This is discernible from the following factors:

(i). When the Lord, the King, brought the beloved, by regeneration, into the inner chambers of His presence in the *heavenly places*, the newborn Israel uses the first person plural pronoun "we," rather than the singular "I," to declare her resolve to follow after Him, saying, "we will run after thee ... we will be glad and rejoice in thee, we will remember thy love more than wine" (1:4).

(ii). In 4:1-5, the Spirit discloses demonstratively how the Lord had been building up the regenerated Israelites into a corporeal entity, the church, during the epochs in her redemptive story that were marked for possessing faith and performance of exploits of faith. Accordingly, the living members of the church, of successive generations, who performed exploits of faith by the operation of the divergent charismatic gifts imparted to them by the indwelling Christ, during such epochs, are not described as personalities, but as parts of the body of Christ, such as, seeing eyes, flowing hair, smiling teeth, rosy cheeks, scarlet thread coloured lips, praising comely mouth, and so on (cf. comment on vv. 4:1-5).

As stated, the description of members of the church, as above, as parts of the body of Christ, occurs in perfect consonance with Paul's description, in 1 Cor 12, of the Spirit-filled church as the body of Christ, and her members who performed divergent functions, for the common good of the church, by the operation of the charismatic gifts imparted severally to them by the indwelling Christ, as parts of the body of Christ.

> For as the body is one, and hath many members, and all the members of that one body, being many, are one body: so also is Christ. 1 Cor 12:12

(iii). According to the Song's disclosure, Israel, the beloved that was born of God, in Jacob, at Peniel, continued to exist, cutting across six major epochs coming within the period of the redemptive history of Israel, which was impossible had she been an individual.

5. *The six major epochs across which Israel, the beloved church that was born at Peniel, continued to exist.*

The following were the six major epochs across which Israel, the beloved that was born of God, at Peniel, continued to exist:

(i) The patriarchal epoch covered in 1:2-17. This was an epoch of simple exemplary faith and trust.

(ii) The four hundred years of Israel's Egyptian captivity, which is alluded to, in 1:13, as an impending night, and in 2:11, as a cold rainy winter season that has come and gone, exactly as the Lord had disclosed beforehand to Abraham in Gen 15:13, (cf. comment on 1:13, with 2:11).

(iii) The three forty year periods of the Mosaic epoch:

The first forty years during which the Pharaoh' daughter brought up Moses as her adopted son, covered in the sub-section, 2:1-6.

The second forty years of Moses' life, which included his flight to the wild regions of the Sinai Peninsula where he had been tending the flocks of Jethro, the Lord's appearance to him in the burning bush, commissioning and sending him to Egypt to deliver Israel from the captivity, and to bring the delivered nation along with him to Horeb (Sinai) to worship Him in the Sinai covenant, covered in the sub-section, 2:8-17.

The third forty years of Moses' life, which included his arrival at Egypt, delivering Israel from the captivity, leading the delivered nation down to Sinai to enter into the covenant relationship with the Lord, the subsequent debacle of Kadesh-barnea, and his wandering with the children Israel in the wilderness until every one of those that had started with him from Egypt died, consequent to the curse, excepting Moses, Joshua, and Caleb, covered in the section, 3:1-8.

(iv). The glorious epoch of possessing faith in the Old Testament dispensation that had extended from the time of the exploits of faith of Joshua and his men, to the end of the Solomonic reign, covered in the section 3:9-4:15.

(v). The nine centuries of Israel's darkened, misty history, which extended from the day of Solomon's demise to the day of Pentecost, alluded to in 5:2 as a prolonged misty night of estrangement between Israel and the Lord.

(vi). The glorious epoch of the primitive Jewish Christian church that had extended from the day of Pentecost to the day the apostles and elders who had gathered at Jerusalem for the first Church Council made the growing Gentile Christian church free from observing the Jewish religious laws and traditional customs, covered in 5:4-8:14

6. *Why does Christ, the Spirit, require a body (the church) to carry out His redemptive work?*

To find out the answer to the question, one must examine it both from the divine and human standpoints.

From the divine standpoint, Christ, the Spirit cannot carry out His redemptive activities for humanity, which exist in the physical realm, unless He abides in physical human bodies. In the Old Testament dispensation, for instance, the pre-incarnate Christ, the Spirit, could not have taken possession of the Promised land for Israel unless He did abide in the hearts of the believers among them and did use their bodies as His own to fight the battles that were involved in the process. So also, in the primitive Christian church period, the Lord could not have spread the gospel even to the ends of the earth unless He did abide in the hearts of the apostles and evangelists of the time and use their bodies as His own. Even today, it is Christ who indwells us who carries out His redemptive activities like giving counseling to needy souls, visiting the sick and suffering, consoling the broken hearted, preaching the gospel and teaching the word of God, and so on. The Lord can perform these redemptive activities only if He abides in the heart of selected individuals who have received Him in their heart by faith and have surrendered to Him their body, soul and spirit absolutely.

From the human standpoint, one must ask the question to himself/herself that Paul asks in 1 Cor 2:11, "For what man knoweth the things of a man, save the spirit of man which is in him?" Only human spirit can understand the aspirations, needs, and problems of fellow human spirits and communicate heartily and effectively with them. We are incapable of understanding the thoughts and aspirations of other creatures or of communicating with them. The communication gulf is a wide chasm when it comes to Christ, the Spirit, and us. For instance, when the Lord manifested Himself over mount Sinai in lightning and thunder, fire and smoke, and a loud trumpet sound, and spoke to the children of Israel, the latter, including Moses, trembled greatly. Consequently, the children of Israel entreated Moses, saying, "Speak thou with us, and we will hear: but let not God speak with us, lest we die" (Exo 20:19). What would have been our plight, if the Lord were to appear to each one of us in the form of the Spirit that He is, at each minute and second in which we seek for His help and guidance?

The facts of the matter being as explained, the normal and appropriate way that the Lord Himself has chosen to carry out His redemptive activities among humanity is by way of abiding in the heart of believers who have lovingly and willingly received

Him in their heart by faith and have surrendered their body, soul and spirit to Him wholly and absolutely, to be used as He will. The Lord takes over the body of such individuals as His own, and abiding within, carries out His redemptive work for humanity. It is from this perspective that the church comprising of such individuals is called the body of Christ.

The foregoing also means the vice versa. That is, the so-called Christian assemblies and congregations consisting of members who have not received the Lord in their hearts as their Lord and Saviour by faith, and have not surrendered their body, soul, and spirit to Him to be used as His own, are neither churches in the real sense of the term, nor are they part of the body of Christ.

a. The Visible and the Invisible Churches in the Song

Discernibly, the persons who appear over the historical arena of the Song, in chronological sequence, in the guise of the beloved (church), are living members of the visible church. For instance, the person who appears in the initial units of the Song, vv.1:2-4, and vv. 5-6, in the guise of the beloved church, is Jacob, the founding father of Israel. The person who appears over the historical arena, in the guise of the beloved, in the succeeding unit, vv. 7-8, is Joseph. The ones who appear in the guise of the beloved, in the rest of the verses of chapter one, vv. 9-17, are the patriarchs and their families, collectively.

There is a gap of the four centuries of Israel's Egyptian captivity between vv.1: 17 and 2:1. The person who comes over the historical arena, in the guise of the beloved, towards the closing period of the Egyptian captivity, i.e. in 2:1, declaring, "I am the rose of Sharon, and the lily of the valleys," is discernibly the baby Moses.

The patriarchs had gone to be with the Lord, prior to the commencement of the Egyptian captivity, after running their race, and finishing their course. Evidently, they had become parts of the invisible church. Therefore they do not appear again in the historical arena in the Song, individually or in groups. This is true of all the believers who appear once over the historical arena, in the successive units, in the guise of the beloved. After having run their race, and finished their course, they had gone to be with the Lord in heaven, and to become parts of the invisible church. It emerges from the above that the invisible wing of the church had been an ever-growing entity, assimilating the believers who were leaving the body, generation after generation, and were going to be with the Lord in heaven. Touching the state of those who have finished their course and gone to be with the Lord, our Lord Himself had made clear, when He countered the Jews who tried to entrap Him in words, saying,

> Have ye not read that which was spoken unto you by God, saying, I am the God of Abraham, and the God of Isaac, and the God of Jacob? God is not the God of the dead, but of the living. Matt 22:31-32.

Discernibly, whenever the Lord addresses His beloved church, which is the body of Christ, to appreciate her over the beauty and comeliness of the parts of her body, namely, of her living members in their acts of faith, as He does, for instance, in 4:1-5, He is addressing the invisible church that had comprised of those who left the body and were present with Him, in heaven. (For details, cf. exegetical comment on vv. 4:1-5, in the commentary section of this book).

b. The Mode of Appearances of the Lovers

Contrary to the prevailing notion, the lovers do not appear in the Song in human form, either literally or figuratively.

i. The mode of appearances of Christ, the Lover

Being an invisible and intangible Spirit, Christ, the Lover, appears in the Song only as such. One needs only to think in terms of the manner in which we speak to the Lord and talk about Him today, in order to understand the way in which the beloved (church) speaks to the Lord, her Lover, and describes the glories of His person. It is the indescribability of His intangible person that prompts her to describe His person in terms of visible objects, such as, "a bundle of myrrh" (1:13); "a cluster of camphire" (1:14); "an apple tree" (2:3); "a roe or a young hart" (2:9), and so on. On most of the occasions when the beloved speaks of the Lord, she speaks of Him only in the third person. A few times when she addresses

Him directly, she uses the second person pronouns, such as, "thy" and "thou" ("thy name," 1:3, "thou art fair," 1:16). For instance, in 1:7, she cries unto Him out of the core of her being, saying, "O thou whom my soul loveth, where, ... where ...." Likewise, in 3:1-4, when she seeks to find Him out, as well as makes enquiries about His whereabouts, she uses the intimate term, "him whom my soul loveth" (3:1-4).

ii. The mode of appearances of the beloved (church).

As the beloved is not an individual but a corporeal entity, namely, the church of the regenerated, she appears in the Song only as such. It is from this standpoint that the Spirit compares her aptly in 1:9, to "a company of horses in Pharaoh's chariots," in 2:2, to "a lily among thorns," in 4:12-5:1, to the Lord's paradisiacal garden, planted in Him, by faith, in the richest soil of His promises, and so on.

Even in the case of individuals appearing over the historical arena in the Song, like Jacob, in the initial units, 1:2-4, and 5-6, Joseph, in the succeeding unit, 1:7-8, and Moses, in the whole of chapter 2, (with the exception of v.2:2), they appear only in the guise of the whole church. (As for v.2: 2, the statement of the Lord, "As the lily among thorns, so is my love among the daughters," it is made with reference to the body of the elect of the time who were undergoing oppression at the hands of the Egyptian taskmasters).

7. *The Salient Points of the Father's Redemptive Scheme that the Lord made known to the Holy Apostles and Prophets, by the Spirit*

A brief outline of the salient points of the redemptive scheme of the Father that the Son had made known by the Spirit to Paul and to other apostles and prophets of his time, are given below:

(i) God, the Father had conceived His redemptive scheme for the salvation of His elect before the foundation of the world.

(ii) The scheme had remained hid in Him, as a mystery, when He created all things by Jesus Christ (Eph 3:9).

(iii) The ultimate goal of the Father's redemptive scheme had not been the salvation of His elect out of the Jewish nation exclusively, as they had misconceived, but the salvation of His elect out of all the nations of the earth, impartially (Gal 3:8; Eph 3:6).

(iv) According to the provisions envisaged in the Father's redemptive scheme, His elect from among the non-Jewish families of the earth were not merely to have had a part in the salvation, but were to be "fellow-heirs, and of the same body, and partakers of his promise in Christ by the gospel" (Eph 3:6).

(v) The Father's redemptive scheme was not merely an emergency remedial measure necessitated by the Fall. The Lamb had been slain from the foundation of the world, and the names of those whom He had predestinated for eternal life had been written in the book of life of the Lamb (cf. 1 Pet 1:19, 20; Rev 13:8; with Rom 8:30; Eph 1:4).

(vi) Christ Himself was the mystery of redemption, or, the Salvation that was hid in the Father when He created all things by Jesus Christ. He is the greatest of all the gifts that the Father gave to humankind. Those who received Him by faith were to have eternal life. Eternal life is Christ Himself; it is not something that He imparts. "For God so loved the world, that he gave his only begotten Son, that whosoever believeth in him should not perish, but have everlasting life" (John 3:16). "I will also give thee for a light to the Gentiles, that thou mayest be my salvation unto the end of the earth" (Isa 49:6). "Christ Jesus … is made unto us wisdom, and righteousness, and sanctification, and redemption" (1 Cor 1:30).

X. THE PLOT OF THE SONG

The hand of the Lord is clearly evident in plotting the disclosure of Israel's redemptive story in the Song. For the disclosure starts aptly with an allusion to the way in which the Lord created Israel, the church of the regenerated, in Jacob, and ends precisely, as it ought, with the portrayal of the scene of the kingdom of God being transferred to the Gentile church, on Israel achieving the goal of the vocation for which she was called, namely, of bringing "the blessing of Abraham ... on the Gentiles" (cf. Gal 3:14).

On accomplishing the vocation for which the Lord had called Israel, He takes away the special grace that was bestowed on her to hearken to His voice and bestows it upon His elect from among the Gentiles.

Hardened from hearkening to the voice of the Lord and dispossessed of her favored status, Israel cries to the Lord from the place of her banishment without, to restore to her the spiritual faculty to hearken to His voice, saying:

Thou that dwellest in the gardens (in the Gentile churches), the companions (the Gentile converts) hearken to thy voice: cause me to hear it. Make haste, my beloved. (Paraphrase mine).

(Cf. detailed exegetical comment on 8:13-14).

XI. THE METHODOLOGY

Though the Song is a prophetic disclosure of the ways in which the Lord fulfilled the promise that He made to Abraham, saying, "I will bless thee, ... thou shalt be a blessing, ... and in thee shall all the families of the earth be blessed," the disclosure is not made in the form of allusions to the landmark events in the redemptive history of Israel, that took place, and were to take place, as one may presume, but in the following artful ways.

1. *The Disclosure is made in the form of the Story of the Birth, Growth and Development unto Maturity of a Female, namely, of Israel, the Church of the Regenerated.*

The disclosure of Israel's redemptive story in the Song is made in the form of the story of the birth, growth and development unto maturity, of a female, which is to say, of Israel, the church of the regenerated that had been both the body of Christ as well as His beloved/spouse. As stated, she was born of God into Israel, the church of the regenerated, at Peniel, in the person of Jacob, and continued to exist and grow, cutting across six major epochs, until, she grew up "unto the measure of the stature of the fulness of Christ" (Eph 4:13).

As the body of Christ, she had possessed only a face, which was 'black, but comely' at the time of her birth (1:5). But by the time the patriarchs were engaged in the service of the Pharaoh of Egypt, she had developed bejeweled cheeks, and golden chains bedecked neck (1:9-10). By the end of the Old Testament dispensation, she had grown up and developed unto a half of the measure of the stature of the fullness of Christ, from the eyes and hair of her head down to her breasts (cf. comment on 4: 1-7).

She had developed finally unto the measure of the stature of the fullness of Christ, inclusive of the other half of her body from feet upwards, only in the latter part of the primitive Jewish Christian church period, when she began to evangelize and win souls from the rest of the nations of the earth.

For instance, she did not possess the "beautiful feet with shoes" of v. 7:1a, which is to say, evangelists, until the primitive Jewish Christian church period. Neither did she develop the strong rounded thigh joints of v. 7:1b, until she began to walk throughout the length and breadth of the lands of all the nations of the earth to proclaim the gospel of peace and reconciliation in Christ. Furthermore, she developed a huge belly of heaps of wheat, only after she had harvested innumerable souls from the ripened Gentile fields and satisfied her God-given hunger for souls. At last, she grew up and consummated unto the "measure of the stature of the fulness of Christ" (Eph 4:13) only during the latter part of the primitive Jewish Christian church period, as described in the vv. 7:3-9. (See exegetical comment on these verses, in the Commentary section of this book).

2. *The Disclosure is made after the Pattern of the Narrative of Jacob's Nightlong Wrestle with the Lord until the Breaking of the Day*

As we have pointed out at the outset, the disclosure of the birth of Israel, the church of the regenerated, and her gradual emergence from the night of spiritual ignorance, that led to her religious bigotry, to the dawn of light of the knowledge of the purpose for which the Lord had called her, is made in the Song after the narrative of the episode of her progenitor Jacob's nightlong wrestle with the Lord, at Peniel, until the breaking of the day (Gen 32:24-32).

This is discernible from the following words and expressions that occur in the Song:

(i) "Until the day break, and the shadows flee away" (2:17; 4:6).

(ii) "I held him, and would not let him go" (3:4).

(iii) "Who is she that looketh forth as the morning" (6:10).

(iv) "Return, return, O Shulamite (princess of peace), return, return, that we may look upon thee. What will ye see in the Shulamite? As it were the company of two armies"- lit.as it were the dance of Mahanaim. (6:13 with Gen 32:1-2).

(v) "The joints of thy thighs" (7:1 with Gen 32: 25, 31,32).

The above stated method used of disclosing the story of Israel's gradual emergence from the night of spiritual ignorance to the dawn of the light of the knowledge of the vocation for which she was called, after the narrative of the episode of Jacob's nightlong wrestle with the Lord until the dawning of the day, paves the way to understand the significance of some of the most inscrutable imageries occurring in the Song.

Let us take, for instance, the inscrutable imagery of 6:10-13. It begins with the vivid picture of Israel, the beloved (church) dawning over the horizon of the (darkened) garden of nut trees, looking "forth like the dawn, fair as the moon, bright as the sun" (NRSV), followed by her statements, "I went down into the garden of nuts ... Or ever I was aware, my soul made me like the chariots of Amminadib."

To understand the significance of the imagery, one has only to bear in mind that the 'beloved (church) dawning over the garden of nut trees' occurs here as the sequel to the dawning of the day that was anticipated both by her own, and by the Lord's, statement that had occurred earlier, in vv. 2:17 and 4:6, respectively, namely, "Until the day break, and the shadows flee away."

The following significant facts emerge, on examining the imagery in the light of the above quoted statement, "Until the day break, and the shadows flee away:"

(i) As Israel, the beloved (church) herself is the one that looks "forth like the dawn, fair as the moon, bright as the sun" at that juncture of her redemptive story, it emerges that the darkness and shadows that had fled away were those that had been ruling her own heart.

(ii) As the statement, "Until the day break, and the shadows flee away," was made by the beloved (church) in 2:17, just after raising her pet slogan that she uses frequently to give vent to her sentiment of religious bigotry, namely, "My beloved is mine, and I am his: he feedeth (only) among (Israel) the lilies" (2:16, paraphrase mine), it emerges that the darkness and shadows that had fled away from her heart, with the dawning of the day, were those of her religious bigotry.

(iii) As the statement, "until the day break and the shadows flee away" is woven into the fabric of the Song, out of the threads taken from the narrative of the Peniel episode, it emerges that the imagery of the beloved (church) dawning over the garden of nut trees, looking "forth like the dawn, fair as the moon, bright as the sun" is patterned after the narrative of Jacob's emergence from Peniel at dawn, with the glory of the Lord, whom he had seen face to face, reflecting over his face, and winning over the hard nuts, to wit, the furious Esau and his four hundred (armed) men.

In order to make the point clear, let us digress for a while to examine the episode of the undreamt-of peace and reconciliation that came about between Jacob and Esau when Jacob emerged from Peniel at dawn.

We need to bear in mind, in this context, that it was the terrifying news that the furious Esau was on his way to meet him with four hundred of his (armed) men that brought Jacob to his knees before the Lord, at Peniel, and impelled him to wrestle with Him throughout the night, saying, "I will not let thee go, except thou bless me (Gen 32: 26). Finally, Jacob obtained the blessing for which he had wrestled with the Lord, namely, "power with God and with men," to overcome the unappeasable ferocious

Esau and his four hundred men with genuine humility and divine love.

At dawn, as Jacob "passed over Penuel the sun rose upon him" (Gen 32:31). Equipped with the newly acquired divine gift of power to overcome with genuine humility and divine love, Jacob, now the newborn Israel, "lifted up his eyes, and looked, and, behold, Esau came, and with him four hundred men" (Gen 33:1). Showing no sign whatever of panic, Jacob advanced toward them courageously "like a prince" with the glory of the Lord, whom he saw face to face, reflecting over his face, and the all-conquering love of God glowing within. As he was approaching Esau, he bowed himself down to the ground seven times with utmost humility, "until he came near to his brother" (Gen 33:3). Seeing this, the hardened heart of Esau, who was watching, melted like wax before the blazing sun, and "he ran to meet" Jacob, and "embraced him, and fell on his neck, and kissed him: and they wept" (Gen 33:4).

It is to this undreamt-of peace and reconciliation that came about between the discordant brothers that the beloved alludes in the imagery under consideration, by her words, "Or ever I was aware, my soul made me like the chariots of Amminadib", followed by the uproarious words, "Return, return ... return, return," by which the so-called nut trees welcome her back. In fact, the ultimate objective of Jacob in wrestling with God throughout the preceding night was that he should find the grace in the eyes of Esau to return in peace to his father's house. (For details, cf. the exegetical comment on 6: 10-13, in the commentary section of this book).

Discernibly, allusion to the above stated episode is made here as the basis for the disclosure of the primitive Jewish Christian church's first ever missionary trip to the so-called garden of hard nut trees, namely, to the Gentiles, with the gospel of peace and reconciliation in Christ, in the episode of Peter's providential trip to the household of Cornelius (cf. comment on 6:10-13, in the commentary section of this book).

3. *Certain Episodes coming within the Disclosure of Israel's Redemptive Story in the Song are Patterned after Parallel Events that took place in Jacob's life-story*

Certain episodes coming within the disclosure of the redemptive story of Israel, the church, are portrayed in the Song after the pattern of the narrative of parallel events that took place in Jacob's life story. (Explained in detail above, under the head, 'CLUES LEADING TO THE INTERPRETATION OF THE SONG ADVANCED THROUGH THIS BOOK.'

4. *Typology is used to Disclose certain Old Testament types that find fulfillment in Antitypes in the Risen Christ and the Primitive Jewish Christian Church*

Typology is used in the Song to disclose certain Old Testament types finding their fulfillment in the risen Christ, and in the primitive Jewish Christian church.

For instance, the expression, "the cunning workman," that occurs in the statement, "the joints of thy thighs are like jewels, the work of the hands of a cunning workman" (7:1b), alludes, first, to the Lord who touched the sinew of Jacob's thigh and put it out of joint; second, to Bezaleel, the "cunning workman" who cut and engraved jewels with the names of the twelve tribes of the children of Israel, "like the engraving of a signet," and set in four rows in the breastplate and ephod of the shoulders of Aaron, the high Priest (cf. comment on 1:10 and 7:1 with Exod 28:9:21 and 31:1-4). Antitypically, the risen Christ was the "cunning workman," and the rounded thigh joints of the church, the body of Christ, stated to be "jewels," were the apostles whom He had gifted with the apostolic ministry gift (Eph 4:11), "of the care of all the churches" (2 Cor 11:28), to ensure that "the whole body" remains "fitly joined together" (Eph 4:16); a ministry that constrained them to walk up and down restlessly, throughout the length and breadth of the Jewish and Gentile lands, to the extent that their thigh joints become beautifully and enduringly rounded.

Likewise, in 8:6, the consummated primitive Jewish Christian church appeals to the Lord, her High Priest, to set herself as the antitype of one of the above stated jewels upon His heart and upon

His shoulders, saying, "Set me as a seal upon thine heart, as a seal upon thine arm: for love is strong as death" (cf. exegetical comment on 8:6).

5. *The Emphasis throughout the Disclosure is on Faith as the Sole Criterion for Salvation*

The emphasis throughout the disclosure in the Song is on faith as the sole criterion for the salvation of souls. It shows demonstratively the beloved (church) growing up and developing as the body of Christ, and her members performing exploits of faith by the operation of the charismatic gifts that were imparted to them severally by the indwelling Christ, during the epochs in her redemptive story that were marked for possessing faith. To the contrary, the ritualistic worship of burning superabundant quantities of incense that she vainly performed, during the epochs in her redemptive story, which were marked for unbelief, is satirically exposed.

XII. THE CONSTANT SHIFT OF MOTIFS IN THE SONG

The constant shift of motifs from unit to unit, or from verse to verse, that takes place in the Song has led to the misconception that the Song is a collection of numerous love poems of the ancient pagan cultures. It is not so. The changing motifs are the backdrop of the historical landmarks in the redemptive story of Israel that are being disclosed in chronological sequence.

Keeping the foregoing in mind, the reader must perceive each unit and verse that occurs in a changed motif as the depiction of the next historical landmark in Israel's redemptive story. As demonstrated, the disclosure begins from the episode of the birth of Israel, the church of the regenerated, in Jacob, and ends with the portrayal of the kingdom of God being taken away from Israel and given over to the Gentiles (cf. Matt 21:43).

No doubt, the disclosures are being made in highly sophisticated figures of speech. Even so, this shall not pose difficulty for those who are cognizant of the principal historical landmarks in Israel's redemptive story. Such shall be able to easily discern, adjudge and identify the events that are portrayed in chronological sequence.

XIII. THE SONG AS A PROPHETIC MONODRAMA IN COMPOSITION

A monodrama is a dramatic composition written in prose or verse for performance by one performer. In other words, in a monodrama one actor plays the parts of all the actors who are given divergent parts to play. This is not to say that the Song is a monodrama; only that its composition is in the form of a monodrama. For one Actor, viz., the Spirit of Christ who was in Solomon, composes and articulates the monologues, dialogues, and exclamatory remarks constituting the Song that are purported to have been spoken by the Lover, the beloved, the daughters of Jerusalem, and onlookers, in alternation.

It needs to be borne in mind, in this regard, that none of the pre-Solomonic historical characters appearing in the guise of the beloved, in the Song, were alive when the Spirit of Christ sang the Song by the mouth of Solomon. They had run their race, finished their course, and had gone to be with the Lord in heaven. Neither were any of the post-Solomonic characters appearing in the guise of the beloved in the Song alive when the Spirit of Christ sang the Song by the mouth of Solomon. They were yet to be born. It emerges from this that all the words and expressions attributed to the different characters in the Song are being constructed and articulated by the Spirit of the pre-incarnate Christ who was in Solomon.

There is no parallel for this type of prophetic monodrama anywhere else in the Scriptures, excepting for the words of the pre-incarnate Christ who speaks about Himself, in the first person singular, found in a number of places in the prophetic books, mainly, in Isaiah.

To cite a few instances, in Isa 48:16, the pre-incarnate Christ speaks prophetically, by the mouth of Isaiah, saying, "Come ye near unto me, hear ye this; I have not spoken in secret from the beginning; from the time that it was, there am I: and now the Lord God, and his spirit, hath sent me." After that, in Isa 49:1-2, He speaks beforehand about His incarnation, saying, "The Lord hath called me from the womb; from the bowels of my mother hath he made mention of my name. And he hath made my mouth like a sharp sword." Again, in Isa 50: 6, He speaks about the unbearable insults and injuries that He was to suffer vicariously, saying, "I gave my back to the smiters, and my cheeks to them that plucked off the hair: I hid not my face from shame and spitting."

All the words and expressions constituting the Song, be it monologues, dialogues, or exclamatory remarks, occur similar to the above quoted prophetic words of our Lord found in the book of Isaiah.

XIV. THE HOUSEHOLD OF GOD

The Heb. word '*bayith*,' translated "house" in the Song can also be translated 'household.' The word occurs only in 3:4 and 8:2. The context shows clearly that the occurrence of the word in both these places is in the sense of a 'household.' In 3:4 the beloved says, "I found him whom my soul loveth: I held him, and would not let him go, until I had brought him into my mother's house(hold)." The beloved who speaks these words is the body of the elect from among the Israelites in the Egyptian captivity. She means, by these words, that she found out the Lord whom she had lost from her hold of faith, during the prolonged period of her captivity, and held Him "within the encircling clutch of her arms"[15] as Jacob did at Peniel, and would not let Him go out of her hold until she had brought Him by force into her mother's house(hold).

On the other hand, in the latter half of the Song, in 8:1-3, the beloved expresses her deep anguish over her total inability to bring the Lord into her mother's house(hold), and be taught by Him therein.

The foregoing episodes clearly show that the beloved belonged to a household whose members were not opposed to her love affair in the first instance, narrated in 3:4, but were totally opposed to it by the time of the second instance, narrated in 8:1-3.

The household is the household of God, namely, of the covenantee. That being the case, all the characters who appear in the Song, as stated, are members of the household of God, with the exception of the "companions" of 1:7, 8:13, and the "friends"

---

[15] G. Lloyd Carr, *op. cit.*, p.110.

or "beloveds" of 5:1. The group of people whom the beloved addresses by the term, "my mother's household," are the natural seed of the covenant; her brethren according to the flesh. The story in the Song is all about the bitter jealousy and strife that arose of the natural seed of the covenant against the (beloved) church, particularly in the latter half of the Song. It is imperative therefore for those who wish to understand the content of the prophetic disclosure in the Song to be equipped with prior working knowledge of the household of God, and of the jealousy and strife that had developed of the natural Israel against the spiritual, described in detail below:

> As we have pointed out earlier, the idea of a household of God had originated and developed as the natural outcome of the covenant concept. The very purpose of God in making the covenant with Abraham and his seed was to generate children unto Him through regeneration. Consequently, God who begot children unto Him in the covenant through regeneration was duly recognized as the Father, and the covenant in which God generated children unto Him was duly recognized as the mother. And the children that were born to Him in the covenant, by regeneration, were duly recognized as the legitimate children of God.

The latter half of the Song discloses the severe doctrinal rift that came to exist between the natural seed of the covenant, who had held that adherence to the stipulations of the Mosaic covenant of the law is the only means of salvation, and the spiritual seed, who had held that faith in Jesus of Nazareth as being Messiah and Lord is the only means of salvation.

In fact, the rift between the natural and spiritual seeds of the covenant had existed from the very beginning for the following reasons, but it surfaced in its vicious murderous form only after the death and resurrection of the Messiah.

1. *The Choice from the Household of Jacob and his Seed exclusively to be the Covenantee gave rise to Jealousy and Strife*

Even though God made the covenant with Abraham and his seed, He had chosen from among the seed of Abraham only Jacob, his grandson in Isaac, and his seed, to live under the covenant. God had made this fact known to Abraham beforehand by saying, "in Isaac shall thy seed be called" (Gen 21: 12). Accordingly, when Rebecca, the wife of Isaac, was great with twins, "that the purpose of God according to election might stand, ... it was said unto her, 'the elder shall serve the younger," (Rom 9:11, 12, with Gen 25:22-23).

2. *The Election of only a few from the Multitude of Jacob's seed to be made Faithful by Regeneration and become the Heirs of Promise gave Occasion to the rest of Israel to Hate and Spite His church that comprised of the Elected and Regenerated Ones*

Though God chose Jacob, and his seed from among the posterity of Abraham to live under the covenant, He had chosen only a few from among them, countless as they had been as the "sand which is upon the seashore," to be made faithful by regeneration, and to become sons and heirs of His promise.

J. I. Packer elucidates the point in the following words:

> While God has chosen the whole nation to live under the privileges of the covenant, he had chosen only some of them (those made faithful by regeneration) to inherit the riches of the relationship to himself, which the covenant held out.[16]

These words of Packer are in perfect consonance with Paul's words in Rom 9: 6-8

> They are not all Israel, which are of Israel: Neither, because they are the seed of Abraham, are they all children: but, In Isaac shall thy seed be called. That is, they which are the children of the flesh, these are not the children of God: but the children of the promise are counted for the seed.

By choosing only a few from among the countless multitudes of the seed of Jacob, which were as the sand of the seashore, to be made faithful by regeneration and become His sons and heirs according to His promise, God Himself, so to say, gave occasion to the rest of Israel, the natural seed of the covenant, to hate and spite the church that comprised of the regenerated ones.

---

[16] J.D. Douglas and others, *The New Bible Dictionary*, Leicester, U.K: The Inter-Varsity Press; Reprinted, Bombay: Pillar Projects, 1990. pp. 315, 316.

3. *The Contrariety of natures between the Natural and the Spiritual Seeds of the Covenant gave rise to further Jealousy and Strife*

The reason for the constant jealousy and strife that had surfaced between the natural and the spiritual seeds of the covenant were rooted in the inherent contrariety of natures between the two, even as Paul writes to the Galatians, "The flesh lusteth against the Spirit, and the Spirit against the flesh: and these are contrary the one to the other" (Gal 5:17). Comparing the natural Israel of his day, which persecuted the church of Christ, to Ishmael who persecuted Isaac, Paul writes, "as then he that was born after the flesh persecuted him that was born after the Spirit, even so it is now" (Gal 4:29).

We know how Joseph's brothers hated him in spite of his innocence, and even went to the extent of killing or selling him. This type of jealousy and hatred of the carnal seed against the spiritual had continued to exist throughout the Old Testament dispensation. The author of the Epistle to the Hebrews cites instances of the cruelties perpetrated upon the children of God, by the unregenerate Israelites in the Old Testament dispensation, saying:

> Others were tortured, not accepting deliverance; that they might obtain a better resurrection: and others had trial of cruel mockings and scourgings, yea, moreover of bonds and imprisonment: They were stoned, they were sawn asunder, were tempted, were slain with the sword: they wandered about in sheepskins and goatskins; being destitute, afflicted, tormented; (of whom the world was not worthy:) they wandered in deserts, and in mountains, and in dens and caves of the earth. Heb 11:35-38

4. *The Addition of the Sinai Covenant to the existing Abrahamic Covenant of Promise gave room for the Natural Seed to gain an upper hand over the Spiritual*

Paul writes categorically that "the law is not of faith" (Gal 3:12), and that "by the deeds of the law there shall no flesh be justified in his (God's) sight" (Rom 3:20). The question arises from the above, if it was not for the purpose of justification before God, for what other purpose, then, was the Sinai covenant of the law added to the existing Abrahamic covenant of promise? Paul himself answers the question, saying; the law "was added because of transgressions, till the seed (Christ) should come to whom the promise was made" (Gal 3:19). He meant to say by this that the Sinai covenant was given as an interim measure to keep transgressors from creating anarchy and havoc in the society; in other words, the law was given to maintain law and order.

The foregoing gives rise to yet another question, to wit, who were those transgressors who had to be kept under control by these externally imposed stringent laws? Were they the children of God who were made faithful by regeneration, or the unregenerate seed of the covenant, who were prone to transgress, countless, as they had been, "as the sand which is upon the seashore"? Certainly, the transgressors were not the children of God, who were but a negligible few. Moreover, they were a law unto themselves. Those who had to be kept under restraint with severe impunity, by the externally imposed stringent laws were the natural seed of the covenant, who are being termed by the beloved in 3:4 and 8:2, as "my mother's house(hold)." They were inclined by nature to betake themselves to violence and crime. The Sinai covenant was added to keep them under restraint with impunity, as Paul clearly states in 1 Tim 1:9-10, saying:

> The law is not made for a righteous man, but for the lawless and disobedient, for the ungodly and for sinners, for unholy and profane, for murderers of fathers and murderers of mothers, for manslayers, for whoremongers, for them that defile themselves with mankind, for menstealers, for liars, for perjured persons, and if there be any other thing that is contrary to sound doctrine.

God's purpose in giving the Sinai covenant will become clearer on viewing it from the standpoint of the exigency that called for its promulgation. In the course of the four centuries of the Egyptian captivity, the children of Israel had multiplied into a great nation, in fulfillment of the purpose for which the Lord had settled them in that country (cf. Gen 15:13,14). After the Lord liberated them from the captivity and brought them down to Sinai, the newly liberated nation required a constitution and a legal code. Over and above, they required a religious code as well since they were the chosen people of God. The Sinai covenant of the law was promulgated to meet these exigencies.

On taking into consideration all the above stated factors, one might safely conclude that the Sinai covenant was no more than an instrument of governance for governing the newly formed theocratic state of Israel.

But the natural seed of the covenant failed to understand that the Sinai covenant was promulgated for the above stated purposes. Instead they took for granted that the law was given as the means for the salvation of their souls. Basing on this misconception, the natural seed of the covenant that kept the law strictly under the stipulations of the Sinai covenant began to pose themselves as more righteous and holier than the rest of the children of Israel with a pharisaical zeal, and to persecute the spiritual seed, which refused to endorse their distorted religious viewpoints. Thus the natural seed gained an upper hand over the spiritual seed with the addition of the Sinai covenant to the existing Abrahamic covenant of promise.

5. ***After the Advent of the Holy Spirit on the day of Pentecost, the bone of contention between the Natural and the Spiritual Seeds turned out to be whether the means of salvation is receiving Jesus of Nazareth by faith as Christ and Lord or observing the stipulations of the Mosaic Law***

After the advent of the Holy Spirit on the day of Pentecost, the primitive Jewish Christian church began to contend with the unbelieving Jews with pricking words, like:

> Be it known unto you all, and to all the people of Israel, that by the name of Jesus Christ of Nazareth, whom ye crucified, whom God raised from the dead, even by him doth this man (the lame man who was made whole) stand here before you whole. .... Neither is there salvation in any other: for there is none other name under heaven given among men, whereby we must be saved. (Paraphrase mine). Acts 4:10-12.

The natural Israel, on the other hand, contended vehemently that meticulous observation of the stipulations of the laws of the Mosaic covenant is the only means for the salvation of souls. Thus the means of salvation became the bitter bone of contention between the primitive Jewish Christian church and the natural Israel whom the beloved (church) addresses by the term, "my mother's house (hold), in 8:1-2.

It was on account of this raging bone of bitter contention over the means of salvation that the rulers of the decadent Judaism, (termed in the Song as "watchmen" and "keepers of the walls), beat and wounded the beloved (church), no sooner did she open the closed door of the decadent Judaism and crossed over the walls (law), in her ardent determination to seek and find out her physically absent risen Lord (cf. comment on 5:7). It was also on account of the selfsame bone of bitter contention that the Judaical rulers strictly debarred the beloved (church) from bringing the Lord (her Lover) into her "mother's house(hold)" as portrayed in 8:1-3 (cf. exegetical comment on 3:4 and 8:2, in the Commentary section of this book).

6. *The Constituent Members of the Household of God appearing in the Song*

a. *The Father/Lover*

The Lord who begets the children of God through regeneration in the Abrahamic covenant of promise is both the Father and the Lover in the Song. As the conception and new birth process take place in the invisible realm of the Spirit, the term "father" does not occur anywhere in the Song. However, in 8:5 the Father recalls the memory of His beloved to the place where her mother (the Abrahamic Covenant) had conceived in Him and gave birth to her, saying, "I raised thee up under the apple tree: there thy mother brought thee forth: there she brought thee forth that bare thee." As the Lord who speaks these words is the Father, it emerges that the Father and the Lover are the Lord Himself. Unfortunately, as pointed out at the outset, under the head, 'The Title and Authorship of the Song,' the passage has been mired in controversy due to the masculine suffixes appearing in the Masoretic Text, instead of the feminine, as found in the Old Syriac Version. (For the proper exegetical comment on the passage, see the Commentary section of this book).

The term, "prince's daughter," that the Lord uses to address the beloved (church) in 7:1 is in recognition of the fact that she has become the true daughter of Jacob, her earthly forbear, who was born of God into an Israel of God at Peniel, by the power he had with God and men as a "prince" and had prevailed (cf. Gn. 32:28).

b. The Mother

Wherever the term, "mother," occurs in the Song, it refers to the Abrahamic covenant of promise. In 8:1 the beloved speaks of the covenant as "my mother," and in 3:4 and 8:2 she speaks of the body of the natural seed of the covenant as "my mother's house(hold)." In 6:9 the Lord speaks of the covenant as "her (the beloved's) mother" and in 8:5 as "thy (the beloved's) mother." (Paraphrase mine). Further, the synonyms for mother occur, such as, "her that conceived me," in 3:4; "her that bare her," in 6:9; and, "she brought thee forth," in 8:5.

Altogether, the term "mother" occurs seven times in the Song (1:6; 3:4; 3:11; 6:9; 8:1, 2, 5). In addition, the synonymous terms and expressions that refer to the mother occur three times (3:4; 6:9; 8:5).

c. The Beloved

(Explained above in detail, under the head, VII, THE THEME OF THE SONG).

d. "My Mother's House(hold)"

As stated above, in 3:4 and 8:3 the beloved uses the term, "my mother's house(hold)" to speak of the body of the natural seed of the covenant.

To reiterate, in 3:4, i.e., in the Old Testament division of the Song, when the beloved found out her missing Lord (her Lover), whom her soul loved, she held Him and would not let Him go, until she had brought Him by force (not by faith), in the Sinai covenant, into her mother's household that had comprised of her brethren according to the flesh. It implies that her mother's household received the Lord without reluctance or resistance of any sort, when the beloved brought Him by force in the Sinai covenant. On the other hand, in 8:1-3, i.e., in the New Testament division of the Song, the beloved's mother's household, namely, the decadent Judaism of the time that had comprised of her brethren according to the flesh, had debarred her from bringing the Lord within. The reason for their refusal was that her Lover was not a prophet "like unto" her brother Moses, as He ought to have been according to the Messianic prophecy of Deut 18:18. Consequently, as Paul does in Rom 9:1ff. the beloved expresses her deep anguish over her inability to bring the Lord into her mother's household, saying,

> O that thou wert as my brother, that sucked the breasts of my mother!
>
> When I should find thee without, I would kiss thee; yea, I should not be despised. I would lead thee, and bring thee into my mother's house.

e. The Watchmen and Keepers of the Walls

The first time that the "watchmen" appear in the Song is in 3:3, i.e., in the Old Testament division of the Song. The context shows that the watchmen who appeared there were Moses and Aaron.

As the beloved was groping in the dark in search of her missing Lord in the streets and squares of Ramses, the capital city of Egypt, the watchmen, i.e., Moses who was commissioned and sent by the Lord from Horeb (cf. 2:17), along with Aaron, found her out. Scarcely had she passed from them that she found him whom her soul loves. Forthwith, she "held him and would not let him go," as Jacob did at Peniel, until she had brought him by force into her mother's household, in the Sinai covenant. (Cf. comment on 2:17, and 3:1-4, in the Commentary section of this book).

On the other hand, in 5:1-7, i.e., in the New Testament division of the Song, "the watchmen," namely, the rulers of the decadent Judaism who sat at that time in the seat of Moses and Aaron, found out the beloved as she opened the closed door of the decadent Judaism, and trespassed the "walls," to wit, the laws. "The watchmen that went about the city (of Jerusalem) found me," she bemoans ruefully, "they smote me, they wounded me; the keepers of the walls took away my veil from me."

This shows that the Jewish rulers who sat in the seat of Moses and Aaron during the primitive Jewish Christian church period were persecuting monsters, in sharp contrast to Moses and Aaron, who had been helpful guides.

f. The Daughters of Jerusalem

The appellative, "daughters of Jerusalem," occur in the Song synonymous with its singular form, "daughter of Jerusalem;" the appellation that occurs frequently in prophetic writings. The plural form is used in the Song to avoid the inconsistency that would arise by according the concept of singularity to them, on account of two reasons. First, the concept, "We, being many, are one body in Christ" (Rom 12:5), is applicable only to the beloved (church). Second, in 6:9, singularity is accorded to the beloved church, by the words, "My dove, my undefiled is but one; she is the only one of her mother, she is the choice one of her that bare her."

The appellative, "daughters of Jerusalem" implies that "Jerusalem" is the name of their mother. However, going by Paul's allegory, their mother is not the "Jerusalem, which is from above," but "Jerusalem which" then was, and is "in bondage with her children" (Gal 4:25). In other words, the so-called "daughters of Jerusalem" were the natural seed of the covenant.

The natural seeds were timid and touchy by nature, contrary to the beloved Spirit-filled church, which was fearless and "terrible" as a triumphant army that marches ahead undauntedly with all of her banners of divine love unfurled (6:4,10). It is to reflect this inherent characteristic of timidity of the daughters of Jerusalem, to wit, of the natural, unregenerate seed of the covenant, that the Spirit pairs them with the characteristically timid gazelles of the field (i.e., of the wilds regions), and causes the beloved church to adjure them, saying, "I charge you, O ye daughters of Jerusalem, by the roes, and by the hinds of the field, that ye stir not up, nor awake my love" 'affair (with the Lord) until it is pleased' (2:7; 3:5; 8:4; paraphrase mine).

However, on viewing the adjuration from the perspective of the adolescent church, she too was timid and touchy, to an extent. Therefore, the purpose of putting the adjuration in her mouth from time to time is also to reflect the degree of timidity, and touchiness that had still ruled her heart (cf. comment on 2:7; 3:5; cf. 8:4).

But, in the New Testament dispensation, the attitude of the daughters of Jerusalem towards the church and vice versa undergoes a positive change. Seeing the watchmen and keepers of the walls beating, wounding, and humiliating the beloved (church), who, in their eyes, was "the fairest among women," the daughters of Jerusalem become sympathetic towards her. Consequently, the beloved (church) seeks their help and cooperation, and begs them urgently that if they happen to find her beloved Lord, (in worship and prayer), they should tell Him that she is sick of love for Him (5:8). The urgency and force with which the beloved church implores for their help and cooperation, coupled with the beauty of the indwelling Lord outshining in the beloved church's person, arouses inquisitiveness in their hearts to know what is so peculiar in her Lover that makes her adjure them so authoritatively. "What is thy beloved more than another beloved, O thou fairest among women?" ask the daughters of Jerusalem, "what is thy beloved more than another beloved, that thou dost so charge us?" This gives the beloved (church) the God-given opportunity to bear a most powerful and effective, spirit-filled witness concerning the glories of the Lord's person and attributes, exactly as did Peter, on the day of Pentecost, "standing up with the eleven," (cf. comment on 5: 10-16, with Acts 2:14). Deeply "pricked in their heart" (Acts 2:37), the daughters of Jerusalem desire to join the beloved church in her (prayerful) search for her physically absent risen Lord, saying, "Whither is thy beloved gone (lit.turned his face), O thou fairest among women? Whither is thy beloved turned aside? that we may seek him with thee" (6:1). (Cf. comment on 6:1, in the commentary section of this book).

Needless to say, the foregoing occurs as a futuristic prophecy concerning the way in which the three thousand Jews of the city of Jerusalem turned to the Lord on the day of Pentecost in response to the apostolic witness and call.

g. The Virgins and Daughters

The terms "virgins," (1:3; 6:8), and "daughters" (6:9), also occur in the Song synonymous with the idiomatic expression, "daughter of Jerusalem," as they occur in 2 Kgs 19:21, "the virgin the daughter of Zion hath despised thee... the daughter of Jerusalem hath shaken her head at thee." Cf. also, "The virgin daughter of my people is broken" (Jer 14:17). "The Lord hath trodden the virgin, the daughter of Judah" (Lam 1:15).

The expression, "without number" (6:8), refers to the 'innumerableness' of the children of Israel, who were countless as the sand of the seashore (Gen 22:17; 2 Sam 17:11). The allied expression, "the daughters saw her, and blessed her" (6:9), occurs parallel to the words of Leah found in Gen. 30:13, "happy am I, for the daughters will call me blessed."

h. The Companions and Friends

The only non–Jewish people who appear in the Song are the "companions" (1:8; 8:13) and "friends" (5:2). These are not members of the household of God, but the elect of God from among the Gentiles. (See comment on vv. 1:7-8; 4:16-5:1, and 8:13).

XV. THE ARTFUL USE OF FIGURES OF SPEECH IN THE SONG

The Song is composed of an assortment of sophisticated figures of speech, as stated at the outset, with a few exceptions. The way in which figures of speech are used in the Song differs drastically from the conventional ways in which they are used in the secular literatures of the world.

1. The Similes in the Song

In the similes occurring in the Song, the objects that the Spirit invokes in the form of figures of speech for comparison are not imaginary, but actual facts pertaining to the redemptive history of Israel taken mostly from the pre-Solomonic books of the Old Testament. On the other hand, the subjects, for the sake of which, such Biblical facts are invoked in the form of figures of speech, are imaginary. This is quite consistent, because literally speaking, Israel, the church of the regenerated, which is the subject of discussion, is not a woman. It is only in an imaginary or ideal sense that the church is pictured as a woman, namely, the bride/ spouse of the Lord. Further, it is in an ideal sense that the church is portrayed in the Song as the body of Christ.

Let us take vv. 4:1b and 2, for instance:

4: 1.b Thy hair is as a flock of goats,
that appear from mount Gilead

2. Thy teeth are like a flock of sheep that are even shorn,
which came up from the washing;
whereof every one bear twins,
and none is barren among them.

The figure of "a flock of goats that appear from mount Gilead" or as NIV, "a flock of goats descending from mount Gilead" (1b) is a figurative description of an actual historic event, namely, of Israel, the flock of God, descending the slopes of mount Gilead poised to cross over Jordan into the Promised Land, under the captaincy of Joshua. Whereas the subject, namely, the flowing hair of the beloved (church), for the sake of illustrating the beauty of which, the said triumphant march of Israel down the slopes of mount Gilead is invoked in the form of a figure, is imaginary. For, literally speaking, the church was neither a woman, nor did it possess hair. For the reason that the flock of God that descended the slopes of mount Gilead had comprised solely of the unregenerate and uncircumcised young men born and brought up in the wilderness, they are described as a flock of black goats.

Likewise, the figure being invoked by the Spirit of "a flock of sheep that are even shorn, which came up from the washing" (2a) occurs as a figurative description of the selfsame flock of God. After having been transformed into a flock of snow-white ewes, in the course of its miraculous passage through the dry bed of the river Jordan, and after having come up from the ravines of the river, the flock of God is now encamped at Gilgal. The expression, "that are even shorn," is a figurative description of the act of Joshua of making sharp knives and circumcising every one of the young men who belonged to the flock, evenly or indiscriminately, during the flock's encampment at Gilgal.

This description of the flock of God, that had achieved its long cherished hope of crossing over Jordan into the Promised Land, and undergone circumcision at their base-camp at Gilgal, as the smiling teeth of the body of Christ, is most befitting. Because, naturally, the mouths of every one of the men that comprised the flock must have been filled with the laughter of spiritual liberty and joyful singing (cf. Ps.126:2). Further, each of them must have been exhibiting the entire rows of their teeth in the course of their spontaneous Spirit-filled laughter and singing.

Literally speaking, Israel, the church of the regenerated did not possess teeth. Neither did she possess the lips, temples, neck, and breasts that are being attributed to her in vv. 4:1-5. Nor did she possess the bodily parts that are being attributed to her in the future sections, 6:4-7 and 7:1-9. It is the 'faithful men' of Israel in performance of the daring acts of crossing over the flooded river Jordan, and going up deep into the Canaanite territory at Gilgal, by the operation of the charismatic gifts of faith and power, on behalf of the whole church, that are described as being the smiling teeth of the body of Christ. As stated, this description occurs precisely in the sense in which Paul describes the Spirit-filled church, as the body of Christ possessed with divergent members according to the charismatic gifts with which they were endued.

The curious statement, "whereof every one bear twins, and none is barren among them," has no relevance whatsoever to the beloved church's teeth or to the men of Israel who are thought of as a flock of sheep. The statement is being made with reference to Rahel (Anglicized as Rachel), the fairer and hence the favourite wife of Jacob, who had been barren.

In fact, there is the presence here of a play on words using the dual meanings of the Heb. word '*rahel.*' Literally, *rahel* means "sheep" or ewe. However, "*Rahel*" (Anglicized as Rachel) was also the name that Laban gave to his younger daughter, whom Jacob later married. As we all know, Rahel happened to be barren. It is with regard to the barren 'rahels' (Heb.*rahelim*) that the Song says, "everyone bear twins and none is barren among them." ("The passive participle feminine plural *qesubot,* is taken here as the poetic equivalent of the common term *rehelim* used in the otherwise identical parallel in 6:6.")[17]

[17] Marvin H. Pope, *The Anchor Bible, Song of Songs:* New York, Doubleday & Company, 1977, p.461.

While Leah went on bearing more and more children unto Jacob and winning his favour, Rahel (Rachel) continued to remain barren. Consequently, the question of bearing larger number of children unto Jacob, and winning his favour thereby became a bone of contention between the two sisters. Discernibly, Rahel and Leah are the "little" and older sisters alluded to in vv. 8:8-10 (cf. Gen 29:31-30:24). While Rachel, the "little" sister had no "breasts" (seed), Leah, the older, boastfully claims that her breasts were as large as towers, adding, "then was I in his eyes as one that found favor" (cf. comment on 8:8-10).

Enraged with jealousy, Rahel finally went to Jacob one day, and quarreled with him, saying, "Give me children, or else I die." Jacob got wild. "Am I in God's stead," he shouted, "who hath withheld from thee the fruit of the womb" (Gen 30:1-2). Finding no way to bear children to be called her own, Rahel, following Leah's example, gave her maid Bilhah to Jacob, and thereby possessed two sons, named Dan, and Naphtali. At last God hearkened to Rahel's prayer and gave her a son, whom she called Joseph. Later on, after Jacob's return to Canaan, the Lord gave Rahel one more son, at whose birth she died. As her soul was departing, she called the child's name *Benoni*, 'the son of my sorrow.' Jacob later renamed him *Benjamin*, 'the son of the right hand.'

The underlying idea of the statement, "every one bear twins, and none is barren among them," is the rejuvenating power of the faith generated in the hearts of every one of the flock of black goats, by the miraculous crossing of Jordan. The rejuvenating power generated in their hearts had been such that it turned every one of them into snow-white Rahels (ewes) that bear twins, none having been left barren among them.

Taking note of this peculiarity in the use of figures of speech in the Song, Robert Gordis, makes the following observation:

> When the poet uses a figure of speech, he often continues to elaborate upon it for its own sake without reference to the subject for the sake of which it was invoked. The figure, so to speak, develops its own momentum, and has its own independent existence.[18]

---

[18] Robert Gordis, *op. cit.,* p. 383.

2. *The Metaphors in the Song*

The metaphors occurring in the Song are far more complex and involved than similes. The simplest among them is the statement, "Your eyes are doves" (1:16; 4:1, RV, NIV, JB). AV's, "thou hast dove's eyes" is interpretative. The symbolic word, "doves," occurs in the Song in the same sense in which it occurs elsewhere in the scriptures, i.e., as a symbol for the Holy Spirit (cf. Matt 3:16). The metaphor signifies that 'the Holy Spirit functions as your eyes,' or that the Holy Spirit of God has opened your eyes of understanding to perceive matters pertaining to God and to the spiritual realm. The metaphor is reminiscent of the words that our Lord spoke to Nicodemus, saying, "Verily, verily, I say unto thee, Except a man be born again, he cannot see the kingdom of God" (John 3:3).

The first occurrence of the metaphor is in 1:15. There it occurs with reference to the acuity of the spiritual vision that the patriarchal church had possessed. Its second occurrence is in 4:1a. There it occurs with reference to the clarity of the spiritual vision possessed by Joshua and his men. However, a "veil" had been remaining before the eyes of Joshua and his men. Cf. "your eyes behind your veil are doves" (4:1, NIV, JB). It signifies that, in spite of the acuity of the spiritual vision that Joshua and his men had possessed, there was still a veil of a certain degree of spiritual ignorance that hindered them from beholding the Lord in the fullness of His glorious person. The reason for this was the fact that they were part and parcel of the Old Testament dispensation of the law. As Paul rightly observes, whenever "Moses is read, the vail" remains upon the reader's heart (2 Cor 3:15). But "when it shall turn to the Lord, the veil shall be taken away" (2 Cor 3:16). Significantly, the figure of a "veil" occurs only here and in 1:7 in the Old Testament division, and in 5:7 and 6:7 in the New Testament division, of the Song. (Cf. exegetical comment on 1:7; 5:7 and 6:7).

The rest of the metaphors occurring in the Song are complex on account of the use of obscure symbolic words and expressions in them. For instance:

> A bundle of myrrh is my wellbeloved unto me;
> He shall lie all night betwixt my breasts. 1:13

Here, the expressions "a bundle of myrrh" and "breasts," are symbolic. That being the case, the metaphor can be deciphered only if the meanings of these symbolic words are ascertained first. (Cf. exegetical comment on 1:13 and notes below on the symbolic word "breasts")

3. *The Symbolism in the Song*

On the advantage of the use of symbolism over allegory in Heb. poetry, Gordis says:

> It is of the essence of poetry that it employs symbolism to express nuances beyond the power of exact definition. .... Symbolism is much more profound than allegory. In allegory the imaginary figures that are chosen are equivalent for real characters and objects involved have no independent reality of their own. The language of symbolism, on the other hand, is superior to literal speech as well, because its elements possess both existential reality, and representational character.[19]

Symbolism is used in the Song more extensively than other types of figures of speech. The symbolic words and expressions occurring frequently in the Song are, lily, henna flower, roes, twins, black, white, goats, sheep, garden, gardens, pomegranate, aromatic spices, ointment, grapevine, clusters, vineyard, tamar, breasts, hair, teeth, neck, and so on. These symbolic words perform the function of alphabets in the symbolic language that is being used in the Song. The keys to understand the intended meaning of each of these symbolic words and expressions are being furnished internally in one of the several places where each of them occurs in the Song. That being the case, attribution of meanings of one's own imaginative ingenuity to them is unwarranted. Let us take for example the symbolic word, "lily."

a. The Symbolic word "Lily"

The symbolic word "lily" occurs eight times in the Song; four times in the Old (2:1, 2,16; 4:5) and four times in the New (5:13; 6:2,3; 7:2) Testament divisions of the Song. Out of these, its occurrence

[19] *Ibid.*, p. 379.

in 5:13 is in association with the Lord, the Lover; "His lips like lilies," If we set this aside for separate study, there remains seven instances where the word "lily" occurs in association with Israel, the beloved. To understand the sense in which the word is used in the Song, we need to examine only the first two occurrences of the word.

The first occurrence of the word is in 2:1, where the beloved says, "I am the rose of Sharon, and the lily of the valleys." By this, it becomes clear that Israel; the Lord's beloved (church) is the lily. This is made clearer in the succeeding verse, v. 2: 2, by the declaratory statement of the Lord (the Lover) concerning Israel (His beloved), "As the lily among thorns, so is my love among the daughters."

In chronological sequence, this statement discernibly occurs at the closing period of the four centuries of Israel's Egyptian captivity, i.e., when the Egyptian taskmasters were oppressing the children of Israel. The figure of a delicate white lily flower being poked from all sides by the surrounding thorns is certainly an apt description of the intolerable oppressions that were being perpetrated upon the children of Israel by the Egyptian taskmasters. The term, "daughters," occurs synonymous to the idiomatic expression found in the prophetical books of the Old Testament and Psalms, to wit, "daughter of Egypt" (Jer 46:11). "Thorns" were a well received symbol in Israel for oppressors (cf.Num 33: 55; Jos. 23:13; Judg 2:3; 2 Sam 23:6).

(To understand the sense in which the word "lily" is used in the rest of the five occurrences of the word, i.e., in 2:16; 4:5; 6:2-3 and 7:2a, see exegetical comment on these verses, in the Commentary section of this book).

b. The Symbolic word "breasts."

The first occurrence of the symbolic word "breasts" in the Song is in a metaphorical form in 1:13:

> A bundle of myrrh is my wellbeloved unto me;
> he shall lie all night betwixt my breasts.

The statement would not pose interpretative problems of any sort to an interpreter who presumes that 'breasts' occur here in the literal sense. But, when the interpreter comes to the next occurrence of the word, in 4:5, he/she gets puzzled,

> Thy two breasts are like two young roes that are twins,
> which feed among the lilies.

The interpreter perceives that a literal interpretation does not apply here. Therefore he/she resorts to a forced interpretation. Taking for granted that the point of comparison is between the physical appearances of the beloved's breasts and that of the young gazelles, the interpreter comments evasively that the ideas of youthfulness and symmetry are meant here. However, still later, when the interpreter comes to vv. 7:7-8 and 8:8-10, he/she comes to the end of his/her wits:

(1) 7: 7. This thy stature is like to a palm tree,
And thy breasts to clusters (of grapes).
8. I said, I will go up to the palm tree,
I will take hold of the boughs thereof:
now also thy breasts shall be as clusters of the vine,
And the smell of thy nose like apples;

(2) 8: 8. We have a little sister, and she hath no breasts:
What shall we do for our sister in the day when she shall be spoken for?
9. If she be a wall, we will build upon her a palace of silver:
And if she be a door, we will enclose her with boards of cedar.
10. I am a wall, and my breasts like towers:
Then was I in his eyes as one that found favour.

These verses are contrived purposefully in the form of abstruse conundrums to bring out profound spiritual truths pertaining to the mystery of Christ esoterically. To be able to decipher them, one needs to be equipped with prior working knowledge of the purpose for which the Lord had called and separated Israel, namely, to make the Gentiles partakers of the blessing that He had promised to Abraham.

(For the solutions to each of these seemingly odd and puzzling, yet fascinating conundrums, see comments on them, in the exegetical commentary section of this book).

Our objective here is confined to show what the symbolic word "breasts" stand for. For the achievement of that objective, we need only to examine what is meant here by the statement of v. 8:9, "If she be a wall, we will build upon her a palace of silver." The Heb. word *bana* rendered "build" is used here in the sense of Gen 16:3, where Sarah prays to Abraham to go unto Hagar, "that I may be builded by her," and of Gen 30:3, where Rachel says to Jacob, "Behold my maid Bilhah, go in unto her that I may 'be built by her'" (cf. AV margin). The Heb. word *bana* used here in the verses of the Song under our present consideration is in the sense of 'to bear children and build up a house out of them.' The silver tower that the apostles and elders of the church who had gathered at Jerusalem for the first Church Council desire to build upon their "little sister," who had "no breasts," was a tower to be built up of the regenerated seed of the Gentiles for a habitation of the Lord. The older sister is Israel, the church of the regenerated, and her breasts which she boasts about, saying, "I am a wall, and my breasts like towers: then was I in his sight as one that found favour," refers to the two symmetrical towers of Judah and Israel that were built up of her spiritual seed, to be the Lord's habitation. These show that "breasts" occurs in the Song as a symbol for the body of the spiritual seed of Israel.

XVI. THE IDENTITY OF THE LOVER

The Lover's identity is disclosed through the figurative description that occurs in 3:9-11 of an object, called 'appiryon,' made by "king Solomon," for himself, followed by a royal proclamation being sent ahead of time to the "daughters of Zion" heralding the arrival of king Solomon, crowned "with the crown wherewith his mother crowned him in the day of his espousals:"

3: 9. King Solomon made himself a chariot of the wood of Lebanon.

10. He made the pillars thereof of silver,
the bottom thereof of gold, the covering of it of purple,

the midst thereof being paved with love, for the daughters of Jerusalem.

11. Go forth, O ye daughters of Zion, and behold king Solomon with the crown wherewith his mother crowned him in the day of his espousals, and in the day of the gladness of his heart.

Most of the commentators have been mistaking the *appiryon* for a literal chariot or some other sort of carriage made by the earthly king Solomon for him to ride in a royal wedding procession to Zion.

But, in reality, *appiryon* is a word of uncertain meaning. It occurs only here in the Old Testament. NIV translates the word "carriage," JB, "throne," and Carr, "palanquin." In the face of the prevailing difficulty to judge the actual meaning of the word, the only option left is to examine the context to find out, (1), whether the name "king Solomon" occurs as an actual or received name? And, (2), to what purpose did the king Solomon make the *appiryon* for himself?

1. Is "King Solomon" an Actual or a Received Name?

It becomes clear from the following facts that "King Solomon" is a received name by which the Lord (the pre-incarnate Christ), appears in the Song:

(i). From the chronological sequence of the events pertaining to the redemptive history of Israel that are described figuratively in the preceding and succeeding sections. The preceding section, 3:6-8, occurs as a satirical expose of the six hundred thousand footmen of Israel who had perished in the wilderness, consequent to the debacle of Kadesh-barnea, and the resultant curse. The first four verses of the succeeding section, 4:1-4, constitute of allusions to the prodigious acts of Joshua, Judges, David and their men, of taking possession of the Promised Land solely by faith. The verse 4:5 that follows occurs as a figurative description of the period of perfect peace and oneness between Judah and Israel that had been ushered in during the reign of the earthly king Solomon, by the exploits of the faith of Joshua, Judges, David and their men, (explained in detail below, and in the exegetical commentary section of this book). This shows that the location where "King Solomon" made the *appiryon* for himself was in the Israelite encampment somewhere over the Moab plateau where Joshua assumed the captaincy over the children of Israel, after Moses' death.

Surprisingly, no mention whatsoever is made of the king Solomon who had made the *appiryon* for himself, over the Moab plateau, nor of the royal proclamation that he had sent to the daughters of Zion, heralding his arrival, until v. 4:6. In v. 4: 6, he appears abruptly at the foot of Zion, the temple mount, declaring, "Until the day break, and the shadows flee away, I will get me to the mountain of myrrh, and to the hill of frankincense." This shows that "King Solomon's wedding procession that had begun from the Moab plateau over three centuries ago has finally arrived at Zion, the temple mount, its destination.

Concerning the significance of this declaration, Delitzsch rightly comments, "the mountain of myrrh and the hill of frankincense put us in mind of the temple where incense ... ascended up before God every morning and evening."[20] In reality, the declaration that the "king Solomon" makes of his resolve that He will get Himself to the mountain of myrrh and to the hill of frankincense, refers to the Lord's resolve to enter into and abide in the Solomonic temple, at the auspicious occasion of its dedication, in accordance with His covenant pledge. The scripture describes this landmark event, in 2 Chr 5:13,14, in the following words:

> When they lifted up their voice with the trumpets and cymbals and instruments of music, and praised the Lord, saying, For he is good; for his mercy endureth for ever: that then the house was filled with a cloud ... for the glory of the Lord had filled the house of God.

This shows that the gracious act of the Lord of condescending to abide among the people whom He had chosen for Himself is

[20] Franz Delitzch, *op.cit.*, p. 78.

the event that was alluded to in v. 3:11 as His wedding. Further, after declaring that He will get Himself to the mountain of myrrh, and to the hill of frankincense, from the succeeding section onwards, i.e., from 4:8 to the end of the Old Testament division of the Song, He changes over the epithet, "my love," by which He had been addressing His beloved (church) until then, to "my sister, my spouse," confirming thereby that His act of getting Himself to the ritualistic temple to abide among His beloved chosen regenerated people was His wedding.

The appearance of the "king Solomon" at the foot of Zion, the temple mount, over three centuries after He had made the *appiryon*, and set out of Israel's encampment over the Moab plateau, declaring that he will get himself to the ritualistic temple of Israel, reveals:

(i) That the "King Solomon" who appears in the Song as the Lover is the pre-incarnate Christ, and not the earthly king who was known by that name.

(ii) That the Lord who appears in the Song by the received name of "King Solomon" had been "the Captain of the host of the Lord" who appeared to Joshua, at a place near Jericho, on the Gilgal Jericho road (Josh 5:14,15) and led the triumphant army of Israel, during those three centuries that it took for it to arrive at Zion, the temple mount, from the Moab plateau.

(iii) That, as the Lord was an invisible, intangible Spirit, He did not travel from the Moab plateau all the way down to the foot of mount Zion in any earthly carriage called "*appiryon,*" but in the hearts of the faithful soldiers of Israel. This, in turn, proves the "*appiryon,*" to be a figurative description of the heart of faith of the soldiers of Israel wherein He abode and captained them during the intervening three centuries. (See exegetical comment on 3:9,10, in the Commentary section of this book).

Moreover, the words that the pre-incarnate Christ picks and uses to declare His resolve, namely, "Until the day break, and the shadows flee away, I will get me to the mountain of myrrh, and to the hill of frankincense," signifies the following profound facts:

(i) That He was weaving these words into the fabric of the Song out of the threads taken from the episode of Jacob's nightlong wrestle with the Lord "until the breaking of the day" (Gen 32:14).

(ii) That, He was using the expression taken from the narrative of the Peniel episode, "until the day break," to show that the Solomonic epoch in which He was getting Himself into Israel's ritualistic temple was a period of spiritual darkness. Further, that He was getting Himself into the ritualistic temple to wrestle in the Spirit, with Israel, the beloved until the day of the true light of the knowledge of Himself and the purpose for which He had called her dawn in her heart.

(iii) That, He was picking the expressions, "the mountain of myrrh," and "the hill of frankincense," and using it in a derogatory sense to expose the dead ritualistic worship of Israel, of burning superabundant quantities of incense, under the stipulations of the Sinai covenant, for which the Solomonic temple was being dedicated.

(iv) That the pre-incarnate Christ who makes the declaration of His resolve to get Himself into the ritualistic temple of Israel, "until the day break, and the shadows flee away," was "the true Light, which lighteth every man that cometh into the world" (John 1:9).

(v) That the ritualistic system of worship of Israel under the stipulations of the Mosaic Law had been only a "shadow of heavenly things" (Heb 8:5) to come, in the fullness of time, when He will incarnate, and arise in the hearts of His elect as the "Day Star," (2 Pet 1:19), after His death and resurrection.

(vi) That He was getting Himself into the Solomonic temple which was being dedicated for Israel's ritualistic worship, fully cognizant of the gruesome fact that He would be humiliated, spat upon, tortured and unjustly crucified cruelly by its rulers after His incarnation, during His earthly ministry, to which reference is being made, in the latter half of the Song (cf. exegetical comment on 8:6-7).

2. *To What Purpose did the Lord make the* Appiryon *for Himself?*

It has already been made clear above that the *appiryon* is a figurative description of the heart of faith of the warriors of Israel prepared by the Lord to abide therein and empower them to take possession of the Promised Land, and turn Israel into a glorious theocracy. The following additional facts go to confirm this fact:

(i) The description of the *appiryon* made by the Lord, who appears as "King Solomon" in the Song, for Himself occurs immediately after the satirical expose of the six hundred thousand footmen of the valiant of Israel who had failed to accomplish the mission of taking possession of the Promised Land for which they had set out from Egypt, and instead, perished in the wilderness consequent to the debacle of Kadesh-barnea, and the resultant curse. It emerges from this, first, that the shocking debacle was the event that stirred "King Solomon" into quick action to make the *appiryon* for Himself, and second, that His purpose of making the *appiryon* for Himself was for Him to abide in the hearts of the soldiers of Israel and impart to them the charismatic gift of faith and power to take possession of the Promised Land.

(ii) The whole of the Promised Land, inclusive of Zion, had been under the occupation of the Canaanites when the "King Solomon" made the *appiryon* for Himself over the Moab plateau and sent out the royal proclamation to the daughters of Zion heralding His arrival with the crown wherewith His mother crowned Him for the day of His espousals. It took the next three centuries for Him to lead Israel to possess the whole of the Promised Land and turn it into the glorious theocratic state of peace and plenty that Israel came to be in the Solomonic era. This shows that the *appiryon* that the He made for Himself, over the Moab plateau was not any earthly carriage, but a model of the hearts of the soldiers of Israel wherein He abode and captained the battles of Israel for possession of the Promised Land during the ensuing three centuries.

(iii) The section 4:1-7 that follows immediately, after the description of the "King Solomon" making the *appiryon* for Himself over the Moab plataeu, occurs as allusions to the prodigious acts of Joshua, Judges, David, and their men, of taking possession of the promised land, part by part, solely by faith, leading to the establishment of the Solomonic theocratic state of peace and plenty. This, along with the fact that the Lord describes Joshua, Judges, David, and their men who took possession of the promised land solely by the power of faith, not as personalities, but as divergent parts of the body of Christ, such as, seeing eyes, flowing hair, smiling teeth, scarlet thread coloured lips, praising comely mouth, rosy-cheeks like halves of a pomegranate, and sturdy neck shows that He had been abiding in their hearts and using their bodies as His own during the days they fought the battles of the Lord by faith.

3. *A List of the People who are described in the Song as parts of the body of Christ.*

A check-list of the men of Israel who are described in the section, 4:1-5, not as historical personalities, but as parts of the body of Christ, is given below:

(i).	The flock of God that had rushed down the slopes of mount Gilead poised to cross over Jordan into the Promised Land.	The downward flowing graceful hair of the body of Christ. 4:1b
(ii).	The very same flock of God at its base-camp at Gilgal, after having been changed by faith into a flock of snow-white sheep, in the course of its miraculous passage by faith through the dry bed of Jordan.	The smiling teeth of the body of Christ. 4:2
(iii).	Rahab, the Canaanite harlot who received the God of Israel, by faith, as her God, and confessed Him with her lips.	The scarlet thread coloured lips of the body of Christ. 4:3a

(iv).	The men of Israel, who took the city of Jericho solely by the power of praise.	The comely mouth of the body of Christ. 4:3b
(v).	The contented generations of the Judges' period.	The temples of the body of Christ that were like halves of a pomegranate. 4:3c
(vi).	David and his thousand mighty men.	The mighty neck of the body of Christ. 4:4
(vii).	The harmoniously co-existing Judah and Israel in enjoyment of the peace and plenty of the Solomonic era.	The two harmonious co-existing breasts of the body of Christ. 4:5

4. ***Why did the Lord pave the midst of the* Appiryon *with love for the daughters of Jerusalem, rather than with love for all the families of the earth?***

To understand this, one must bear in mind the following facts:

(i). The *appiryon* made by the Lord for Himself was actually an alternative for the Ark of the Covenant. An alternative was necessitated, as the Ark of the Covenant was merely a container meant to ensconce and preserve the tables of stone engraved with the Ten Commandments given in the Sinai covenant. According to the provisions of the Sinai covenant, the invisible Lord had promised to manifest His presence only over its top cover, called the Mercy Seat, in the visible form of the *Shekinah,* and that because His Law engraved on tables of stone were ensconced within it. This means that the Ark of the Covenant was only typical of the New Covenant that the Lord had promised to make with Israel, in Jer 31:31-34 and Ezek 36:26-27, according to which He promised to write His law in their hearts by giving them a "new heart" and a "new spirit." In fact, being an invisible, intangible Spirit, the Lord normally abides only in the hearts of His faithful people, not in inanimate objects, and that to enable them to live godly lives and perform exploits of faith. The debacle of Kadesh-barnea owed to the fact that the Lord had no place to abide in the hearts of the unbelieving six hundred thousand footmen of Israel. That is why a preparation of the hearts of the soldiers of Israel was necessitated for the Lord to abide therein and captain them in their battles to take possession of the Promised Land.

Further, as Paul makes it lucid in Rom 13:10, the love of God with which Christ paves the hearts of the believers, is the fulfillment of all the laws of God. And Christ Himself is the Love of the Father. When Christ, the Spirit comes into the midst or core of the heart of believers and paves it with Himself, the law of God finds its fulfillment in them.

(ii). The *appiryon*, as we have seen, was a model of the heart of the faithful men of Israel wherein the Lord dwelt and captained them in all of their battles to take possession of the promised land by faith alone.

(iii). The appellative, "daughters of Jerusalem," occurs, as explained, as an idiomatic term for the generality of Israel.

From the above perspectives, to say that the Lord paved the midst of the *appiryon* with the love for the daughters of Jerusalem, is the same as saying that He paved the heart of the faithful men of Israel with His love for the generality of Israel; in other words, with love for their own people.

The questions arise from this as to what prompted the Lord to pave the heart of the men of Israel with the Lord's love for their own people? Should He not have paved the midst their hearts with the love for all the families of the earth as He had paved the heart of Abraham, Isaac, and Jacob, and of the apostles, prophets, evangelists, pastors and teachers of the New Testament church?

The answer is that the men of Israel, like Joshua, Judges, David, and the men under their command were not called to make all the families of the earth blessed with the blessing of Abraham, but to possess the lands of the Canaanite nations for themselves and their own people, termed here idiomatically as "the daughters of Jerusalem." The seemingly unjust task involved pulling down and destroying the cities and villages of the innocent and ignorant multitudes of the Canaanites mercilessly, and after annihilating them, seizing their lands and possessions, for the sake of their own people. Performance of heartless tasks of this nature required strong self-will and self-love and an inhuman disposition. Nevertheless, the exigency of the purpose for which they were called had demanded it.

OUTLINE OF CONTENTS COMMENTARY

I. THE TITLE 1:1

PART ONE
THE PATRIARCHS
("The fairest among women")

II. JACOB, JOSEPH, JOSEPH'S BROTHERS AND THEIR FAMILIES 1:2-17

1. Israel, the newborn Church, breaks forth into singing 1:2-4
2. Having come under conviction, Israel, the newborn Church, openly confesses the contrariety between her life with and without Christ 1:5-6
3. The infant church cries out to the Lord to tell her where He pastures His flock and makes it to rest 1:7-8
4. Israel, the Lord's 'mare,' harnessed to Pharaoh's Chariots 1:9-11
5. The brevity of the period of time Israel continued to remain as a sweet-smelling savour unto the Lord and to the Egyptians 1:12
6. The patriarchs express their firm belief that their posterity will keep the Lord in close embrace of faith throughout the impending night of the Egyptian captivity and apostasy 1:13
7. The Patriarchs foresee the Gentile pedigree of the coming Messiah 1:14
8. The patriarchal age: A dramatic finish 1:15-17

PART TWO
THE MOSAIC PERIOD
2:1-3:8

III. THE FIRST FORTY YEARS OF MOSES' LIFE DURING WHICH HE WAS BROUGHT UP BY THE PHAROAH'S DAUGHTER 2:1-6

(the first forty years of Moses' life)

1. An adorable child 2:1
2. Israel, the lily, among poking thorns 2:2
3. Moses shelters himself under the shadow of the Lord Almighty 2:3
4. The Lord Leads Moses to the Baptism in the Spirit 2:4-6

IV. MOSES FLEES TO THE WILD REGIONS OF THE SINAI PENINSULA, WHERE THE LORD APPEARS AND COMMISSIONS HIM TO GO TO EGYPT AND DELIVER ISRAEL FROM CAPTIVITY 2:7-17

(the second forty-year period of Moses' life)

1. Moses goes into hiding in the wild regions of the Sinai Peninsula 2:7
2. The Lord appears to Moses in the burning bush, in the vicinity of Horeb, "the mountain of God," 2:8-9
3. The Call 2:10-13
4. Moses behaves like a timid 'rock-dove' that withdraws and hides itself within the cleft of rock, and advances lame excuses that act virtually like crafty 'little foxes' that spoil the vines 2:14-15
5. Moses who appears in the guise of the beloved is convinced and confesses the Lord as his own God and Shepherd. 2:16
6. Moses bids farewell to the Lord on the eve of his departure from Horeb to Egypt 2:17
7. On Arrival at Ramses, Moses and Aaron find out the Beloved groping in the dark in search of the missing Lord, and show her the way to find Him out 3:1-4

V. THE FORTY YEARS OF ISRAEL'S WANDERING IN THE WILDERNESS 3:5-8
(the third forty-year period of Moses' life)

1. The wilderness journey begins 3:5
2. The debacle of Kadesh-barnea, and Israel's wandering in the wilderness until every one of those that started from Egypt perished 3:6-8

PART THREE
FROM JOSHUA TO SOLOMON
3:9-11 and 4:1-7

VI. ISRAEL, THE OLD TESTAMENT CHURCH, GROWS UP AS THE BODY OF CHRIST UNTO HER DESTINED MEASURE OF HALF OF THE STATURE OF THE FULLNESS OF CHRIST 3:9-4:7

1. The *Appiryon* made by King Solomon for Himself 3:9-11
2. Israel, the Old Testament Church of the regenerated, Grows Up as the Body of Christ unto Half of the Measure of the Stature of the fullness of Christ 4:1-5
   a. Joshua and his men: the seeing eyes of the body of Christ 4:1a
   b. The flock of God that rushed down the slopes of mount Gilead, poised to cross over Jordan into the Promised Land: the flowing graceful hair of the body of Christ 4:1b
   c. The flock of sheep that came up from the ravines of the river Jordan, in encampment at Gilgal: the smiling teeth of the body of Christ 4:2
   d. Rahab, the harlot, who believed in the God of Israel, and confessed with her lips, and the men of Israel who took Jericho by the power of praise: the lips and mouth of the body of Christ 4:3a,b

e. The contented generation of the Judges' period: temples of the body of Christ 4:3c

f. David and his thousand mighty men: the sturdy neck of the body of Christ 4:4

g. The unity and oneness of Judah Israel: the two breasts of the body of Christ 4:5

3. The Lord declares His resolve to get Himself into the ritualistic Solomonic temple over Zion, the temple mount 4:6

4. The Perfected Bride 4:7

VII. ISRAEL, THE MARRIED SPOUSE OF THE LORD 4:8-15

1. Israel, the Married Spouse of the Lord Takes Possession of the Last Vestiges of the Promised Land by the Power of the Indwelling Christ 4:8

2. The Lord Eulogizes the Praiseworthy Aspects of His Consummated Spouse 4:9-15

a. Of the efficacy of her faith 4:9

b. Of the mirth of her love 4:10

c. Of the sweetness of her words 4:11

d. Of the chastity of her life 4:12

e. Of the productivity of her life 4:13,14

f. Of her virtue as a life-giver 4:15

VIII. THE WEDDING FEAST 4:16-5:1

PART FOUR

THE LATTER HALF OF THE SONG

(Futuristic Prophecies)

5:2 – 8:14

IX. THE OBSCURE NINE CENTURIES BETWEEN SOLOMON AND CHRIST

(Considered as a prolonged night of estrangement between the Israel and the Lord, the newly married couple)

THE MESSIANIC AGE

X. THE LORD AROUSES AND DRAWS AFTER HIMTHE SLUMBERING REMNANT OF ISRAEL, AFTER NINE CENTURIES OF KNOCKNG AND CALLING 5:2-7

SIMILARITIES

DIFFERENCES

XI. THE PRIMITIVE JEWISH CHRISTIAN CHURCH BEARS WITNESS TO THE GLORIES OF THE RISEN LORD TO THE CURIOUS CROWDS OF JERUSALEM 5:8-6:3

1. Curiosity and interest arise in the hearts of the generality of the Jews of the city of Jerusalem to know more about the person and glories of the risen Christ 5:8-9
2. The apostles bear witness to the glorious Christ to the crowd of Jews of the city of Jerusalem that came running to the upper room on the day of Pentecost 5:10-16
3. "Pricked in their heart" by the church's challenging word of testimony, three thousand of the Jews out of those who came running to the upper room wish to know where the Lord has gone so that they may join her in her search for the risen Lord. 6:1
4. The beloved (Church) answers 6:2-3

XII. THE CHURCH TRIUMPHANT NOW MARCHES INTO THE REGIONS OF SAMARIA AS AN ARMY WITH BANNERS, AND ASSIMILATES THE SAMARITANS WHO BELIEVED INTO THE BODY OF CHRIST 6:4-9

1. The Church's conquest of the Samaritans by the love of Christ likened to the conquest of Canaan by the army of Joshua and the Judges 6:4-7
2. The constituent members of the household of Christ classified. 6:8-9

XIII. THE DAY OF THE FULLNESS OF THE KNOWLEDGE OF HER CALLING DAWNS IN THE COLLECTIVE HEART OF ISRAEL, (THE CHURCH), AND SHE, IN TURN, DAWNS OVER THE HORIZON OF THE DARKENED GENTILE WORLD 6:10

1. The Maiden Missionary trip of the church to the Gentiles, in the person of Peter 6:11-13

XIV. THE CHURCH GROWS UP UNTO THE MEASURE OF THE STATURE OF THE FULNESS OF CHRIST, WITH THE INCORPOREATION OF GENTILES INTO THE BODY OF CHRIST 7:1-6

1. Evangelists: the beautiful, shod feet of the body of Christ 7:1a
2. The apostles who walked throughout the length and breadth of the Jewish and Gentile lands: the rounded thighs of the body of Christ 7:1b
3. The Spirit-filled members of the church: the navel of the body of Christ, like a large bowl that wanteth no liquor 7:2a
4. A bumper harvest of Gentile souls: the belly of the body of Christ, like a heap of wheat set about with lilies 7:2b
5. The unity and the oneness of the Jewish and Gentile believers: the two breasts of the body of Christ, like twin young roes 7:3a
6. The body of believers in enjoyment of spiritual rest and liberty: the neck of the body of Christ 7:4a
7. Tearful intercessors: eyes of the body of Christ, like the fishpools in Heshbon by the gate of the daughter of multitudes 7:4b
8. Apostle Paul: the nose of the body of Christ, like the tower of Lebanon that looketh toward Damascus 7:4c

9. Crist, the Head of the church: like mount Carmel, in majesty and excellency 7:5a

10. The youthful vicarious death of Christ, the Head: the purple coloured hair of the Head of the church, like hanging threads of the weaver's loom after he has cut off the finished product 7:5b

11. The consummated primitive Jewish-Gentile Christian church 7:6

XV. THE LORD DECREES THAT THE GENTILES SHOULD BE "FELLOWHEIRS, AND OF THE SAME BODY, AND PARTAKERS OF HIS PROMISE, BY THE GOSPEL," 7:7-9

XVI. THE CHURCH SETS HER MIND ON WINNING THE GENTILES FOR CHRIST, ON THE JEWS' REFUSAL TO ACCEPT THE MESSIAHSHIP OF JESUS OF NAZERETH 7:10-13

XVII. HAVING BEEN EXCOMMUNICATED FROM JUDAISM, THE BELOVED (CHURCH) EXPRESSES HER ANGUISH OVER HER INABILTY TO BRING THE LORD TO HER BRETHREN ACCODING TO THE FLESH WITHIN JUDAISM 8:1-4

XVIII. THE ENDS OF THE TANGLED STORYLINE 8:5-7

XIX. A FIGURATIVE DESCRIPTION OF THE ONGOING DELIBERATIONS IN THE JERUSALEM CHURCH COUNCIL ON WHETHER OR NOT TO IMPOSE THE JEWISH LAW UPON THE GENTILE CONVERTS 8:8-10

XX. HEIRS OF THE LORD'S VINEYARD OF FAITH VERSUS KEEPERS OF HIS VINEYARD OF THE LAW 8:11-12

XXI. THE TRANSFERRAL OF THE KINGDOM OF GOD TO THE GENTILES 8:13-14

COMMENTARY

COMMENTARY

I. THE TITLE, 1:1

The Song of Songs

The title, "the Song of Songs," is a common idiomatic expression in the Hebrew language, similar to "the King of kings," "the Lord of lords," "the heaven of heavens," "vanity of vanities," etc, to denote the best, highest or profoundest of a class or kind. Here the expression, "the Song of Songs," denotes that, in thematic content, this Song is the profoundest of all the prophetic songs found in the Old Testament books.

Which is Solomon's

Which was composed by the heavenly Solomon and sung by Him, by the mouth of the earthly Solomon. The relative clause, "which is Solomon's," recurs in 3:7, where it refers to the Ark of the Covenant of the Lord, typified in the antecedent clause, as "His," i.e. the heavenly Solomon's, "bed."

PART ONE
THE PATRIARCHS
("The fairest among women")

II. JACOB, JOSEPH, JOSEPH'S BROTHERS, AND THEIR FAMILIES, 1:2-17

This first major section of the Song, 1:2-17, discloses prophetically the redemptive story of the founding fathers of Israel. It begins with an allusion to the turn of events through which the Lord brought Jacob to Peniel and regenerated him into an Israel of God. This is followed by allusions to a series of the turn of events through which the Lord exalted Joseph to the position of the grand Vizier of Egypt, and the subsequent arrival and settlement of Jacob and his sons and families in that country. The section concludes with the serene picture of the Lord's flock enjoying physical and spiritual rest in "the green pastures" (1:16; cf. Ps 23:2), prepared for it by the Lord, at Goshen, in the manifest company of the Lord Himself, its Shepherd.

As stated at the beginning, the Song reckons that it was Israel, the church of the regenerated that was born of God in Jacob at Peniel.

1. *Israel, the newborn Church, breaks forth into singing, 1:2-4*

"He brought me up also out of an horrible pit... and set my feet upon a rock,... and he hath put a new song in my mouth, even praise unto our God" (Ps 40:2, 3), says David. The Song commences likewise, with the new song of praise unto the name of her Redeemer King that the Lord had put in the mouth of the newborn Israel, as follows:

1: 2. Let him kiss me with the kisses of his mouth:
for thy love is better than wine.
3. *Because of the savour of thy good ointments*

Thy name is as ointment poured forth,
Therefore do the virgins love thee.
4. *Draw me, we will run after thee:*
The king hath brought me into his chambers:
We will be glad and rejoice in thee,
We will remember thy love more than wine:
The upright love thee.

The following pertinent facts come to light on closely scrutinizing these words of the song that proceed from the female partner's mouth.

(i). That she is deeply immersed emotionally in praising and adoring the name of the Lord and worshipping Him.

(ii). The spirit of her worship and the words and expressions that proceed from her mouth show that she is a true worshipper worshipping the Lord "in spirit and in truth" (John 4:24). For instance, she speaks out to the Lord, in prayer and worship that His love filling her heart is more titillating than that of the literal wine, just as the disciples felt on the day of Pentecost when they were filled by the Holy Spirit. Likewise, the sweetness of the aroma of His name, she tells Him, is filling her heart, like the fragrance that emanates when precious anointing oil is poured out of its container. Moreover, she appeals to the Lord to keep on drawing her graciously after Him by the strong cord of His divine love, so that she could run after Him, along with her seed of all times to come, throughout her lifetime, and be glad and rejoice in Him. We know that this is how one feels when worshipping the Lord in the fullness of the Spirit.

(iii). She furnishes additional proof to substantiate the fact that she is worshipping the Lord "in spirit and in truth" when she asserts, saying, "the King hath brought me into His chambers." It means that she is worshipping the Lord, who is an invisible Spirit, face to face, within the inner chambers of His presence *in the heavenly places.*

We know that, being an invisible Spirit, the Lord does not abide in any literal chambers, neither does He require space of any sort to abide in. What she really means is that the Lord has granted her access by the Spirit into His spiritual presence (cf. Eph 2:18). In other words, that she is born of God. For, to be born of God, and to be brought by the Lord, the Spirit, unto His glorious presence, by the Holy Spirit, refer to one and the same experience. None but those to whom the Lord grants access unto His glorious presence by the Spirit, graciously, would be able to worship Him in spirit and in truth.

(In contrast, in vv. 3:6-8 and 4:6 the Spirit makes a satirical expose× of the futile ostentatious worship of the Israelite worshippers who vainly burn superabundant quantities of incense in the name of religious worship).

(iv). The name that she adores is the name of "the Lamb that was slain from the foundation of the world" (Rev. 13:8). This is what she actually means by the use of the figurative expression, "Your name is as ointment (anointing oil) poured forth."

Typically, the plural form "chambers," refer to the sanctum and the sanctum sanctorum of the tabernacle and the temple. The children of Israel were debarred by the stipulations of the Sinai covenant from entering into these holy apartments of the tabernacle and the temple. While access into the holy place was granted to the priests, access into the most holy place was granted only to the high priest, and that once in a year, i.e., on the Day of Atonement, to atone for the sins of his people before the Holy God. Evidently, the beloved is not speaking of these literal chambers, because, in the first place, she is not a high priest, and, second, the high priest who entered the most holy place once in a year, did so merely to perform the ritual of atoning for the sins of his people, not to worship the Lord in spirit and in truth, as she does here, and thirdly, she is not worshipping the Lord according to the stipulations of the Sinai covenant but according to the Abrahamic covenant of promise, by faith.

Let him kiss me with the kisses of his mouth (2a).

It appears that the expressions, "kisses of his mouth" and "savour of thy good ointments," allude to the words spoken by Isaac while kissing Jacob and bestowing the paternal blessing and birthright upon him. "Please come close and kiss me, my son," said Isaac, "See, the smell of my son is as the smell of a field which the Lord hath blessed" (Gen 27:26, 27). In reality, the smell that Isaac smelled was not the smell of his younger son Jacob, as he blindly believed, but the smell of the "goodly raiment" of Esau, which Rebekah had taken stealthily and put upon Jacob, the imposter. Esau was a "cunning hunter," "a man of the field,' (Gen 25:27). It was natural, therefore, that his raiment smelled "the smell of a field." *"The aromatic odors of the Syrian fields and meadows, often impart a strong fragrance,"* notes JFB Commentary, and adds:

> The long white robe-the vestment of the firstborn,...transmitted from the father to the son and kept in a chest among fragrant herbs and perfumed flowers used much in the East to keep away moths, his mother provided for him.[21]

The relevance of the above stated episode of Isaac, of kissing and bestowing the blessing and birthright upon Jacob, the imposter is not direct here, but in that the kisses that Isaac bestowed on Jacob unknowingly were factually the kisses of the Lord who had foreknown and predestinated him to be "the heir of promise," in the covenant. For the episode of Rebekah coercing Jacob to subvert his father's deliberate plan to sidestep the known purpose of God and bestow the blessing upon Esau, the elder, had not taken place without the Lord's permissive will.

The third person pronoun "him" refers to the third person "the king" of v.4, namely, to the Lord (the Lover), who had regenerated Jacob into an Israel of God, from his inborn sinful nature of having been 'black as the tents of Kedar,' and brought him into the antitypical inner chambers of His presence, to wit, into the actual Sanctum, and Sanctum Sanctorum of His presence in *"the heavenly places."*

However, as stated, viewed from the Song's perspective, it was Israel, the church of the regenerated, that was born of God at Peniel; not Jacob, an individual. Having brought the newborn church into existence, the Lord kissed her with the kisses of His

---

[21] Rev. Robert Jamieson, et. al., *Commentary on the whole Bible*, Grand Rapids, Michigan: Zondervan Publishing House, 1978, p. 33.

mouth and brought her into the inner chambers of His presence, in *the heavenly places*. The Heb. word *peh* translated "mouth" can also mean, 'word,' 'speech,' 'command,'[22] "Kisses of His mouth" appears to be a felicitous expression for the gracious promises of God.

Kissing or warmly hugging a person and bringing him/her into the inner chamber of one's own house are the Song's symbolic expressions for acceptance (cf. comment on 3:4; 8:1,2). In the present context, the expression, "let him kiss me with the kisses of his mouth," should be understood to be an expression of the returned and graciously kissed and accepted prodigal's (Jacob's) desire to be kissed more and more (cf. Luke 15:20ff.).

For thy love is better than wine (2b)

For, because. It is when the sinner realizes that the redeemer's love for him/her surpasses his/her sins and sinfulness that he/she resolves to return to the Lord.

The Heb. word *dodim,* rendered love, is in the plural form, 'loves.' It is the form used when speaking of the love between the opposite sexes.[23] The existing analogy between the titillation of divine love and wine recurs in vv.4, and 4:10

> The shift from **kiss me** to **his mouth** to **your mouth** appears awkward to us, but such a sequence of shifting pronouns is a common phenomenon in biblical poetry (e.g. Amos 4:1; Mic 7:19; cf. Song 4:2;6:6).[24]

Because of the savour of thy good ointments, thy name is as ointment poured forth, (3)

The context shows that the name that the newborn church adores is the exalted name of Christ, the Lamb of God that was "slain from the foundation of the world" (Rev13:8). In fact, the

---

[22] James Strong, The New, *Strong's Exhaustive Concordance of the Bible,* Nashville, Tennessee: Thomas
Nelson Publishers, 1995, p.113.

[23] H. W. F. Gesenius, *Gesenius' Hebrew-Chaldee Lexicon to the Old Testament,* Grand Rapids, Michigan: Baker Books, 1979, p.191.

[24] G. Lloyd Carr, *op.cit.,* p. 72.

Father had highly exalted the name of His Son "from the foundation of the world," "that at the name of Jesus every knee should bow ... and ...every tongue should confess that Jesus Christ is Lord" (Phil 2:9,10,11)

Instead of AV's *"the savour of thy good ointments,"* RSV has *"Your anointing oils are fragrant."* The Heb. word *"Messiah"* means "the Anointed One," and the word "ointment," Heb. *shemen*, refers here to the typical holy anointing oil. The Lover is the *Messiah*, the "Anointed One." The newborn church knows that the name that she adores is the name of the Holy One of Israel, the *Messiah*. The sacred oils used for anointing kings, priests, and prophets of Israel, were typical of the Holy Ghost. The act of anointing one who was set apart for any of the above stated ministries with the holy anointing oil was part of the person's investiture to that office, before the people. But, the Lord's act of anointing the person with the Holy Spirit that often followed the ritualistic anointing was proof of the Lord's approval of the ministry for which he was anointed. For instance, our Lord took the book of Isaiah, and standing before the doubting people of his own city, read the words of 61:1, in the hearing of them all, "The Spirit of the Lord is upon me, because He hath anointed me to preach the gospel to the poor" (Luke 4:18). He did this to prove His claim that He was the *Messiah*, the Anointed One. The underlying thoughts of the beloved's words of adoration are those of Ps 45: 7-8: "Thy God, hath anointed thee with the oil of gladness above thy fellows. All thy garments smell of myrrh, and aloes, and cassia, out of the ivory palaces, whereby they have made thee glad." The diffusing fragrance of the Lord's name spread far and wide during His earthly ministry. It multiplied manifold upon His vicarious death, resurrection and His continued presence in the church, consequent to the outpouring of the Holy Ghost.

Thy name is as ointment poured forth.

Better as Gesenius renders, "thy name is poured forth like ointment."[25] The Lord's name was poured forth like the anointing oil poured forth out of its container upon His chosen

---

[25] H.W.F. Gesenius, *op. cit,*, p. 763.

ones. The statement is fraught with far-reaching significance. The beloved (church) has in mind here the act of the Lamb slain from the foundation of the world, of pouring out his life unto death as a ransom for the souls of His elect. The sweet savor of the aroma of His precious name had been spreading far and wide throughout the world, ever since He poured out His life as a ransom for the world of sinners, just as the fragrance of the alabaster box of costly ointment that the sinful woman poured upon our Lord's head had filled the whole room. To redeem means to purchase with a price. The price of redeeming human souls and setting them free was not anything less than the Redeemer's own life-blood.

Therefore do the virgins love thee (3c)

In that, 'your name is as fragrant as the holy anointing oil poured forth out of its container do the virgins love thee.' (For details on the identity of the virgins, see the note on 'Virgins and Daughters,' under the heading, 'The Household of God,' in the introductory section of this book).

Draw me (4a)

"No man can come to me, except the Father which hath sent me draw him" (John 6:44), stated our Lord, and, "I, if I be lifted up from the earth, will draw all men unto me" (John 12:32; cf. Jer 31:3; Hos 11:4). The Lord had already drawn the beloved by the strong cord of His sacrificial love and brought her graciously into the inner chamber of His glorious presence in *the heavenly places*. She is making the present prayerful appeal while being with Him, in His glorious presence, in *the heavenly places*. She appeals to Him, to keep drawing her constantly and continuously by the inseparable cord of His love which is "strong as death" (8:6), until the end of her earthly pilgrimage, without which she would not be able to run after Him, wholeheartedly, as she ought, and be glad and rejoice in Him, and maintain the remembrance of His love which is far more intoxicating than wine. That one can run after the Lord only by His gracious act of drawing by the strong cord of His love, constantly and continuously is not only one of the fundamental teachings of the scriptures, but also a fact well known to each and every believer who has been trying wholeheartedly to run after the Him.

We will run after thee (4a).

As stated, the use of the plural form of the first person pronoun, "we," proves that Israel, the church of the redeemed, and not Israel, an individual, was born of God through regeneration, at Peniel. This fact is crucial for the study of the Song. (Cf. detailed notes on this, under the head, 'The THEME OF THE SONG,' in the introductory section of this book)

The King hath brought me into his chambers (4b)

The Heb. word *cheder* means inner chamber. As stated, typically, the plural form "chambers" refer to the holy and the most holy places of the tabernacle and temple. The innermost chamber, the most holy place, was the dwelling place of the Lord in the typical system of temple worship in the Old Testament dispensation. A thick, gorgeous veil hung up at the entrance of the most holy place debarred the worshippers from entering unto the Lord's presence within, according to the stipulation of the law. The worshippers were to worship the Lord only in the outer court of the temple proper. There were also middle walls of partition in the court that stood between the male and the female, and the Jewish and the proselyte worshippers.

When our Lord died on the cross, the veil which stood at the entrance of the most holy place of the temple in Jerusalem was rent in twain (Matt 27:51), signifying thereby that, through His death, the Lord has removed once for all, all the hurdles that stood between the Father and the worshippers, and has opened a "new and living way" unto Him for the true worshippers to worship Him "in spirit and in truth" (Heb 10:20; John 4:23-24).

When Paul wrote to the church in Ephesus that Christ has "broken down the middle wall of partition between us ... to make in himself of twain one new man, so making peace" (Eph 2:14-15), he had meant to say that the Lord had removed all the legal barriers that stood not only between the Father and the worshippers, but also that which stood between the Jews and the Gentiles worshippers, and made both the Jewish and Gentile worshippers who worship Him in the inner chamber of His dwelling in the heavenly places, in spirit and in truth, "one new man" or "creation" (cf. 2 Cor 5:17). At present there are no more middle walls of any kind between the worshippers to whom the Lord has granted access to the Father graciously, by the Spirit. All those to whom the Father has granted access to His presence within the sanctum sanctorum of His dwelling place in *the heavenly places* are one in Christ..

There is, however, a room for misgiving in the foregoing explanation. While drawing the existing sharp contrast between the system of worship in the Old and the New Testament dispensations, Paul had only the typical system of ritualistic worship of the natural Israel in the Old Testament dispensation in mind. In other words, he was contrasting the difference between the ritualistic worship under the stipulations of the Sinai covenant in the Old Testament dispensation with the true worship in spirit and in truth in the New Testament dispensation. Therefore, the question arises as to whether there was any difference in God's sight between the Old Testament worshippers who had worshipped the Lord in spirit and in truth, under the Abrahamic covenant of promise, and the New Testament worshippers who had also worshipped Him in spirit and in truth. The answer to the question is crucial for the study of the Song, for the Lord's beloved (church) in the Old Testament division of the Song belongs to the former category.

Our answer to the question is that we do not find the possibility of drawing any sharp line of difference between those who had worshipped the Lord in spirit and in truth in the Old and in the New Testament dispensations. As explained under the head 'The Structure of the Song,' the Song is divided into two co-equal parts: one dealing with the church in the Old, and the other dealing with the church in the New, Testament periods. But the Song does not differentiate the Lord's beloved (church) of the Old and the New Testament dispensations in any way. The beloved (church) continues to be the same in the Old and the New Testament periods, though with different levels of enlightenment. The day of the fullness of the light of the knowledge of the Lord dawned upon the church only in the latter part of the primitive Jewish Christian church period, as described figuratively, in 6:10.

Notwithstanding the differences in the levels of enlightenment, there was only one church, and one heaven. In this connection, it is better to recall the words spoken by our Lord to the people when He heard the words of the Roman centurion, and marveled at his faith, saying,

> many shall come from the east and west, and shall sit down with Abraham, and Isaac, and Jacob, in the kingdom of heaven" (Matt 8:11).

We will run after thee...we will be glad and rejoice in thee: we will remember thy love more than wine (4a,c)

The newborn church's longing desire to run after the Lord and be glad and rejoice in Him, throughout her existence on earth, is being expressed here prophetically. It found fulfillment in the beginning of the New Testament dispensation, in the manner in which she rejoiced in the Lord and remembered His love which was far more titillating than wine, when the Holy Spirit was poured upon her on the day of Pentecost. On seeing the one hundred and twenty disciples, on whom the Holy Spirit came, filled with the love of God in Christ, behaving like drunken people on that day, it had appeared to the multitudes of Jews who came running to the upper room that the disciples were truly drunk with "new wine." Significantly, the word *samach* rendered "rejoice" is "used for louder expressions of joy, as of those who make merry with wine."[26] Likewise, the Heb. word *giel* rendered "glad" is derived from the "effervescing" of lime when put in water.[27]

> And they, continuing daily with one accord in the temple, and breaking bread from house to house, did eat their meat with gladness and singleness of heart, praising God, and having favor with all the people. And the Lord added to the church daily such as should be saved (Ac. 2:46-47)

The upright love thee, (4d)

That is, the upright from among the "virgins" of v.3. None but the upright can know the Lord genuinely and love Him un-

---

[26] H.W.F. Gesenius, *op. cit.*, p. 791.
[27] *Ibid.*, p. 169.

feignedly. "Lord, who shall abide in thy tabernacle?" asks the Psalmist, "who shall dwell in thy holy hill?," and answers himself, "He that walketh uprightly, and worketh righteousness, and speaketh the truth in his heart."

2. *Having come under conviction, Israel, the newborn Church, openly confesses the contrariety between her life with and without Christ, 1:5-6.*

The sense of the words that a person speaks is dependent mostly upon the nature of his/her person. In the present context, if the speaker of the words, 'I am black as the tents of Kedar, but comely as the curtains of Solomon,' is a literal woman caught in a worldly love affair, as commonly presumed, she must then necessarily be speaking about the colour of her skin and complexion. On the other hand, if she is Israel, the newborn church of the regenerated, who was brought by the Lord graciously to His glorious presence, she must of necessity be openly confessing the duality of her natures, as to what she has been and still is, in herself alone, and what she has become from the time Christ came to dwell in her heart.

1: 5. I am black, but comely, O ye daughters of Jerusalem,
as the tents of Kedar, as the curtains of Solomon

6. Look not upon me, because I am black,
because the sun hath looked upon me:
My mother's children were angry with me;
they made me the keeper of the vineyards;
but mine own vineyard have I not kept.

"Woe is me! for I am undone; because I am a man of unclean lips, ... for mine eyes have seen the King, the Lord of hosts," cried out Isaiah, when he encountered the Lord of glory in the full splendor of His majesty, in His temple. In like manner, when brought by the Lord face to face within the innermost chamber of His dwelling place *in the heavenly places*, and thereby having come under conviction of her inborn sinful nature, Israel, the newborn church, openly confesses the state of her life with and without Christ, saying, "I am black, but comely, O ye daughters of Jerusalem, as the tents of Kedar, as the curtains of Solomon."

I am black, ...O ye daughters of Jerusalem, as the tents of Kedar (5)

Grace is the mercy that God extends freely to an unworthy sinner, on the ground of His own righteousness and goodness. "Where sin abounded, grace did much more abound" (Rom 5:20). Here, the beloved (church) likens the depth of the blackness of her inborn sinful nature to that of the black goat-hair tents of the tribe of her first cousin Kedar, so that she may not be mistaken for saying that her sins were swarthy.

Kedar was the second in order of the sons of Ishmael, analogous to Jacob, who was the second in order of the sons of Isaac. Thus, in solidarity of kinship, both were equal in their relationship to Abraham, in that both were his grandsons, in Ishmael and Isaac, respectively. Even so, their status and standing before God had become irreconcilably opposite on account of God's own prerogative in election and choice. While God had chosen Jacob to become the heir of promise, in the covenant, purely by virtue of His gracious election, Kedar had become a cast-out in His sight. As a result, while Kedar and his posterity were wandering about in the wilderness of Arabia Petraea with their black goat-hair tents, Jacob was born of God to emerge glorious as the tabernacle of the Lord, the King Solomon of the Song.

On the question of the color of the tents of Kedar, Delitzsch writes:

> Ohel is the house of the nomad. ... to the present day the Beduin calls his tent his 'hair-house,' ... for the tents are covered with cloth made of the hair of goats, which are mostly black colored or gray.[28]

In depth, the color of the goat-hair covering cloth of the tents of Kedar that is intended here were not gray or swarthy, but black as the black hair of an Oriental beauty. (Cf. comment on "Thy hair is as a flock of (black) goats," 4:1c).

But comely ...as the curtains of Solomon. (5)

The Heb. word *yeriah* translated "curtains," refers to the tabernacle of the Lord. Carr points out that, "forty-one of the forty-

---

[28] Frans Delitzsch, *op. cit.*, pp. 25, 26.

eight uses of this word in the Old Testament are in connection with the tabernacle which Israel constructed in the wilderness."[29] The word occurs here as a synonym for the tabernacle itself in the sense in which it is used in Jer 4:20; 10:20; 49:29; Heb 3:7. The intended meaning is clear. She claims that she has become comely as the tabernacle of the Lord from the time Christ came to dwell in her heart.

The analogy between her inborn and reborn natures and the tabernacle of the Lord is cogent. Outwardly and inwardly, the tabernacle of the Lord was black. Outwardly it was covered with the black badgers' skins. Inwardly, the sanctum sanctorum of the tabernacle was a pitch-dark room. However, it was filled with the glory of the Lord, the King Solomon of the Song, from the time He came down in the visible form of the glorious *Shekinah* and abode in it, over the Mercy Seat. It is in these senses that the beloved claims that she is comely as the tabernacle of the Lord.

Applied to Jacob personally, the core of his heart had been black as the goat-hair tents of Kedar, as evident from the fact that he had covered himself deceptively with the (black) skins of "two good kids of the goats" (Gen 27:9), and duped his own aged, blind father, for personal gain. But from the moment he was born of God, the glorious Lord, the King Solomon of the Song came down to dwell in him. It is from this perspective that he, in the guise of the beloved, says, 'I am comely as the tabernacle of Solomon.'

Look not upon me, because I am black, because the sun hath looked upon me: my mother's children were angry with me, (6a,b)

The Heb. verb *raah* translated *"look"* in *"look not upon me"* is a word carrying double meanings. The normal nuance of the word is "look," as rendered in the AV. But, when the statement is read in the sense of its other nuances, such as, 'consider,' or 'regard,' it connotes the opposite meaning, namely, 'regard me not that I am black, that the sun has looked upon me.'[30] In actuality, the beloved is punning here using this double nuance of the word.

---

[29] G. Lloyd Carr, *op. cit.*, p. 78.
[30] Franz Delitzsch, *op. cit.*, p. 26.

Parallelism of thought is a distinctive feature of Heb. poetry. When the thought that occurs in one line of a poem is repeated in the succeeding line, either in literal or figurative sense, it is viewed as a parallelism of thought. In the case of the statement under our consideration, the beloved personifies the sun as an angry woman who scorches with her infuriated consuming look, in order to make the thought of the statement parallel to that of the succeeding line. "My lady the sun"[31] "The looking is thought of as scorching." (Delitzsch).[32] Thus the thought of this line makes a parallelism of thought with the infuriated consuming looks of her "mother's sons," described in the succeeding line. "My mother's sons were angry with me." The Heb. verb used for the brother's anger is also one which connotes the 'burning of anger, "to burn inwardly"(Delitzsch).[33] "There is similarity with the heat of the sun and the heat of the brothers" (Carr).[34]

After all, who could be the persons at whom the beloved (here Jacob) points her finger, saying, 'my mother's sons scorched me with their angry looks?' The answer is, Esau and his brethren. Because, as stated above, when Isaac said later to the weeping Esau, *"Behold, I have made him thy lord, and all his brethren have I given to him for servants ... what shall I do unto thee, my son?"* (Gen 27:37), he had made plain as to whom he had meant, when he pronounced the blessing upon Jacob, saying, *"Be lord over thy brethren, and let thy mother's sons bow down to thee"* (Gen 27: 29).

They made me keeper of the vineyards, but mine own vineyard have I not kept, (6c)

(Cf. notes under the head, vi. 'The identity of the Lovers,' in the Introductory Section of this book (pp.7-11), and exegetical comment on 8:11,12).

---

31 *Ibid.*, p. 27.
32 *Ibid.*, p. 26.
33 *Ibid.*, p. 28.
34 G. Lloyd Carr, *op. cit.*, p. 79.

3. *The infant church cries out to the Lord to tell her where He pastures His flock and makes it to rest, 1:7-8*

One of the most outstanding redemptive works performed by the Lord after the creation of Israel, the church, was settling the infant church in Egypt, to nurture her and let her multiply into a great nation, under the protective wings of the mighty Egyptian Empire. The paradoxical way in which the Lord performed this is common knowledge. He showed in a dream to the young lad Joseph that his father, mother, and brothers would bow down before him one day. When He showed the dream, the Lord foreknew that the young lad would innocently blurt out the contents of the dream before his brothers and would become the helpless victim of their jealousy and hatred. However, the consequent horrendous sufferings that awaited the lad, at the hands of his own heartless brothers was the Lord's predestinated paradoxical way for his exaltation to the position of the Grand Vizier to the Pharaoh, and to get His own people settled in Egypt, under Joseph's care and protection, in accordance with that which He had made known to Abraham, beforehand, saying,

> Know of a surety that thy seed shall be stranger in a land that is not theirs, and shall serve them; and they shall afflict them four hundred years; ... and afterward shall they come out with great substance. (Gen 15:13-14)

The unit under our present consideration (vv.7-8) shows the Lord leading the lad Joseph 'blind-folded,' to Egypt, to prepare the feeding and resting places for Israel, the Lord's flock, as was envisaged in His Father's redemptive scheme.

As the lad Joseph was wandering about in the fields around Shechem in search of his brothers and their flock, with frustration writ large on his face, a Shechemite shepherd found him and enquired inquisitively, "What seekest thou?" "I seek my brethren," answered Joseph, "Tell me, I pray thee, where they feed their flocks" (Gen 37:15-16).

Assuming that the appeal was not made by Joseph, but by the infant church, and not to the Shechemite shepherd, but to the Lord whom her soul loves, the Spirit rephrases the words of

Joseph, as follows:

> 1: 7. Tell me, O thou whom my soul loveth, where thou feedest,
> where thou makest thy flocks to rest at noon:
> for why should I be as one that turneth aside
> by the flocks of thy companions?

Tell me (7a)

The Lord had discreetly withheld the name of the place from Abraham, when He foretold him that his seed would be a stranger in a land that is not theirs for four hundred years. Hence the cry, "Tell me, ... where...where...?

What makes this otherwise simple petition crucial is that the lad had raised it when the Lord was leading him 'blind-folded' to Egypt, to prepare the physical and spiritual feeding and resting places for His flock that His Father had envisaged in His redemptive scheme before the foundation of the world.

O thou whom my soul loveth (7b)

This profound phraseology occurs in the Song only here and in 3:1-4. It is used in 3:1-4 to indicate that the passionate thirst to find out the God of her fathers had remained unquenched in the elect's soul throughout the dark epoch of the Egyptian captivity. Cf. "Love no flood can quench, no torrents drown" (8:6,JB).

Naturally, there exists a thirst deep down in every human soul to search and find out its Creator and Owner and unite with Him in heavenly bliss.

Where thou feedest, (7c)

The question is not where the Lord feeds His flock at the time of asking, but always: in keeping with His covenant pledge. The Spirit's purpose in putting the question in the mouth of the infant church at this initial juncture of her redemptive story is to make room in the succeeding sections of the Song to disclose Himself and His redemptive plans to successive generations of Israel progressively, until He reveals Himself fully, by way of His incarnation, death, resurrection and ascension. The light of the knowledge of God, which was to be imparted progressively to the church was intended to be the spiritual manna for the souls of the posterity of all times to come to feed on and live.

Where thou makest thy flock to rest (7d)

Spiritual rest comes to the Lord's flock through feeding it with the balanced spiritual provender. Pastured with the balanced provender of the 'Living Manna,' the flock is sure to enter into and enjoy the desired spiritual rest. Cf. "He maketh me to lie down in green pastures...He restoreth my soul" (Ps 23:2-3). In the coming section, vv.1:15-17, the Spirit portrays vividly the serene picture of the patriarchal flock enjoying the spiritual and physical rest, commensurate with the Lord's progressive self-disclosure of Himself and His redemptive plans to her, during the time of her prolonged settlement at the verdant pasture land of Goshen. The church realized the full and final degree of spiritual rest only at the end of her redemption story, i.e., during the latter part of the apostolic age, when she had learned to lean on confidently, in absolute faith and trust, on the gracious bosom of the loving Lord, as depicted tellingly in 8:5a, cited below:

> Who is this that cometh up from the wilderness,
> leaning upon her beloved?

At noon (7e)

The forward looking thought that is being introduced here of the coming of a hot noon of scorching heat, during which the Lord's flock would need to be sheltered under the shadows of spreading leafy trees finds its fulfillments, first, in the serene picture of 1:15-17, of the fully fed patriarchal flock lying down and resting over the green grassy bed of Goshen, under the shadows of the tall and mighty firs and cedars of the Egyptian hierarchy, and second, in Moses sheltering himself under the shadow of the Apple Tree, to wit, under the shadow of the Lord Almighty, as depicted in 2:3.

For why should I be as one that turneth aside (7f)

RSV, "Like one who wanders"; NIV, "like a veiled woman."

The thoughts of both 'wandering about' and of being 'veiled' are present here. Literally, the lad Joseph was wandering about in the fields around Shechem, in his bid to locate the place where his brothers were encamping along with their flocks. Spiritually, the lad was 'veiled' in that the harrowing as well as marvelous things that were going to happen to him in the near and far future respectively were hidden from his spiritual perception.

By the flocks of thy companions (7g)

Factually, Joseph was wandering about by the side of the flocks of the Shechemite shepherd, and perhaps by that of other flocks of strangers like him.

The term "companions," Heb. *cheber,* (lit. an associate, a companion, fellow)[35] is introduced here designedly. Though, the term refers, in the present context, to the Shechemite shepherd, a Gentile, who furnished Joseph with pointers to locate the place where his brothers were encamping with their flock, the real purpose of introducing the term here is to show, first, that the Gentiles were the Lord's "companions" or "friends" and, second, to use the word at the end of the Song to describe the transferal of the kingdom of God to the Gentiles. (Cf. exegetical comment on, 5:1, "Eat, O friends; drink, yea, drink abundantly, O beloved(s), and on 8:13, "The companions hearken to thy voice").

The answer

The narrative in the Genesis record of the answer given by the Shechemite shepherd reads, "The man said, they are departed hence; for I heard them say, Let us go to Dothan. And Joseph went after his brethren, and found them in Dothan" (Gen 37:17). Assuming that the Lord, and not the Shechemite shepherd, responded, not to Joseph's, but to the infant church's, appeal for direction, the Spirit rephrases the answer furnished by the Shechemite shepherd, as follows:

1: 8. If thou know not, O thou fairest among women,
Go thy way forth by the footsteps of the flock,
And feed thy kids beside the shepherds' tents.

---

[35] H.W.F. Gesenius, *op. cit.,* p.259.

If thou know not (8a)

'You ought to have known the answer to your question, but if you do not, then, you go your way, following the footprints of the flock.' With these words, the Spirit lays the foundation for disclosing the way in which the Lord dispelled the darkness of ignorance from the church's soul by imparting the light of the knowledge of God and of His way of Salvation, progressively. (Cf. comment on 2:17 and 4:6, "until the day break, and the shadows flee away.").

O thou fairest among women (8b)

The Spirit addresses only the patriarchal Church, as here, and the apostolic church as in 5:9 and 6:1 as "the fairest among women"

Individually, Joseph was certainly the fairest among the saints in the Old Testament dispensation, inasmuch as chastity and purity were concerned.

Go thy way forth (8c)

The calling of the church is to go forth "into all the world (of sinners), and preach the gospel to every creature" (Mark 16:15) and not to pose herself "holier" than the rest of the world and confine herself within the rigid walls of her rightly or wrongly framed dogmas and creeds.

By the footsteps of the flock (8d)

The term, "footsteps" is used here with reference to the legacy of the life of faith left by the fathers. The posterity of all times to come was to follow the footprints of Abraham, Isaac, Jacob, and others like them who went before. The Bible is the compilation of the 'print outs' of those "footprints" of the fathers' walk of faith. One can know God the Father, the Lord Jesus Christ, and the Holy Spirit only from the life story and testimony of the fathers found written down in the books of the Holy Bible. It is the final, unquestionable authority for all matters pertaining to God and faith. Meddling with them is equivalent to the mischief of digging out and scattering around the sacred foundation stones of the faith of the fathers on which the church, collectively, and each of us, individually, stand.

And feed thy kids (8c)

The prayer of the church was, "tell me, O thou whom my soul loveth, where thou feedest, where thou makest thy flock to rest at noon?" While furnishing the answer to the prayed for matters, the Lord gives a command regarding a matter unasked for, i.e., how she should feed her "kids."

"Kids" refer to the natural posterity. Kids become lambs only when they are born of God. The church comprises only of sheep and lambs. Goats and "kids" are outside the church until they are born of God. Hence the injunction, "go thy way forth and feed thy kids."

As the late David du Plessis, the father of the modern day worldwide charismatic movement, used to preach, "God has no grandsons." He has only sons. Each of the "kids" born naturally to Christian parents ought to be nourished and brought up with the balanced provender of spiritual manna, so that the kids are born again into lambs. The prevailing phenomena of the dynamic denominational churches, which were founded once by the Spirit-filled ardent men of God, through incessant labours of love, in the face of stiff opposition, turning out in course of time into dead organizations, retaining nothing but the name and form thereof, without the original power of God and vitality, are the outcome of the failure of their members to feed their kids with the living manna of the word of life.

The Israelites were commanded to teach the law of God to their children and grandchildren, and ensure thereby that the light of the saving knowledge of the God of the forebears continue to remain undiminished in the hearts of the children and children's children, generation after generation, (Gen 18:19; Deut 6:7). The very same commandment is given here figuratively.

Beside the shepherds' tents (8d)

The term "shepherds" refers to pastors and teachers. The Church had never been, or ever will be, without God-given shepherds. In the present context, the term refers to the patriarchs. It appears that the term is borrowed from the answer that the patriarchs gave to the Pharaoh, when he asked them, "What is your occupation?" To this they had answered, "Thy servants are shepherds, both we, and also our fathers" (Gen 47:3).

The Heb. word *miskan* translated '"tents" is used in the books of Exodus and Leviticus for the tabernacle of the Lord. Out of one the hundred and twenty-eight uses of this word in the Old Testament, one hundred and nineteen times it is translated as "tabernacle," thirteen times as "dwelling place" or its synonyms, and five times as "habitation." It becomes clear from the above that the command being given by the Lord to the Church is that she must bring up her posterity in the sound teaching of the revealed truth of God, under the God-given shepherds who served Him in the tabernacle.

"Tents" can also be taken as a symbol for 'pilgrimage.' For Abraham "sojourned in the land of promise, as in a strange country, dwelling in tabernacles with Isaac and Jacob, the heirs with him of the same promise: ... And confessed that they were strangers and pilgrims on the earth" (Heb 11: 9,13).

4. *Israel, the Lord's 'mare' harnessed to Pharaoh's chariots, 1:9-11*

1: 9. I have compared thee, O my love,
to a company of horses in Pharaoh's chariots.
10. Thy cheeks are comely with rows of jewels,
thy neck with chains of gold.
11. We will make thee borders of gold
with studs of silver.

The motif shifts from the pastoral imagery of the preceding unit to the milieu of the Egyptian Pharaoh's palace, denoting that the patriarchal flock has shifted its dwelling place from the pasture lands of Palestine, to a location somewhere near the Pharaoh's palace.

I have compared thee, O my love, to a company of horses in Pharaoh's chariots (9).

AV's, "company" is not present in the original text. However, the use of the term is befitting, because Jacob, his sons and families whom the Lord brought down and settled in Egypt were only a small company of seventy souls. In his official position as the Grand Vizier to the Pharaoh, Joseph rode in the second chariot of the Pharaoh, and Joseph's brothers served the Pharaoh as "keepers of his flock" (Gen 47:6). Evidently, the Lord has Joseph predominantly in mind when He compares His beloved (church) to His mare harnessed to Pharaoh's chariots. It appears that He had Jacob and company also in mind who had traveled all the way from Canaan to Egypt in horse-wagons dispatched by the Pharaoh (cf. Gen 45:19, 27).

Thy cheeks are comely with rows of jewels (10a)

The portrayed cheeks are not of the mare to which the Lord compares His beloved (church) in the preceding verse (v.9), but of the church, the body of Christ, which is the beloved in the Song. The purpose of comparing the church in the preceding verse to the Lord's mare harnessed to Pharaoh's chariots was limited to highlight the fact that the Lord had purposefully given over His beloved (patriarchal church) to the service of the Pharaoh according to His predestinated purpose and plan.

As stated, as the body of the indwelling Christ, the church had possessed only a face, which was black but comely at the time of her birth. But, by now, she has developed golden chains adorned cheeks and neck.

The cheeks of the church are adorned with rows of jewels. The rows of jewels allude in fact to the twelve patriarchs. The root meaning of the word *tor* translated "rows" in AV, is "one's turn." (Carr)[36] Twelve jewels, each bearing the name of one of the patriarchs of the tribes of the children of Israel, were set in four rows, according to each "one's turn" or ranking, upon the breastplate of the high priest of Israel. (This shall become crystal-clear as we advance to the study of the section 4:1-7).

The first row, a sardius, a topaz, a carbuncle.
The second row, an emerald, a sapphire, a diamond.
The third row, a ligure, an agate, an amethyst.
The fourth row, a beryl, an onyx, a jasper. *(Exod 28:17-21)*

[36] *G. Lloyd Carr, op. cit.,* p. 83.

These jewels were cut and engraved, by Bazaleel, "the cunning workman," with the names of each of the patriarchs, "like the engravings of a signet." (Cf. exegetical comment on vv. 7:1; 8:6, with Exod 28:11,21;31:15). In the present context, when the Spirit describes the patriarchs as jewels in their turn, He implies them to be the works of the hands of the Lord, "the cunning workman," as described in 7:1.

Thy neck with chains of gold (10b)

Joseph who shouldered the entire responsibility of the care and protection of patriarchal church during the time of her settlement in Egypt was truly her neck. This description of Joseph as the patriarchal church's neck is based on the fact that the Pharaoh arrayed Joseph "in vestures of fine linen, and put a gold chain about his neck," on the occasion of his investiture to the position of the Grand Vizier of Egypt (Gen 41:42-43). What is described in the book of Genesis, as "a gold chain about his neck," appears to have been a massive assemblage of numerous chains of gold. This is the impression one gathers from a drawing on Paser's tomb, of his investiture to the position of Vizier, reproduced in the New Bible Dictionary.[37]

We will make thee borders of gold with studs of silver (11)

The Lord assures the patriarchal church that they, the triune God, will make her "borders of gold with studs of silver." The same Heb. word *tor,* of the preceding verse, meaning, 'one's own turn' is translated here "borders." The word occurs only two more times in the Old Testament, i.e., in Esth 2:12, 15. Both of these times it occurs in the sense of one's own turn. On the assumption that "turn" refers to circles, NIV and JB mistranslate the word as "earrings."

To know the original meaning of the Lord's statement, one has only to find out whether the triune God intends 'to turn the patriarchal church into,' or 'to make for her.' NASB has "make for you." On the other hand, Robert Jamieson, et al, in the JFB

[37] J. D. Douglas, et. al., *op. cit.,* p. 619.

Commentary comments, "make-not merely give, (Eph 2:10)."[38] Eph 2:10 reads, "For we are his workmanship, created in Christ Jesus unto good works." In 8:6, the beloved (church) appeals to the Lord to set her upon His heart, and upon His arm, as the antitype of one of these jewels, which were engraved with the names of the twelve tribes of Israel, like the engraving of signets or "seals," and set on the breastplate and ephod of the shoulders of Aaron, the high priest, saying, "Set me as a seal upon thine heart, as a seal upon thine arms: for love is strong as death." On comparing that portrayal with the present one, it appears that the triune God's intention is to turn each one of the patriarchs, according to their turn, into a jewel or signet ring of His own workmanship, to be worn as His eternal wedding ring. (Cf. exegetical comment on 8:6 for further enlightenment on the subject).

5. ***The brevity of the period of time Israel continued to remain as a sweet-smelling savour unto the Lord and to the Egyptians, 1:12***

> 1: 12. While the king sitteth at his table,
> my spikenard sendeth forth the smell thereof.

The motif continues to remain set in the milieu of the Pharaoh's palace.

> "While, 'until:' not the end of the period as such, but the whole length of the period; 'so long as,' " (Delitzsch).[39]

The king.

The term "king" occurs here in dual senses. It refers spiritually to the Lord, and literally, to the Hyksos king who had exalted Joseph.

Sitteth at his table.

The Heb. word *mesab* rendered "table" occurs only three more times in the Old Testament (1 Kgs 6:29; 2 Kgs 23:5; Job 37: 12).

---

[38] Jamieson, et. al, *op. cit.*, p. 491.
[39] Franz Delitzsch, *op. cit.*, pp. 35, 36.

In each of these contexts, the word is rendered "round about.' Carr says, "the Hebrew root used means 'surround' and is perhaps best understood here as 'among his own surroundings.'"[40] The emerging meaning is, 'so long as the king was round about.'

My spikenard sendeth forth the smell thereof, (12b)

The idea underscored by the expression, "my spikenard" is, 'my fragrance.' 'To be a sweet savour unto God and men,' is the emerging sense; the very same sense in which Paul writes,

> Now thanks be unto God, which always causeth us to triumph in Christ, and maketh manifest the savour of his knowledge by us in every place. For we are unto God a sweet savour of Christ, in them that are saved, and in them that perish.
>
> 2 Co. 2:14,15

The idea underscored here, of becoming a sweet savour unto God and to men, assumes significance, in the context of Israel's (the church's) calling, which was to become a sweet savour of the Lord's name among all the families of the earth. (Cf. Comment on vv. 4:13-14 and on vv.4:16-5:1). The emerging sense primarily is, so long as the Lord, the King was around, Israel sent forth the fragrance of her spikenard to the Egyptians.

Secondarily, so long as the Hyksos king who exalted Joseph was 'round about' or 'was in power,' the patriarchal church continued to be a sweet savour unto him and to the Egyptians. But, about sixty years after the death of Joseph, the Hyksos, which was a foreign dynasty, was over-thrown through a local uprising, and with that the kingdom reverted to a native line of kings. The native rulers, just like the Egyptians in general, counted Israel and other Asiatic shepherd tribes who came to settle among them as a sort of "loathsome" people (cf. Gen 46:34). The church has obviously this in mind when she asserts that she gave forth the fragrance of her spikenard only so long as the king was round about.

---

[40] G. Lloyd Carr, *op. cit.*, p. 84.

6. ***The patriarchs express their firm belief that their posterity will keep the Lord in close embrace of faith throughout the impending night of the four centuries of the Egyptian captivity and apostasy, 1:13.***

> 1: 13. *A bundle of myrrh is my wellbeloved unto me;*
> *He shall lie all night betwixt my breasts.*

Foreboding an impending night of the Egyptian captivity and apostasy, the patriarchal church gives expression to her firm belief that her posterity will maintain her unrelenting hold on the Lord close to her bosom in the embrace of faith during the sleepy hours of the night.

A bundle of myrrh (13a)

"A bundle." RSV, "a pouch"; NIV, "a sachet." Myrrh is a resin that exudes from the bark of a tree. Therefore, it cannot be bundled. Out of the six more uses of the word *tseror* in the Old Testament, three times it is translated "bag" (Job 14:17; Prov 7:20; Hag 1:6), and three times "bundle" (twice in Gen 42:35, and once in 1 Sam. 25:29). A pack, or parcel of myrrh capable of being enfolded and kept close to one's bosom suits the context better. The sense of this figurative description is made clear in 3:4 where the beloved enfolds the Lord, with "the encircling clutch of her arms,"[41] on finding Him out at the final hours of the dreaded night of the four centuries of captivity and apostasy (cf. comment on 3:4).

Myrrh was in use as a perfume, in ancient days. It was one of the principal ingredients of the holy anointing oil (Exod 30:23-25). The wise men brought it as a gift to the newborn King (Matt 2:11). Nicodemus brought a hundred pound of a mixture of myrrh and aloes and anointed the body of our Lord, in demonstration of his love for Him. (John 19:39). Myrrh was highly prized in Egypt, the so-called land of mummies, this being the principal spice employed in embalming dead bodies.

Well-beloved (13b)

There is the possibility of the presence of an allusion here to Christ as the David who was to come (cf. Ezek 34:23;24;37:24,25;

---

[41] *Ibid.*, p. 110.

Hos 3:5). The name David literally means "well-beloved"; or, beloved (cf. Smith's Bible Dictionary).[42]

Is my well-beloved ... he shall lie.

The variation in the tense of the verbs is noteworthy. While the former clause occurs in the present tense, the latter happens to be in the imperfect tense. "He shall lie all night;" the night is yet to come: it shall not come until after v.17. Disregarding this distinction, modern Versions render both of the clauses of the verse in the present tense. RSV, and NIV omit the words "all night." Carr, on the other hand, upholds the correctness of AV's rendering. He says, "The sense of the main verb is correctly rendered by the AV *shall lie all night.*"[43] The context favours Carr's viewpoint.

Betwixt my breasts (13c)

The word "breasts" occurs in the Song as a symbol for seed or posterity. (Cf. notes on 'The Symbolic word Breasts' under the head, 'The Artful use of Figures of Speech in the Song' in the introductory section of this book). Here, as stated, the patriarchal church gives expression to the firm hope she had been cherishing that her posterity will certainly continue to keep the Lord within the close embrace of faith throughout the impending night of the four centuries of the Egyptian captivity.

Historically, this refers particularly to the certainty of the hope that had been cherished by both Jacob and Joseph concerning the Lord's promise that He will give the land of Canaan for an inheritance to their faithful posterity.

When Jacob sensed that the end of his earthly pilgrimage was at hand, he called Joseph to his bedside, and appealed to him in child-like manner: "Bury me not, I pray thee, in Egypt: But I will lie with my fathers ... carry me out of Egypt, and bury me in their buryingplace ... Swear unto me" (Gen 47:29-31).

Joseph, likewise, exacted an oath from his brothers to the effect that they would certainly carry his "bones" (i.e., mummy) to

---

[42] William Smith, *A Dictionary of the Bible*, ed. F.M. and M.A., Pelouvet, Iowa Falls: Riverside Book and Bible House, 1979. p. 137.

[43] G. Lloyd Carr, *op. cit.*, p. 85 .

Canaan, on the day the Lord takes them there as promised, saying, "God will surely visit you, and bring you out of this land unto the land which he sware to Abraham, to Isaac, and to Jacob... and ye shall carry up my bones from hence" (Gen 50:24, 25).

Significantly, only the bodies of Jacob and Joseph were mummified and preserved in the hope of their posterity's deliverance from Egypt. The mummified body of Jacob was carried in a great and dignified funeral procession to Canaan and buried there in the ancestral burial place. In the case of Joseph's mummified body, the children of Israel had carried it along with them at the time of their Exodus from Egypt.

The mummifying process consisted of the removal of internal organs and filling the cavity with "pure myrrh pounded, cassia and other aromatics."[44] The "bundle" or pack of myrrh to which the beloved compares the Lord in the present imagery refers to the packs of myrrh that were placed in the chest cavity of Jacob and Joseph, in the process of embalming and preserving their bodies. (For proof of the fact that this is the meaning intended here, cf. comment on v. 2:13a, "the fig tree putteth forth her green figs.").

7. *The Patriarchs foresee the Gentile pedigree of the coming Messiah, 1:14*

1: 14. My beloved is unto me as a cluster of camphire in the vineyards of En-gedi.

A cluster

The word, "cluster," (Heb. *eschcol*) alludes to the huge clusters of grapes that the spies cut from the brook of *eschcol* and brought down with them to Kadesh-barnea, bearing it "between two upon a staff" (Num 11:23) as proof of the fruitfulness of the Promised Land. It recurs in 7:7-8. There the 'breasts' (i.e. seed) of Israel, the consummated church, which was planted in the Lord by faith, are compared to clusters of the palm tree and of the grapevine.

---

[44] William Smith, *op. cit.*, p. 170.

Camphire

Heb word '*koper*' is commonly understood as henna; "a tree or shrub, *lawsonia inermis,* of Asia and northern Africa, having fragrant white or reddish flowers."[45] The lexicons list at least four different nouns with this form and spelling. This shrub grows wild in the spring season and covers the landscape in Palestine with fragrant whitish flowers that grow in clusters like the grapes."[46] "The verbal root ... is used most frequently of 'atonement,' i.e. 'covering sin'."[47] The word recurs in v. 4:13 and v. 7:11. The AV translates the word *koper* that occur v. 7:11 as "villages," while the NEB translates the same as "among the henna bushes." The context favours the NEB rendering. The recurrence of 'henna bushes in 7:11 is discernibly as a symbol for the Gentile nations, as against Israel, the "lily." From the perspective of the Song's overall theme of making the Gentiles partakers with the Jews of the promised blessings in Christ, the present figure of "a cluster of henna flowers," to which the beloved likens the Lord, could possibly be with reference to the Gentile pedigree of Christ, the promised seed of David.

En-gedi

Situated in the wilderness of Judah, halfway down the dead-sea shore, this scenic oasis had been a travellers' delight from time immemorial. The welcoming features of En-gedi include, among other things, an inviting waterfall and pool. With its fresh-water springs and lush greenery, En-gedi presented a sharp contrast with the endless rock and wastelands that formed the Judaean desert. David and his men had hid themselves from Saul in the "strongholds at En-gedi" (1 Sam 23:28,29).

8. *The patriarchal age: A dramatic finish,1:15-17*

1: 15. Behold, thou art fair, my love; behold, thou art fair;
Thou hast doves' eyes.

---

[45] Robert Illson, (ed), *The Great Illustrated Dictionary,* New York: The Readers' Digest Association, 1985, p. 108.

[46] Lloyd Carr, *op. cit.*, p. 165

[47] *Ibid.*, p. 165.

16. Behold, thou art fair, my beloved,
Yea, pleasant: also our bed is green.
17. The beams of our house are cedar,
And our rafters of fir.

The imagery comes under four heads:

1. "Eyes like doves (15)
2. Blackness to fairness
3. A bed of green grass (16)
4. A house formed of the bowers of cedar and fir trees, (17)

Behold, thou art fair, my love; behold, thou art fair, thou hast doves' eyes. (15a)

Instead of AV's, "thou hast dove's eyes," RSV and IV render the statement metaphorically, as it occurs in the original text, "your eyes are doves."

As Paul writes to the Corinthians, a believer's life changes into the very image of the Lord not by any amount of own efforts, but by beholding by faith the glory of God in the face of the Lord Jesus Christ with unveiled eyes, as in a glass:

> But we all, with open face beholding as in a glass the glory of the Lord, are changed into the same image from glory to glory, even as by the Spirit of the Lord. 2 Cor 3:18

In the present verse the Lord appreciates the acuity of the spiritual vision of His beloved (patriarchal church) to behold Him in the fullness of His glorious person, whereby her life has been transformed into His glorious image.

Behold, thou art fair, my beloved, yea, pleasant: also our bed is green, (16)

The use of the affirmative word "yea" in these words that are being spoken by the beloved (patriarchal church), in response to the Lord's approbatory words of the preceding line, shows that she is acknowledging the Lord's approbation, saying, 'yes, you are right, my beloved (Lord), you are truly fair in my spiritual vision, yes, pleasant: also the bed of our spiritual rest is green.'(Paraphrase mine). She is, in fact, affirming the Lord's approbation, that the change, which has taken place of her person, was truly the result of her beholding Him in the fullness of His glorious face.

The ultimate goal of the believers' life-long pursuit of faith after the Lord is to be changed into His glorious image, and to enter into and enjoy the spiritual rest that comes about thereby.

The metaphorical statement," your eyes are doves," refers to her eyes of understanding that have been opened by the Holy Spirit, the heavenly Dove.

For AV's "pleasant," JB has "delightful," NIV has "charming." "RSV's truly lovely captures intensive force of the particle" (Carr).[48]

The 'green bed' occurs here in the selfsame sense in which David writes in Ps 23:2, "He maketh me to lie down in green pastures." Literally, the 'green bed' refers to Goshen, the verdant pastureland that the Pharaoh gave to the children of Israel to be their dwelling place. Goshen is pictured as though it were a soft mattress of green grass that had extended over vast areas for the well-fed and satisfied Lord's flock to lie down and rest.

Delitzsch points out that the Heb. word rendered "green" is:

> Not a word of colour, but signifies to be extensible, and to extend far and wide... We have no word such as this, which combines in itself the idea of softness and juicy freshness, of bending and elasticity, of looseness.[49]

The "bed" occurs in the Song as a symbol for spiritual rest. The word recurs in v. 3:1 as "my bed" and in v. 3:7 as "his bed." In 3:1, the beloved speaks of the bed as "my bed" to denote the absence of the Lord from the bed and of the spiritual rest forfeited by her consequently.

The occurrence of the plural form of first person possessive pronoun "our": "our bed," "our house" and "our rafters" signifies the companionship of the Lord being experienced palpably by the patriarchal church at this juncture of her history.

The beams of our house are cedar, and our rafters of fir (17)

The pastoral motif of vv.7-8 and 16 continues. The word rendered "house" is in the plural number, "houses." Carr points

---

48 *Ibid.,* p. 86.
49 Franz Delitzsch, *op. cit.,* p. 39.

out that the word "house" refers to "the whole garden with its many-shaded bowers."[50] Delitzsch concurs by saying, "cedar tops will form the roof of the house in which they dwell, and the cypresses its wainscot."[51]

The time is the spiritual noonday that was presaged in v.7. The patriarchal flock is lying down and resting on an extensive cushion of green grass, under the shadow of the "many shaded bowers" of the cedar and fir trees of Goshen, showing thereby that the flock has been fed with the spiritual provender to its full satisfaction. The cedar and fir trees occur possibly as symbols for the protection and safety that the Lord provided for His flock in Egypt.

The description of the Lord's flock lying down and resting under the bowers of the cedar and fir trees of the lush green pasture land of Goshen occurs as the answer to the beloved's own question that she had raised in v.7, "Tell me, O thou whom my soul loveth, where thou feedest, where thou makest thy flock to rest at noon?"

It is the spiritual rest entered into and enjoyed by the patriarchs and their families by grace, through faith, that is portrayed in this manner. Both Jacob and Joseph were still alive and the Lord's presence with this little flock of simple faith and trust was very real and palpable.

The present depiction contrasts with the former portrayal, in 1:7-8, of the wandering state of the Lord's flock, and of the ensuing portrayal in 3:1-3. The vv. 3:1-3 depict the beloved groping about in the dark in the streets and broadways of the city of Ramses, in search of the Lord who had gone missing from her hold of faith and from the bed of her complacency during the four centuries of the night of captivity and apostasy.

The Song regards the spiritual rest enjoyed by the church during the lifetime of the patriarchs as the model to be followed by the Lord's flock of all ages to come.

---

50 G. Lloyd Carr, *op. cit.*, 87.
51 Franz Delitzsch, *op. cit.*, p. 39.

PART TWO
THE MOSAIC PERIOD 2:1 - 3:8

III. THE FIRST FORTY YEARS OF MOSES' LIFE DURING WHICH HE WAS BROUGHT UP BY THE PHAROAH'S DAUGHTER 2:1-6

(The first forty-years of Moses' life)

After remaining in an embryonic state for four centuries of the Egyptian captivity, portrayed in 1:13 as an impending night and in 2:11 as a cold winter that has come and gone, Israel, the beloved appears in the historical arena, declaring herself as the "rose of Sharon" and the "lily of the valleys" that have blossomed with the onset of the Spring season. (Cf. comment below on 2:11, 12a,"For, lo, the winter is past, the rain is over and gone; the flowers appear on the earth.").

According to 3:1, the elect had been groping in the dark "all night long" in search of him whom her soul loves. In chronological sequence, the one who appears over the historical arena, in the guise of the beloved, declaring, "I am the rose of Sharon, and the lily of the valleys," is the baby Moses. This assertion may appear presumptuous at this juncture. However, it will become crystal-clear when we come to the study of the succeeding sections, 2:8-3:8, and 8:2-4.

1. *An adorable child, 2:1*

2: 1. *I am the rose of Sharon,*
and the lily of the valleys.

Moses, we are told, was possessed with a beauty that was almost proverbial. "Beauty," it is said, "was regarded by the ancients as a mark of the divine favour."[52] It was because the child

---

[52] Rev. Robert Jameison, et. al., *op. cit.*, p. 54.

was "exceeding fair," lit. "fair to God" (Acts 7:20), that Moses' mother hid him for three months. For no other reason did Pharaoh's daughter adopt the child despite knowing that he was of the servile Hebrew stock. "The beauty of the child was so remarkable and natural to him," writes Josephus, that every time when he was being carried along the road, "it detained the spectators, and made them stay longer to look upon him."[53]

Rose of Sharon

The Heb. word *chabatstseleth,* is inapplicable to the rose. The meadow saffron, or the narcissus, is among the flowers that are suggested. The word occurs in Isa 35:1-2, in association with Sharon. "The desert shall...blossom as the rose...the glory of Lebanon shall be given unto it, the excellency of Carmel and Sharon."

In the Heb. language, "Sharon" means a level place or "plain country." The use of the definite article indicates that a particular plain or level place is meant. The plain country of Sharon, which was situated in the Mediterranean coast, was "remarkable for the fertility of its fields and pastures."[54] This Palestinian Sharon is said to have been "in ancient times ... a swampy area." [55] However, this region does not appear to be the one meant here. For, the Spirit of God invokes only facts taken from the redemptive history of Israel as figures of speech in the Song. As the historical facts portrayed in this unit are set in Egypt, the "swampy area" wherein the figurative rose of Sharon blossoms also has to be located in Egypt itself. The particular marshy place that was situated somewhere in the Nile delta, wherefrom Pharaoh's daughter picked the baby Moses, suits the context better.

And the lily of the valleys, (1b).

Lily is the Song's symbol for Israel as opposed to henna blossoms, which occur as the symbol for the Gentiles (cf. comment on vv.2 below and 7:11). As stated, the person who self-introduces

---

[53] Flavius Josephus, *Josephus' Complete works,* trans. William Whiston, Michigan, A.M. Kregel, 1960, p. 57.

[54] H. W. F. Gesenius, *op. cit.,* p. 850.

[55] G. Lloyd Carr, *op. cit.,* p 87.

himself, saying, "I am ...the lily of the valleys" is the baby Moses. The word "valley" appears to denote Moses' humble origin from the slavish Israelite family.

2. *Israel, the lily, among poking thorns,* 2:2

2: 2. *As the lily among thorns,*
so is my love among the daughters.

The word "daughters" occurs here in the sense in which the idiomatic term, "daughter of Egypt," is used in the prophetic writings, to speak of the people of Egypt in general. With regard to the rationale for using the plural form, "daughters," instead of the singular form, "daughter," see comment, under "The Daughters of Jerusalem," in the Introductory Section of this book.

Thorns.

"Not the thorns of the flower-stem, but the thorn-plants that are around," (Delitzsch).[56] The word "thorns" is commonly used in the Old Testament as a symbol for the oppressive people among whom Israel dwelt (cf. Num 33:55; Judg 2:3; 2 S 23:6). The Egyptians among whom Israel dwelt had oppressed her as the surrounding thorn bushes kept poking at a lone lily. Significantly, in chronological sequence this verse occurs at the time when the children of Israel were groaning under the intolerable oppression perpetrated upon them by the Egyptian taskmasters.

The context shows that the succeeding verses, vv. 3-6, occur as the figurative descriptions of a series of spiritual blessings with which the Lord blessed His elect, particularly Moses, during the time when Israel had been undergoing severe oppression at the hands of the Egyptian taskmasters, like a "lily among thorns, as described in v.2.

3. *Moses shelters himself under the shadow of the Lord Almighty,* 2:3

2: 3. *As the apple tree among the trees of the wood,*
so is my beloved among the sons.
I sat down under his shadows with great delight,
and his fruit was sweet to my taste.

As the apple tree…is my beloved (2a).

She leaves no room for ambiguity. The apple tree occurs as a figurative description of the Almighty Lord, her Lover.

Among the trees of the wood … among the sons.

The trees of the wood occur parallel to the thorns of the preceding verse. Carr points out that the Heb. word *yaar* which is translated wood occurs 59 times in the Old Testament, and "is always translated 'forest' or 'thicket,' or some synonym for these," except at 5:1, and 1 Sam. 14:26, where it is rendered "honeycomb."[57] The word, he says, comes from a root, meaning, and "a rugged, mountainous place."[58] Obviously, the word "wood" refers here to the Egyptian court along with the officials thereof.

The sons

The "sons" occur parallel to the daughters of the preceding verse. While the daughters were the surrounding poking brambles, the "sons" are a thicket of wild trees. The points of contrast between the Lord, the Lover, and the sons are two-fold. In the first place, the sons are leafless trees that do not provide the required shadow to the beloved to protect herself from the scorching heat. In the second place, they are barren trees that do not provide the fruits required by the beloved to satisfy her spiritual hunger. These are clearly implied from the description of the beloved sitting down under the shadow of the Lord, her Apple tree with great delight, and relishing His fruits so sweetly to the full satiation of her spiritual hunger.

Those described as a thicket of barren, leafless trees are the men of the Egyptian court who were all around Moses in his daily life. If Josephus' remarks in this regard are trustworthy, there were always conspirators in the Egyptian court who wanted to kill Moses and rid the Egyptians of the possible threat posed to the hierarchy by his education and status.[59]

---

[56] Franz Delitzsch, *op. cit.*, p. 41.
[57] G. Lloyd Carr, *op. cit.*, p. 129.
[58] *Ibid.*, p. 89.
[59] Flavius Josephus, *op. cit.*, p. 59.

I sat down under his shadow with great delight (3b)

The underlying thought of the statement is the same as that of Ps 91:1-2:

> He that dwelleth in the secret place of the Most High shall abide under the shadow of the Almighty. I will say of the Lord, He is my refuge and my fortress: my God; in Him will I trust.

There was a cry for the shadow of shady trees from the commencement of the storyline. It had surfaced first in 1:6 under the motif of the vinedresser exposed to sunburn out of the sun's infuriated look. It had surfaced again, in v. 7, under the changed motif of sheep and shepherd, "Tell me, O thou whom my soul loveth, where thou makest thy flock to rest at noon?" The answer to that quest for shadow was found in the well-fed patriarchal flock lying down and resting over a soft cushion of juicy green grass of the pasture land of Goshen, under the bowers of the tall and shady cedars and firs of the Egyptian hierarchy, as portrayed in vv. 1:51-17. Later on, when the patriarchs disappeared from the earthly scene, the posterity ("kids") had lost her hold of faith in the Lord, and with that she ceased to abide under the shadow of the Lord Almighty. Instead, the beloved, i.e. the elect of God from among the posterity, began to grope about in the dark, in search of Him whom her soul loves, as depicted in 3:1. Judging from the above, the present portrayal of the elect sheltering herself under the shadow of the Lord, the Apple Tree, towards the closing period of the Egyptian captivity, cannot be otherwise than that of Moses sheltering himself "under the shadow of the Almighty."

We are not given to know much about the kind of religious life that Moses led during the days he lived in the Egyptian palace as the adopted son of Pharaoh's daughter. He received "a training at home," opines *Smith's Bible Dictionary*, "in the true religion, in faith in God, in the promises to his nation ... a training which he never forgot."[60]

The light of the knowledge of the God of his fathers would have come to Moses, as it does normally, in due course of time.

---

[60] William Smith, *op. cit.*, p. 48.

"When he was come to years," that is, when he attained the required maturity to make decisions for himself, he "refused to be called the son of Pharaoh's daughter; choosing rather to suffer affliction with the people of God, than to enjoy the pleasures of sin for a season" (Heb 11:24). He did so because he was "seeing him who is invisible (Heb 11:24ff) "The Hebrews depended on him," writes Josephus, "and were of good hopes that great things would be done by him." The Egyptians, on the other hand, were suspicious of Moses, fearing that he would "raise a sedition, and bring innovations into Egypt."[61]

The comparison of external threats to the smiting of the sun occurs here as in Ps 121:5-6, and the grace of God to the cooling shadow as in Ps 17:8; 36:7; 63:7; and 91:1.

And his fruit was sweet to my taste (3c).

"His fruit" that is, the fruit of the Apple tree, which occurs here as a symbol for the Lord Almighty. The fruit of the symbolic Apple tree, namely, "apples," ought to be occurring as a symbol for the promise of God (cf. 2:5; 7:8). Eating His fruit sweetly signifies relishing the promises of God sweetly through faith. God's promises are more sweetly relished when the soul is gripped with spiritual hunger. And they become sweeter to one's spiritual palate when he/she is born of God. The "great delight" with which Moses shelters himself under the shadow of the Lord Almighty, and the sweetness with which he relishes God's promises appear to be the natural outcome of regeneration. This ought to be so, seeing that the succeeding verses (vv 4-6) describe the Lord filling Moses with His Spirit.

4. *The Lord Leads Moses to the Baptism in the Spirit, 2:4-6*

2: 4. *He brought me to the banqueting house,*
and his banner over me was love.

5. *Stay me with flagons, comfort me with apples:*
for I am sick of love.

6. *His left hand is under my head,*
and his right hand doth embrace me.

---

[61] Flavius Josephus, *op. cit.*, pp. 57, 58.

He brought me into the banqueting house (4a).

Banqueting house is literally "the house in which wine is drunk."[62] But, its occurrence here is not in the literal sense. It refers, figuratively, to the wine house of divine love. Because, when brought within the banqueting house, the beloved did not get drunk with literal wine, but with the wine of divine love, as made candid by the beloved's statements, "his banner over me was love," coupled with, "I am sick of love."

The existing analogy between the titillation of divine love and wine has figured twice before. First in 1:2, "Thy love is better than wine." Thereafter, the beloved had expressed her longing desire, saying, "we will remember thy love more than wine" (1:4) The longing desire of the newborn Israel to remember the love of God in Christ had found its fulfillment on the day of Pentecost when the waiting band of disciples were filled by the Spirit sent from on high. The emotional exuberance of the disciples on that occasion led the onlookers to say one to the other, "These men are full of new wine" (Acts 2:13). The present portrayal is that of the Lord bringing Moses to the banqueting house of the Lord's love, in the baptism in the Holy Spirit. The baptism in the Spirit is in reality the baptism in divine love. (Cf. "The love of God is shed abroad in our hearts by the Holy Ghost which is given unto us" Rom 5:5).

His banner over me was love (4b)

"He brought me ... his banner ... was" occurs parallel to the underlying thought of vv. 6:4,10, of Christ, the Captain and the banner-bearer of His church, marching her ahead against all odds "terrible as an army with banners" (cf. comment on vv. 6:4,10). Moses himself was the originator of the idea that the love of the Lord flutters over His chosen people like a banner. To commemorate the miraculous way in which God enabled Israel to triumph over the Amalekite army, (as long as Moses held up his hand in faith), Moses erected an altar at Rephidim and called its name *Jehovah-nissi*, meaning, "the Lord is my banner" (Exod 17:15).

---

[62] Franz Delitzsch, *op. cit.*, p. 43.

Stay me with flagons, comfort me with apples (5a).

Delitzsch says that the meaning of the intensive form of the Heb. word *samak*, rendered "stay," is "to prop up, support," or, "to under-prop, 'uphold."[63] Likewise, with regard to the intensive form of the Heb. word *raphad*, rendered "comfort," he says that it means, "to raise up from beneath... to furnish firm ground and support."[64] Carr thinks that *raphad* refers to preparing "any kind of supporting couch or bed (i.e. a place of restoration from sickness, fatigue, etc)."[65] It emerges from the foregoing that the beloved is appealing here for support lest she falls down out of the imbalance brought about by inebriation with divine love. The depiction in the succeeding verse, of the beloved lying down in the lap of the Lord, with His left hand under her head, and His right hand caressing her, shows clearly, that this was what she had appealed for.

However, in spite of the above stated explanations, a serious anomaly still remains. For raisin cakes are not meant for propping up drunkards from falling down; nor are apples spread as a "couch" to relax upon.

Prompted, probably by the necessity to avoid the emerging absurdity, almost all the modern versions, following AV, employ words and expressions, which could apply, more or less, to love-sickness, rather than to drunkenness. Thus RSV renders, "sustain me with raisins; refresh me with apples; for I am sick with love."

However, the anomaly continues to remain in spite of translating the Heb. words *samak* and *rafad* as sustain and refresh respectively. Because, raisin cakes and apples are not the answer for a woman who is 'sick of love' but the caresses of her lover even as she remains within his loving embrace, as described in the succeeding verse. The passage, therefore, needs to be interpreted from its spiritual perspective, namely, that the love sickness refers to that which is associated with the Lord's love. It occurs again in 5:8, where the beloved charges the daughters of

---

[63] *Ibid.*, p. 43.
[64] *Ibid.*, p. 43.
[65] G. Lloyd Carr, *Op. cit.*, p. 92.

Jerusalem, saying, "I charge you, ... if ye find my beloved, that ye tell him, that I am sick of love."

Apples (Heb. *'tappuach'*) are the fruits of the apple tree (Heb. *'tappuach'*). "As the apple tree ... is my beloved... I sat down under his shadow with great delight, and his fruit (i.e. *tapuach*) was sweet to my taste" (2:3). In v. 7:8, the smell of the beloved's nose is stated to be like apples. In both of these contexts, 'apples' occurs in a figurative sense, as a symbol for the promises of God.

Flagons are dried grapes pressed together into cakes. A flagon was part of the gift that David gave to each of those present upon the auspicious occasion of bringing up the Ark of the Covenant to Zion (2 Sam 6:19). Occurring parallel to apples, flagons ought to be the symbol for some sort of similar spiritual provision.

If AV's "comfort me with apples" has textual support, it becomes meaningful, in that our Lord used the expression "the Comforter," Gk. *'paracletos,'* (One who stands along-side the believer, to help, and comfort), as a synonym for "the Spirit of truth," "the promise of the Father," whom He had promised to receive of the Father and send (John 14:16, 26; 15:26; 16:7; Acts 1:4; 2:33, 39).

His left hand is under my head, and his right hand doth embrace me (2:6).

The beloved is lying down in the Lord's lap. In quick response to her cry for help and support, the Lord had propped her up and laid her down gently. He pillows her head with his left hand and embraces her with his right. With regard to the significance of the expression, "his right hand doth embrace me," Delitzsch says, "the situation here is like that at Gen xxix. 13, xlviii.10; where...it is meant of loving arms stretched out to embrace."[66] Significantly, in the passage of Gen 48:10 the act of embracing is coupled with the act of kissing. In Gen 29:13, there is the additional thought of kissing and bringing home, as was implied in vv.1:2,4 and clearly stated in vv3:4; and 8:1-2 of the Song.

---

[66] Franz Delitzsch, *op. cit.*, p. 45.

The description of the Lord supporting the elect's head from beneath with His left hand recalls the words of Deut 33: 27, of the blessing Moses pronounced upon the children of Israel, saying, "The eternal God is thy refuge, and underneath are the everlasting arms."

IV. MOSES FLEES TO THE WILD REGIONS OF THE SINAI PENINSULA, WHERE THE LORD APPEARS AND COMMISSIONS HIM TO GO TO EGYPT AND DELIVER ISRAEL FROM CAPTIVITY, 2:7-17

(The second forty-year period of Moses' life)

1. *Moses goes into hiding in the wild regions of the Sinai Peninsula, 2:7.*

2: 7 I charge you, O ye daughters of Jerusalem,
by the roes, and by the hinds of the field,
that ye stir not up, nor awake my love, till he please.

The scene shifts from the royal banqueting house to a wild region, which is the regular habitat of the wild gazelles. The expression "of the field" means, 'of the wild region.' The description in the succeeding unit (vv.2:8-9), of the Lord's appearance to Moses in the burning bush, in the vicinity of Horeb, "the mountain of God" (Exod 3:1), shows that the depicted wild region of the present verse is the same. Fearing that the Pharaoh would take revenge upon him for slaying an Egyptian, Moses had fled to the wild regions of the Sinai Peninsula and had been tending the flock of Jethro, his father in law.

The present adjuration has been interposed in this historical juncture of the disclosure as a device to reflect the panic of fear and touchiness that had reigned in Moses' heart, in the absence of absolute faith and trust in the Lord. The "roes and hinds of the field," (i.e., of the wild region) being characteristically timid and touchy, the adjuration is framed in their name, to reflect the panic of fear that had ruled the heart of Moses.

The AV rendering, "my love, till he please" is obviously based on the assumption that "love" stands for the lover. On the other hand, NASB's, "my love, until she pleases," is based on the assumption that "love" refers to the female partner. Differing from both, NRSV, takes "love" in the abstract sense, and renders, "do not stir up or awaken love until it is ready." But what is actually meant here appears to be, 'do not stir up or meddle with my love affair, until it pleases.'

There is the possibility of the presence of a distant allusion here to the episode of Esau selling his birthright to Jacob, binding the transaction with an oath, and later, conceding to his father's wishes, breaking his oath and trying to retake it for himself by means of the "savoury" dish of venison brought from the field. Esau was "a cunning hunter," and was also "a man of the field" (Gen 25: 27-33). Once he had readily sold out his birthright and confirmed the sale by a binding oath, he had no more right to claim it back for himself. But, as the matter was finally for God to settle, He saw to it that Jacob, whom He had predestinated to be the heir of promise, becomes the legitimate heir of the birthright. After all, as Esau was a carnal seed, he also was timid, like the gazelles of the field. Most of his youthful days he had been quietly lying in wait to hunt after these timid gazelles. A mild stir or movement was sufficient to drive the gazelles away. Hence the adjuration, "stir not up, nor awake."

The Heb. verbs rendered "stir" and "awake" are different forms from *ur;* a common root, meaning, 'astir' or 'disturb.'

2. *The Lord appears to Moses in the burning bush, in the vicinity of Horeb, "the mountain of God," 2:8-9*

2: 8. The voice of my beloved! behold, he cometh
Leaping upon the mountains, skipping upon the hills

9. My beloved is like a roe or a young hart:
Behold, he standeth behind our wall,
He looketh forth at the windows,
Shewing himself through the lattice.

Except for the presence of a mountain range at hearing distance, the scene remains set in the wild regions of the preceding verse. From an imaginary prison cell, its windows latticed, the beloved hears the approaching voice of her Lover, as He rushes down the mountain towards her. She likens His rushing down the mountain to that of an uncharacteristic act of a timid wild roe or a young hart, which emerges openly out of its lurking place in some crag over the mountain range: throws all of its characteristic timidity and fears to the winds, and rushes down, "leaping upon the mountains and skipping upon the hills." The points of comparison are between the characteristic natures of both the Lord and the young gazelle of remaining concealed and unseen over the mountain, on the one side, and of their uncharacteristic act of openly disclosing themselves to the utter surprise of the beloved (here Moses).

The beloved has other valid reasons as well for resorting to this type of seemingly bizarre figure of speech to describe the Lord's appearance. In the first place, the Lord's person and movements are indescribable in human terms, for the reason that He is an invisible, intangible, Spirit. In the second place, Horeb was believed to be "the mountain of God" (Exod 3:1). It is thought that the Lord had been abiding over it unseen and concealed, unconcerned of the incessant groaning cries of His beloved people that had been rising to Him for centuries, just like one of the innumerable timid young gazelles that had been remaining unseen and concealed within the crags, over the rugged rocky mountain.

The prison house occurs as a figure for Israel's Egyptian captivity. However, in the present context, Moses, a self-immured prisoner, alone had been the captive Israel.

The voice of my beloved, (8a).

The Lord being an invisible Spirit, Moses did not see Him, only heard His "voice." Note the repeated stress on the "voice" of the Lord, in vv.5:2, and 8:13.

Behold, he cometh, (8b).

The Lord was coming down from His Mountain, in response to the groaning cries of Israel that had been rising unto Him, for deliverance from the oppression of the Egyptian taskmasters.

Leaping upon the mountains, and skipping upon the hills, (8b).

This is how gazelles normally go from one place to another, particularly, when they have to rush down a rugged rocky mountain like Horeb, which is replete with crags and fissures. One must not mistake that the young gazelle is pictured here as though it were leaping from one mountaintop to the other, and skipping from one hilltop to the other. Taken as the modern Sinai range, Horeb is stated to be "steep mountains, first red and brown sandstone, and then bronze-red granite, terrifying, yet beautiful."[67] Walking is impracticable in such "fantastic rock formations... above narrow twisting valleys."[68]

My beloved is like a roe or young hart, (9a).

That is, in two respects: first, in that the Lord had been abiding over His mountains, unseen and concealed, similar to a pretty young gazelle that had been living thereon in one of its numerous crags. And second, in His present stunning theophany, which was in sharp contrast to His characteristic nature of remaining hidden. The point of comparison is not between the physical appearances of the Lover (the Lord) and the young gazelles. In that the Lord was a Spirit, the question of comparing Him with the physical appearance of a gazelle did not arise.

Behold, he standeth behind our wall, (9b).

Note the use of the plural form of the first person pronoun "our." The "wall" is that of Israel's common "prison." Moses notices that, after having arrived, the Lord was standing behind the wall of Israel's common prison cell, in the manner of an intimately domesticated young gazelle.

He looketh forth at the windows, shewing himself though the lattice, (9c).

By now, the Lord has come close to the latticed window through which the beloved had been watching. "Shewing himself" means disclosing Himself. In fact, the statement in Exod 3:2, "The angel of the Lord appeared unto him in a flame of fire," literally means, "The angel of the Lord shewed himself."

---

[67] Gardner, Joseph L: *Atlas of the Bible,* New York: Reader's Digest Association Inc., 1981, p. 67.

[68] *Ibid.,* p. 67.

3. *The call, 2:10-13.*

2: 10. My beloved spake, and said unto me,
Rise up, my love, my fair one, and come away
11. For, lo, the winter is past, the rain is over and gone;
12. The flowers appear on the earth;
the time of the singing of birds is come,
and the voice of the turtle is heard in our land;
13. The fig tree putteth forth her green figs,
and the vines with the tender grape give a good smell.
Arise, my love, my fair one, and come away.

The approaching voice of the Lord that the beloved had been hearing over the distant mountaintop was the "voice" of these words that He was speaking aloud, as He was rushing down the mountain, towards her.

Now after the arrival at the imaginary prison cell, the Lord discloses Himself, in the manner of an intimately domesticated, meek and lowly young gazelle that presses its lovely face against the lattice and reveals itself to Moses.

Having shown Himself, in the dazzling theophany, the Lord calls upon the captive Israel, through Moses, to muster faith, "rise up" from the captivity, and "come away" to take possession of "our land," i.e., the Promised Land (vv.10, 12). He reinforces His words with compelling reasons to drive home to her the urgency of the need for her to rise up forthwith and come away. The gist of His arguments: "the winter is past ... the time ... is come." The winter refers to the four hundred years of her Egyptian captivity, the coming and going of which was a foregone conclusion, as the Lord had made known beforehand the surety of its coming and going (cf. Gen 15:13, 16). "The time" refers to the period that was envisaged in the Father's redemptive scheme for His chosen people to come out of Egypt and take possession of the Promised Land.

For lo, the winter is past, (11a).

The imagery is framed after the onset of a promising bright spring season, after the passing of a cold rainy winter. Accordingly, the time of Israel's exodus from Egypt had coincided with the onset of the spring season, i.e., in the month of Abib (Nissan), corresponding to March-April of our Christian calendar.

The rain is over and gone, (11b).

The winter rain, "*geshem* from *gashem*, to be thick, massy,"[69] imply darksome clouds, foggy weather, and biting cold. "The winter is thought of as a person who has passed by" (Delitzsch).[70] "The three verbs almost personify the winter rain as a traveler who has passed through and has gone" (Carr).[71] This, as stated above, refers to the surety of Israel becoming a "stranger in a land that is not theirs" and "the fourth generation" returning to the Promised Land, as the Lord had foretold Abraham, in the covenant, (cf. Gen 15:13-16).

The flowers appear on the earth, (12a).

Appearance of flowers on the earth occurs as the natural outcome of the winter rains that have come and gone, followed by the onset of the spring season. (cf. exegetical comment above on v.1, "I am the rose of Sharon and the lily of the valleys").

The appearance of flowers occurs as the precursor of a fruitful season.

The time of the singing of birds is come, (12b).

The time of singing refers to the time of rejoicing over the miraculous deliverance that was round the corner. "Of birds" is not present in the Heb. text, as indicated by the italics in the AV. "The Heb. word *zamir* is not normally used of bird-songs."[72] However, the singing of birds is certainly implied in the imagery, as spring season is the time when birds begin to sing.

The voice of the turtle is heard in our land, (12c).

The *turtle* is a migratory bird, which arrives in Palestine early in the spring and remains throughout the following summer.

---

69 Franz Deleitzsch, *op. cit.*, p. 50.
70 *Ibid.*, p. 50.
71 G. Lloyd Carr, *op. cit.*, p. 97.
72 *Ibid.*, p. 97.

The cooing of turtledoves is the precursor of the onset of springtime.

Historically, the cooing of the turtledove alludes to the groaning cries of the children of Israel that rose up unto the Lord, under the cumbersome burdens imposed on them by the Egyptian taskmasters. Cf. "The children of Israel sighed by reason of the bondage, and they cried, and their cry came up unto God ... And God heard their groaning" (Exod 2: 23-24).

The Lord who was to incarnate as the Seed Par Excellence of Abraham, in the Abrahamic covenant, and His beloved, to wit, the body of the regenerated seed of Israel were the joint-heirs of the promised inheritance. Hence the use of the first person possessive plural pronoun, "our," to speak of the Promised Land as, "our land."

The fig tree putteth forth her green figs, (13a).

"In fig trees, by this time the green of the fruit formation changes its colour" (Delitzsch).[73] Carr points out that the verb *chanat* translated "putteth forth" occurs "only four other times in the Old Testament" and each time it is translated "embalm."[74] Significantly, all the other four occurrences of the verb are in the same chapter (Gen 50:2, 3, 26), and in the same context of embalming the bodies of both Jacob and Joseph. Carr sees no link whatsoever between the ripening of figs and the embalming of human bodies, "unless it has to do with the change of colour of the skin that is associated with embalming process."[75] Pope concurs with Carr, saying, "the verb *hnt* is used elsewhere in the Scripture only in Gen 50: 2, 26 where it is applied to embalming of Jacob and Joseph in Egypt. No suitable sense is suggested by this usage."[76] However, viewed from the standpoint of our line of interpretation, Carr's observation turns out to be of immense spiritual significance. An allusion had already been made in 1:13

[73] Franz Deleitzsch, *op. cit.*, p. 51.
[74] G. Lloyd Carr, *op. cit.*, p. 99.
[75] *Ibid.*, p. 99.
[76] Marvin Pope, *op. cit.*, p. 397.

to the sachet of myrrh used for embalming and preserving the bodies of both Jacob and Joseph, as the token of the sure hope they had cherished that their posterity will certainly be delivered from Egypt and take possession of the Promised Land, as the Lord had foretold Abraham. It is, therefore, quite consistent for the Lord to advance the 'reddening' of the mummified bodies of the patriarchs to prove to the posterity that the time for their deliverance from Egypt and taking possession of the Promised Land has come.

The vines with the tender grape give a good smell, (13b).

NIV's "blossoming vines" is preferable to AV's "vines with the tender grape" for the simple reason that the tender grapes do not give out fragrance.

The budding and blossoming of vines, pomegranates and figs are the Song's symbols for budding forth of faith and blossoming of a sweet-smelling spiritual life (cf. comment on 6:11; 7:12). One must bear in mind here that the vines that blossom and give a good smell at present are of the selfsame symbolic "vineyard," concerning which Jacob had ruefully bemoaned in 1:6, saying, "mine own vineyard have I not kept."

4. *Moses behaves like a timid 'rock-dove' that withdraws and hides itself within the cleft of rock, and advances lame excuses that act virtually like crafty "little foxes" that spoil the vines, 2:14-15*

2: 14. O my dove, that art in the clefts of the rock,
in the secret places of the stairs, let me see thy countenance,
let me hear thy voice; for sweet is thy voice,
and thy countenance is comely.

2: 15. Take us the foxes, the little foxes, that spoil the vines:
for our vines have tender grapes.

The scene continues to remain set in the vicinity of Horeb, the rocky mountain. It will remain so until 2:17. In spite of the Lord's dazzling self-disclosure of Himself to Moses as the God of Abraham, the God of Isaac and the God of Jacob, Moses was neither convinced, nor was he ready to proceed to Egypt in obedience to the divine commission to bring the light of the knowledge of the God of their fathers to Israel, and deliver them from the captivity. Instead, he began to invent all sorts of lame excuses one after the other to be bailed out from the cumbersome task, and to draw back and continue to remain in the very same hiding place that he had made for himself somewhere in the side of a rocky cliff. The reason for Moses' reluctance to proceed to Egypt was the fear of the Pharaoh's revenge for slaying an Egyptian. The Lord therefore aptly likens Moses to a timid rock dove, which for fear of humankind has flown off to a far away mountainous region and made its dwelling place in the cleft of some rocky cliff. With regard to the lame excuses that Moses was inventing and advancing one after the other, the Lord likens them to crafty "little foxes" that spoil the blossoming vines of the faith that He was trying to germinate in his heart, and impede its growth and fruition.

Moses' first reaction to the Lord's, saying, "Come now therefore, and I will send thee unto the Pharaoh" had been the blunt retort, "Who am I, that I should go unto Pharaoh, and that I should bring forth the children of Israel out of Egypt?" In sympathetic response, the Lord reassured him, saying, "Certainly I will be with thee." (Exod 3:11,12). "Behold, they will not believe me," answered Moses, "nor hearken unto my voice: for they will say, 'The Lord hath not appeared unto thee' " (Exod 4:1).

It was then that the Lord endowed Moses with the ability to perform signs and wonders, saying, "if they will not believe thee, ... they will believe ... the sign" (cf. Ex. 4:8,9). "O my Lord, I am not eloquent," answered Moses, "neither heretofore, nor since thou hast spoken unto thy servant: but I am slow of speech, and of a slow tongue" (Ex. 4:10). "Who hath made man's mouth? ... have not I the Lord," answered the Lord, "now therefore go, and I will be with thy mouth" (Exod 4:11,12). "O my Lord, send, I pray thee, by the hand of him whom thou wilt send," replied Moses.

At this, the anger of the Lord was kindled against Moses, and then only did Moses agree to go. However, instead of going straight to Egypt, he set his face towards the house of Jethro, his father-in-law. The Lord appeared to Moses there again, and commanded him, "Go, return into Egypt: for all the men are dead which sought thy life" (Exod 4:19). Only after this did Moses dare to go into Egypt and face the next Pharaoh.

O my dove, (14a).

The Heb. word *yona* translated "dove "actually means, a 'rock dove.' There is due recognition here on the Lord's part that Moses was guileless like a dove despite the fact that he lacked the required courage to go and face the Pharaoh, in obedience to the divine call and commission. "The Lord is merciful and gracious ... He knoweth our frame" (Ps 103: 8, 14).

That art in the clefts of the rock, in the secret places of the stairs, (14a).

The expression, "the secret places" refers to the hiding-places that Moses had constructed to remain hidden from the Pharaoh. The Heb. word, *madregah,* translated "stairs" is said to be an Aramaic loan-word derived from the root meaning, "to go step by step or to lift."[77] The word can apply also to "steps (cut in rocks)," or to a "mountain path."[78] LXX takes it for a "fortification wall."[79] Significantly, none of these meanings apply to the simple cleft of a rock in which a rock dove makes its nest. They apply only to secret hiding places prepared laboriously by a human being-here Moses.

Let me see thy countenance, let me hear thy voice, (14b).

NIV, JB, "Show me your face, let me hear your voice."

It appears that these words are framed with the following two-fold reactions of Moses in mind. First, "Moses hid his face," when the Lord appeared to him in the burning bush, "for he was afraid to look upon God" (Exod 3:6). Second, he had said, "O my Lord, I am not eloquent."

---

[77] *G. Lloyd Carr, op.cit.,* p. 101.

[78] William L. Holladay: *A Concise Hebrew and Aramaic Lexicon of the Old Testament,* Michigan: Eerdmans Publishing Company, 1980, p. 183.

[79] G. Lloyd Carr, *op. cit.,* p. 100.

For sweet is thy voice, and thy countenance is comely, (14c).

These statements are being made by the Lord with the future prospects that He foresaw in Moses, rather than the present state of his voice and countenance. For the Scriptures bear unrivalled testimony to the fact that "the Lord spake unto Moses face to face, as a man speaketh unto his friend" (Exod 33:11). And, concerning Moses' countenance, the scripture bears unparalleled witness to the fact that "the man Moses was very meek, above all the men which were upon the face of the earth" (Num 12:3).

Take us the foxes, the little foxes, (15a).

NRSV, "catch us," from the Heb, root *akhaz.* "The verb form is imperative, masculine plural, but there is no indication whether the speaker is male or female" (Carr).[80] The context clearly shows that the Lord is the speaker.

The Heb. word *shualim* translated foxes is from the root *shagal,* "to go down, or into the depth" (Delitzsch).[81] Foxes are crafty creatures. As stated, they are brought into the picture to reflect the sly defense and lame excuses that Moses had been inventing and advancing one after the other to bail himself out from the risky task of facing the Pharaoh. Just as little foxes craftily burrow under the vines and impede their growth and productivity, Moses was undermining and impeding the growth of the faith that the Lord was germinating in his soul.

For our vines have tender grapes, (15b).

The Lord who speaks these words is the Seed Par Excellence of Abraham, in the Abrahamic covenant of promise (cf. comment on 3:11). His beloved to whom He speaks these words is also the seed of Abraham, in the same covenant. The symbolic vineyard is their common heritage. It is from these standpoints that the Lord uses the first person plural pronoun to speak of the vines as "our vines." (Cf. exegetical comment on 8:12, "My vineyard, which is mine, is before me: thou, O Solomon, must have a thousand."

---

[80] *Ibid.,* p. 101.

[81] Franz Deleitzsch, *op. cit.,* p. 54.

5. *Moses, who appears in the guise of the beloved, is convinced finally and confesses the Lord as his own God and Shepherd, 2:16*

2: 16. *My beloved is mine, and I am his:*
He feedeth among the lilies.

Moses, who appears in the guise of the beloved, is finally convinced that the God of his fathers has truly owned Israel as His chosen people and has come down to deliver her from the captivity, and accordingly confesses Him with his mouth. The substance of the words of the beloved's confession is that the Lord belongs (exclusively) to Israel, that Israel belongs (exclusively) to the Lord, and that the Lord (her Shepherd) feeds (only) among (Israel), the lilies (paraphrase mine).

We shall see, as the study continues, that this slogan, which he raises now and then is one sided and biased (cf. comment on 4:5 and 6:3). For, if the Lord belongs exclusively to Israel, and He feeds only among Israel, the lilies, to whom does the rest of the nations of the world belong, and who will feed them?

My beloved is mine, and I am his, (16a).

As stated, these statements occur as the beloved's confession of faith in the sense of the words of Paul, in Rom 10:9-10, "If thou shalt confess with thy mouth the Lord Jesus, and shalt believe in thine heart ... thou shalt be saved." See the recurrence of the expression "mine" that the beloved uses to assert her claim that the Lord and His vineyard of promise belong to her exclusively (1:6c; 6:3; 8:12).

He feedeth among the lilies, (16b).

The pastoral motif of the former units vv.1:7-8 and vv. 15-17 resumes. The statement occurs as the beloved's answer to her own question that she had raised in 1:7, "Tell me, O thou whom my soul loveth, where thou feedest?" Literally, the Heb. verb *raah* rendered "feed" occurs in the sense of 'to pasture.' However, in 4:5, the verb is being used in the sense of 'to browse,' in the statement, "two young roes that are twins, which feedeth among the lilies."

The word "lily" occurs here in the sense in which it occurs in Ho. 14:5, "I will be as the dew unto Israel: he shall grow as the lily."

6. *Moses bids farewell to the Lord on the eve of his departure from Horeb, to Egypt, 2:17*

> 2: 17. Until the day break, and the shadows flee away,
> Turn, my beloved, and be thou like a roe or a young hart
> Upon the mountains of Bether

The scene still remains set in the vicinity of Horeb, "the mountain of God." The Lord had come down from Horeb, His mountain, "like a roe or a young hart," to reveal Himself to Moses, in the burning bush; to commission him to deliver Israel from the Egyptian captivity and to return to the selfsame place, along with the delivered nation, to worship Him in the Sinai covenant. Now, on the eve of his departure to Egypt, Moses appeals to the Lord to "turn," that is, return, to His mountain, and remain concealed and unseen, as He had always been, "like a roe or a young hart," until he returns along with the delivered nation.

Until the day break, and the shadows flee away, (17a)

This curious statement recurs again in 4:6, in the form of a refrain. Evidently, the refrain is being woven into the fabric of the Song out of the threads taken from the episode of the nightlong wrestle between the Lord and Jacob that took place at Peniel "until the breaking of the day."

In the present context, the use of the expression, "until the day break and the shadows flee away," implies:

(i). Moses' conceited belief that when he returns along with the delivered nation and worships the Lord in the Sinai covenant, the day of fullness of the knowledge of God will dawn in his, and Israel's heart, and the lingering shadows of doubts and fears will flee away.

(ii). That a certain amount of wrestling in the Spirit is required for the Lord to bring the light of the knowledge

> of God in the hearts of the children of Israel, just as a wrestle had to take place between the Lord and Jacob until the breaking of the day. (Cf. comment on 6:10).

The thought of "daybreak" occurs here in the sense in which Peter writes in 2 Pet 1:19, "Until the day dawn, and the day star arise in your hearts."

Upon the mountains of Bether," (17c).

NIV, "rugged mountains." NRSV, "cleft mountains." AV. Margin, "of divisions."

Delitzsch thinks that the mountains of *Bether* mean "mountains of separation, i.e. the riven mountains, which thus presents hindrances, but which he, 'the swift as gazelle' easily overcomes."[82] Luther, as quoted by Delitzsch, takes mountains of Bether, for "mountains with peaks, from one of which to the other one must spring."[83] In fact, Horeb is thought of here as being a craggy mountain, which affords innumerable crags for the gazelles to live hidden from humankind. In that the Lord is an unseen Spirit, He also is thought of as living hidden and unseen over Horeb, His Mountain, like one of those gazelles.

The word *"Bether"* occurs only two more times in the Old Testament. First, in Gen 15:10, in connection with the sacrificial animals that were cut or divided by Abraham, and passed between the parts, on the occasion of confirmation of the covenant. Second, in Jer 34:18, again with reference to the ritual of cutting "a calf in twain" before God, and passing between the parts to confirm the covenant made with Him. Basing probably on these, JB renders "mountains of *Bether*" as "mountains of the covenant." The presence of this additional meaning is possible here, in that Horeb is being called here as the "mountains of Bether," in connection with the making of the Sinai covenant.

---

[82] *Ibid.*, p. 55.
[83] *Ibid.*, p. 56.

7. *On Arrival at Ramses, Moses and Aaron find out the Beloved groping in the dark in search of the missing Lord, and show her the way to find Him out, 3:1-4*

3: 1. By the night on my bed I sought him whom my soul loveth:
I sought him, but I found him not.

2. I will rise now, and go about the city in the streets, and in the broad ways I will seek him whom my soul loveth:
I sought him, but I found him not.

3. The watchmen that go about the city found me:
to whom I said, saw ye him whom my soul loveth?

4. It was but a little that I passed from them,
but I found him whom my soul loveth:
I held him, and would not let him go,
until I had brought him into my mother's house,
and into the chamber of her that conceived me.

The scene shifts from the vicinity of Horeb to a large metropolis having numerous streets and broadways. The city, no doubt, is Ramses, the capital city of Egypt.

The beloved's misfortune of missing of the Lord from her bed in the dead of the night occurs as a sequel to the premonition of an impending night that the patriarchal church had, and the firm hope she had cherished that the posterity will certainly keep the Lord close to her bosom in the embrace of faith throughout the coming night (1:3). But, when the night did come, the posterity finds out to her dismay that the hope cherished dearly by the patriarchs did not come true. She sought for the Lord on her bed of complacency throughout the night and finds out that He is missing from her bosom. Alarmed and anguished, she sets out at night and gropes in the dark in the streets and broad ways of the city of Ramses, in search of Him whom her soul loves.

The description of the watchmen going about in the city and finding out the beloved as 'she groped about in the dark in search of Him whom her soul loves' occurs as the sequel to the depiction of the preceding verse, 2:17. In 2:17, as explained, Moses had bidden farewell to the Lord and had departed from the vicinity of Horeb to bring the light of the knowledge of the God of the fathers to the body of the elect from among the captive Israel which had been groping in the dark in Egypt. We know from the Biblical records that Moses took Aaron, his brother, along with him, according to the Lord's counsel. Hence the plural form, "watchmen."

By night, (1a).

In the Masoretic Text, the Heb. word *lailoth* rendered night is in plural number; "nights." "NIV, all night long catches the force of the Hebrew plural 'nights' as well as NEB night after night" (Carr).[84]

On my bed, (1a).

"Bed" refers to spiritual rest. The "bed," which the beloved describes here as "my bed" is the very same bed that she had described in 1:16 as, "our bed." Because the Lord's presence with her in her bed was palpable during the patriarchal age, she had described the bed as "our bed" at that time. On the contrary, as the Lord is missing from her bed now, she describes the bed here as "my bed."

In a literal sense, as in 1:16, the "bed" alludes to Goshen, the verdant pastureland that the Pharaoh gave to Israel for her dwelling place.

I sought him whom my soul loveth, (1b).

The beloved had addressed the Lord by this significant term in 1:7. This is the second time that she uses the term. It denotes the inherent longing that every human soul has to seek and find out the Lord, its Creator and Owner, and unite with Him in the heavenly bliss and rest.

I sought him, but I found him not, (1c).

The beloved's search for the Lord whom her soul loves occurs in three stages. The statement before us refers to the first stage.

---

[84] G. Lloyd Carr, *op. cit.*, p. 105.

This stage of her search for the Lord whom her soul loves had been throughout the night, while yet being in her bed. Because it had been a complacent and passive search, it had ended up in failure and frustration, as she indicates by saying, "I sought him, but I found him not."

I will rise now, and go about the city in the streets, and in the broad ways will I seek him whom my soul loveth: I sought him, but I found him not, (2).

This refers to the second stage of her search for her missing Lord. Unlike the first stage, this had been an active and resolute one. Saying to herself, "I will rise now, and go about the city," she went about groping in the dark, in the streets and broadways of the city in search of him whom her soul loves. Even so, this stage of her search also ended up in anguish and frustration. She indicates this by repeating the same phraseology that she had used in v.1, saying, "I sought him, but I found him not" (v.2).

The watchmen that go about the city found me: to whom I said, Saw ye him whom my soul loveth? It was but a little that I passed from them, but I found him whom my soul loveth, (3,4a).

This statement refers to the third and the final stage of her search for him whom her soul loves. Unlike the former stages of her search, this turned out to be fruitful. "The watchmen that go about the city found me," says she, with a sigh of relief. The watchmen were Moses and Aaron who were commissioned and sent by the Lord from Horeb. She enquires of them saying, "saw ye him whom my soul loveth?" It is not mentioned here as to what sort of answer the watchmen gave her. However, the fact that the counsels they gave had been the faith-generating living word of God is evident from her statement, "it was but a little that I passed from them, but I found him whom my soul loveth" (4a).

The Lord can be found out and received only by faith. And faith cannot be produced artificially; rather it must "come." For as Paul writes, "faith cometh by hearing, and hearing by the word of God" (Rom 10:17). This shows also the reason why the second stage of her search for him whom her soul loves had ended up in frustration. For, as Paul writes in Rom 10:14-15:

> How shall they believe in him of whom they have not heard? And how shall they hear without a preacher? And how shall they preach, except they be sent? as it is written, How beautiful are the feet of them that preach the gospel of peace.

I held him, and would not let him go, (4b).

One must bear in mind here that the imagery is cast out of the words and expressions taken from the scriptural narrative of the episode of Jacob's nightlong wrestle with the Lord at Peniel. It is now the last watch of the night. The beloved had been wrestling with the Lord, from the time she found Him out, all the way to her mother's house. For unless the Lord had said, as He said to Jacob, "let me go, for the day breaketh," the beloved need not have stated, "I held him and would not let him go, until I had brought him into my mother's house."

The objective of incorporating this clause taken from the narrative of the Peniel episode here is to show that the law was not of faith. Israel did not receive the Lord in the Sinai covenant voluntarily out of conviction and faith. Rather, they were terrorized into accepting Yahweh as their God and obey the stipulations of the Sinai covenant, by the fear generated in their hearts by the "thunders and lightnings, and a thick cloud … and the voice of a trumpet exceeding loud" (Exo 19:16), and the horrible penalties pronounced on the disobedient and violators. The whole affair involved a great deal of spiritual tussle. The underlying thought is best understood by the words of the writer of the Epistle to the Hebrews, found in 12:18-21:

> For ye are not come unto the mount that might be touched, and that burned with fire, nor unto blackness, and darkness, and tempest, and the sound of a trumpet, and the voice of words; which voice they that heard entreated that the word should not be spoken to them any more: (for they could not endure that which was commanded, And if so much as a beast touched the mountain, it shall be stoned, or thrust through with a dart: And so terrible was the sight, that Moses said, I exceedingly fear and quake:)

Until I had brought him into my mother's house, (4c).

The couple had been wrestling all the way, until somehow she managed to bring the Lord into her mother's house. This is certain, because the word "until" is used in Gen 32:24 to indicate that Jacob and the Lord had wrestled with each other throughout the night, "until the breaking of the day." In the case of the Peniel episode, it was the Lord who began the wrestling bout. Cf. "And Jacob was left alone; and there wrestled a man with him until the breaking of the day."

The excessive use that the beloved makes of the first person pronouns, "I," "my," and "me," twenty times in all, in the course of narrating the story of her seeking, finding, and bringing the Lord into her mother's house reflects the egoism and use of force involved in the whole affair.

As explained in the Introductory Section of this book, under the head, 'The Household of God,' the expression "my mother's house" refers exclusively to the entity of the natural seed of the covenant. In saying that she brought the Lord to her mother's household, she means to say that she brought Him by force in the Sinai covenant to the entity of the natural seed of the covenant. Not to be forgotten, the Abrahamic covenant of promise is the mother throughout the Song. As the Sinai covenant was not a covenant of the grace of God and faith, it did not have the power to generate children unto God through regeneration. Therefore, the Sinai covenant was not a mother in the intended sense of the term.

Into the chamber of her that conceived me, (4d).

This curious expression, "the chamber of her that conceived me," refers to the position of the saving faith by which the beloved (church) was born of God, in the Abrahamic covenant of promise. Even though the beloved claims that she restored the entity of the natural seed of Israel in the Sinai covenant to the very same position of saving faith with the Lord, by which she was born of God in the Abrahamic covenant of promise, the story of the debacle of Kadesh-barnea that had involved the six hundred thousand footmen of Israel who perished in the wilderness, described in the succeeding section, vv.6-8, shows that they did not possess the saving faith.

V. THE FORTY YEARS OF ISRAEL'S WANDERING IN THE WILDERNESS, 3:5-8

(The third forty-year period of Moses' lifetime)

1. *The wilderness journey begins, 3:5.*

3: 5. I charge you, O ye daughters of Jerusalem,
By the roes, and by the hinds of the field,
That ye stir not up, nor awake my love, till he please.

This verse is just a facsimile of the refrain of 2:7. (See exegetical comment on 2:7). It is interposed here between the story of the beloved bringing the Lord to the children of Israel in the Sinai covenant, described in the preceding unit, (3:4), and that of the six hundred thousand footmen of Israel who had perished in the wilderness, despite the fact that they had collectively agreed to obey the Lord in the Sinai covenant of the law, to show:

(i). That Israel's wilderness journey has begun.

(ii). That, due to the absence of faith, panic of fear had ruled the hearts of the six hundred thousand footmen of Israel who had conceded to obey the Lord in Sinai covenant of the law.

2. *The debacle of Kadesh-barnea, and Israel's wandering in the wilderness until every one of those that started from Egypt perished, 3:6-8.*

A brief account of the debacle.

When the children of Israel arrived at Kadesh-barnea, Moses commanded the six hundred thousand footmen of Israel who were under his command, "Behold, the Lord thy God hath set the land before thee: go up and possess it ... fear not, neither be discouraged" (Deut 1:21). But, it appeared reckless and foolish to the rationalistic minds of the soldiers to venture against the army of an unknown people without assessing the might thereof, and ascertaining whether their land was worth possessing. "We will send men before us, and they shall search us out the land, and bring us word" (Deut 1:22), they answered. But the word brought back by the men whom they had sent turned out to be quite contrary to what they had been expecting to hear.

"We saw the giants," they had declared, "the sons of Anak, which come of the giants: and we were in our own sight as grasshoppers, and so we were in their sight" (Num 13:33). Totally demoralized and dismayed, the whole congregation of Israel "lifted up their voice, and cried; and ... wept" (Num 14:1) throughout the night.

Grieved at the people's' unbelief, the Lord damned the generation, saying, "As truly as I live ... your carcases shall fall in this wilderness; and all that were numbered of you ... shall not come into the land ... which I sware to make you dwell therein" (Num 14: 28-30). The consequence was devastating. The curse took a quick toll of the men who had brought the demoralizing words of disbelief and disheartened the people.

Terrified, the soldiers came back to Moses, having "girded on every man his weapons of war," saying, "we have sinned against the Lord, we will go up and fight, according to all that the Lord our God commanded us" (Deut 1:41). Knowing this, the Lord commanded Moses to tell the men, "Go not up, neither fight: for I am not among you" (Deut 1:42). But the men would not listen. They "rebelled against the commandment of the Lord, and went presumptuously up into the hill. And the Amorites, which dwelt in that mountain" chased them as bees do, and destroyed them in mount Seir, even unto Hormah (Deut 1:43-44).

The unit which we are about to examine is a satirical exposé of the vain ritualistic worship that the men, who were cursed to die in the wilderness, performed during the forty years of their wandering about in the wilderness, and that despite the word of the Lord that came to them categorically, saying, "I am not among you" (Deut 1:42).

3: 6. Who is this that cometh out of the wilderness
like pillars of smoke, perfumed with myrrh and frankincense,
with all powders of the merchant?

5. Behold his bed, which is Solomon's;
threescore valiant men are about it, of the valiant of Israel.

6. They all hold swords, being expert in war:
every man hath his sword upon his thigh because
of fear in the night.

Who is this? (3:6a). NASB, "What is this?"

The cynosure of attraction is not a person, but a thing. This is made clear by the remark of one of the intrigued onlookers, "Look! It is Solomon's carriage" (v.7, NIV). Or, as NRSV, "Look, it is the litter of Solomon." The Heb. word *mitta* translated "bed" in AV is "a common word for a place to sleep." [85] The room for ambiguity as to whether a person or a thing is the cynosure of attraction arises from the demonstrative pronoun "this" which occurs in the feminine singular number in the Hebrew text. In such a grammatical construction, the pronoun can refer either to the beloved or to the *mitta*.

The context shows that the object that the intrigued onlooker mistakes for Solomon's *mitta* is actually the God-forsaken Ark of the Covenant, (explained below).

The Ark of the Covenant was virtually a mobile carriage or a reclining bed of Yahweh. The invisible Yahweh rested on its top cover, called the "Mercy Seat," in the visible form of the glorious *Shekinah*. The Ark was provided with handles, like those of palanquins, to facilitate the Levitical priests to carry Yahweh from place to place wherever Israel pitched their camp, in the course of their wandering in the wilderness. At times, out of superstitious belief, they carried the Ark even to the war fronts.

That cometh out of the wilderness like pillars of smoke, perfumed with myrrh and frankincense, (6a).

NRSV, "that coming up from the wilderness, like columns of smoke."

This shows that the cynosure of attraction was not only the *mitta*, but also the columns of perfumed smoke mushrooming up into the sky from all around the *mitta*.

---

[85] *Ibid.*, p. 109.

Delitzsch attributes the rising columns of smoke to the burning of incense.[86] Carr says that the word rendered "perfumed with" is the passive form of a verb meaning "go up in smoke," or "make a sacrifice (go up) in smoke."[87] In fact the perfumed columns of smoke were those of the superabundant quantities of incense burnt by the soldiers of Israel before the Ark of the Covenant, in ritualistic worship.

Frankincense was one of the ingredients of the holy incense according to those mentioned in Exod 30:34. However, myrrh is not mentioned among them. The fact that Zion, the temple mount, is being contemptuously spoken of in 4:6 as "the mountain of myrrh, and the hill of frankincense" implies that myrrh was also burnt as one of the aromatic powders, in the ostentatious, ritualistic worship of Israel.

With all powders of the merchant, (6b).

The Heb word, *rakahl,* means 'a trafficker,'[88] i.e., 'a roving merchant.' The word trafficker is used to denote especially one who carries on "illegal trade."[89] "Burning aromatic powders purchased from roving merchants, as holy incense, was sacrilegious. Only the incense powder made of the stipulated ingredients under the divine sanction was used in the tabernacle and temple worship. Whosoever makes or uses the incense powder like unto it was to be "cut off from his people" (Exod 30:37-38). On viewing the ongoing ritualistic worship of the soldiers of Israel from that perspective, it emerges to be sacrilegious. Burning such superabundant quantities of aromatic powders of all kinds purchased from a trafficker to the extent that the perfumed smoke thereof mushroomed up into the sky like tall pillars was an exercise in futility.

---

[86] Franz Delitzsch, *op. cit.,* p. 61.

[87] G. Lloyd Carr, *op. cit.,* p. 108.

[88] Francis Brown, S.R. Driver, Charles A. Briggs, *Brown-Driver-Briggs Hebrew and English Lexicon,* Massachusetts: Hendrickson Publishers, Inc., 2004, p. 940.

[89] Readers' Digest, *The Great Illustrated Dictionary, op. cit.,* p.1751.

Behold his bed, which is Solomon's, (7a).

(See exegetical notes above, under "What is this").

Three score valiant men are about it, of the valiant of Israel, (7b).

The footmen of Israel who came out of Egypt with Moses and remained with him at this juncture of Israel's redemptive history were six hundred thousand, (Exod 12:37; Num 11:21). For the sake of proportionate representation, their number is being brought down to a symbolic sixty, taking one for every ten thousand. The expression, "of the valiant of Israel" means that the men were the choicest from among the valiant of Israel.

The men are stated to be "about" or around the Ark of the Covenant, described contemptuously as Solomon's bed.

They all hold swords, (8a). RSV, "All girt with swords."

Delitzsch says that the sense of the expression, "all girt with swords," in the Hebrew language is, "held fast by the sword."[90] The underlying idea is that the men were held fast by their swords to the extent that the swords would not let them be free. In other words, the men had become slaves of their own swords. It was fear that made them to be so.

Carr sees a close correspondence between the senses in which the term, "I held him," was used in 3:4, and the present description of the sheath of the swords "belted on." In 3:4, the beloved clung to the Lord with the "encircling clutch of her arms,"[91] saying, "I will not let him go." In the present case, the sheaths of the swords, which were belted on, hold fast the men, as though they were saying that they would not let them free.

Being expert in war, (8a)

By earthly standards the men were regarded as experts in warfare. It was the men's conceited belief in their expertise in warfare that drove them to put their whole trust on their swords, instead of on God. The underlying idea is that as they were unable

---

[90] Franz Delitzsch, *op. cit.*, p. 63.
[91] G. Lloyd Carr, *op. cit.*, p. 110.

to leave their dependence on their swords, they could not put their trust wholly on God and His word.

Every man hath his sword upon his thigh because of fear in the night, (8b).

The Heb. word *pachad* rendered "fear" occurs 78 times in the Old Testament of which 67 times it is translated "fear" as here. Of the rest, 6 times it is translated "terror" or "dread." The word "alarms" used in most of the modern Versions, instead of AV's "fear," does not convey the intended sense accurately. What is intended is the inconsistency of the choicest of the valiant men of Israel being fear-gripped. Fear is the antonym of faith. Hence fear and faith do not go hand in hand. Genuine courage and daring comes only through faith in God, at His word.

PART THREE

FROM JOSHUA TO SOLOMON

3:9-11 and 4:1-7

VI. ISRAEL, THE OLD TESTAMENT CHURCH, GROWS UP AS THE BODY OF CHRIST UNTO HER DESTINED MEASURE OF HALF OF THE STATURE OF THE FULLNESS OF CHRIST, 3:9-4:7.

We prefer to treat the sections, vv. 3:9-11 and 4: 1-7, together, because vv. 4:1-7 alludes to the conquest of the Promised Land, and vv. 3:9-11, to the preparatory steps taken by the Lord for that event.

1. *The* Appiryon *Made by King Solomon for Himself, 3:9-11*

3: 9. King Solomon made himself a chariot of the wood of Lebanon.

10. He made the pillars thereof of silver, the bottom thereof of gold, the covering of it of purple, the midst thereof being paved with love, for the daughters of Jerusalem.

11. Go forth, O ye daughters of Zion, and behold king Solomon with the crown wherewith his mother crowned him in the day of his espousals, and in the day of the gladness of his heart.

4: 1. Behold, thou art fair, my love; behold, thou art fair; thou hast doves' eyes within thy locks: thy hair is as a flock of goats, that appear from mount Gilead.

2. Thy teeth are like a flock of sheep that are even shorn, which came up from the washing; whereof every one bear twins, and none is barren among them.

3. Thy lips are like a thread of scarlet, and thy speech is comely:

thy temples are like a piece of a pomegranate within thy locks.

4. Thy neck is like the tower of David builded for an armoury, whereon there hang a thousand bucklers, all shields of mighty men.

5. Thy two breasts are like two young roes that are twins, which feed among the lilies.

6. Until the day break, and the shadows flee away, I will get me to the mountain of myrrh, and to the hill of frankincense.

7. Thou art all fair, my love; there is no spot in thee.

King Solomon made himself a chariot of the wood of Lebanon, (9).

Carr translates the verse as below, on the plea that "most of the translations fail to catch the poetic parallelism in the verse,"

A palanquin made for himself the king,
Solomon from the wood of Lebanon.[92]

We have proved conclusively that Solomon is a received name by which the Lord appears in the Song as the Lover of Israel, the church. (Cf. Notes on 'the identity of the Lover' in the introductory section of this book)

Of the wood of Lebanon, (9a).

The *appiryon* made by the Lord for Himself was a replacement for the Ark of the Covenant. The replacement was necessitated because the Lord, the Spirit, abides normally in the hearts of His faithful people to revive them and to enable them to perform His will. But, in the case of the Ark of the Covenant that was made by Moses in the wilderness according to the stipulations of the Sinai covenant, the Lord could abide only symbolically, as He did, over its top cover, called the Mercy Seat. The debacle of Kadesh-barnea was due to the fact that the Lord did not abide in the hearts of the faithless six hundred thousand foot men of Israel who entered into the covenant relationship with the Lord at Sinai to obey the

92 *Ibid*, p. 111.

law, out of fear of the unbearable penalties that were pronounced against violators.

The choice of the hard wood of Lebanon, instead of the softer acacia wood with which the Ark of the Covenant was made, was in view of its incorruptibility and lasting nature. Significantly, the hardwood of the cedar and fir trees of Lebanon was the choice of the earthly king Solomon for building the temple of God. Cedar and fir trees figure in the Song in 1:17, and boards of cedar in 8:9. The importance given to Lebanon in the Song is evident from its recurrence in 4:8, 11, 15; 5:15 and 7:4).

He made the pillars thereof of silver, (10b).

The symbolic significance of the materials used by the Lord to construct the *appiryon* should be traced from the pre-Solomonic books of the Bible, or else, from any one of the places where they occur in the Song. For instance, silver occurs in the book of Exodus, and in v. 8:9 of the Song.

In Exodus, silver occurs as a type of the price paid by our Lord for the redemption of souls. Every Israelite male of over twenty years of age was required to pay half a shekel of silver unto the Lord as "ransom for his soul." The total amount of silver thus collected as ransom money was "one hundred talents, and a thousand seven hundred and three score and fifteen shekels." Out of this, one hundred talents were used to cast the sockets of the tabernacle, and the sockets of the veil. The remaining one thousand seven hundred and seventy five shekels were used for making hooks for the pillars of the tabernacle. Thus, the entire amount of silver collected from Israel as ransom money was used for the construction of the tabernacle (Exod 30:12-16; 38: 25-28).

It is in the very same sense that silver occurs in 8:9, which reads, "if she (the "little sister") be a wall, we will build upon her a palace of silver." The "little sister" refers to the growing Gentile church, and the older sister to Israel, the church of the regenerated. As to what should be done to the growing Gentile church when she attains the required maturity and be spoken for marriage to the Lord was the topic of discussion that took place in the Jerusalem Council, according to the Song's imagery. The silver tower that the apostles and elders of the Jewish Christian church desire to build upon the little sister refers to the church of the regenerated that they wished to build up exclusively of the ever-growing numbers of Gentile converts to Christianity.

Delitzsch suggests that the pillars of silver that the King Solomon made for the *appiryon* could have been to support its canopy. Or else, it must be that the *appiryon* was "silver legged," or that it was provided with a "silver pedestal."[93]

The bottom thereof of gold, (10c)

The Heb. word *repidat* translated "bottom" is from the root *raphad*, 'to lie back,' 'to stretch out.' The same word is used in 2:5, to signify 'to raise up from beneath.'

The Heb. words for gold occur five times in the Song; in 1:11, here, 5:11, 14, and 15). In 1:11, the triune God discloses their resolve to make the patriarchal church into "borders of gold with studs of silver." All the other occurrences of the word for gold in the Song are in chapter 5, in connection with the figurative descriptions of the attributes of the risen, glorified Christ. Purified gold occurs in the Bible as a symbol for the lives sanctified through fiery trials. Interestingly, the word *zahab*, normally translated "gold" is rendered "golden oil" in Zech 4:12, with reference to the holy anointing oil.

The covering of it of purple, (10d).

The Heb word *merkab* translated "covering" occurs only two more times in the Old Testament, i.e., in Lev 15:9 and 1 Kgs 4:26. In Lev 15: 9, the word is translated "riding seat," and in 1 Kgs 4:26, "chariot." It is in the sense of 'riding seat,' or 'saddle' that the word occurs here. Delitzsch suggests, a "divan ... arranged on an elevated frame, serving both as a seat and a couch."[94] "Here it is upholstered with purple, i.e. cloth, usually wool or linen, dyed with an expensive purple dye.... The colour is usually associated with royalty" (Carr).[95]

---

[93] Franz Delitzsch, *op. cit.*, p. 64.
[94] *Ibid*, p. 67.
[95] G. Lloyd Carr, *op. cit.*, p. 112.

The overall idea that emerges from these descriptions of the purple cloth covered riding seat and sofa-like provision to lie back is that they were made by the heavenly King Solomon Himself to facilitate Him to take control of the reigns of the figurative object called *appiryon* from within and ride in it from place to place.

The midst thereof being paved with love, for the daughters of Jerusalem, (10e).

The key to the entire mystery of the *appiryon* lies in this statement. Love, whether divine or human, cannot be paved on inanimate objects. It can be 'paved' only in broken and contrite hearts. As for divine love, Christ who appears as the heavenly King Solomon in the Song Himself is the Love of the Father manifested in human form. He, the Supreme Spirit, comes down from on high and 'paves' the hearts of those who are of a contrite and humble spirit, with Himself. Cf. "For thus saith the high and lofty One that inhabiteth eternity, whose name is Holy; I dwell in the high and holy place, with him also that is of a contrite and humble spirit, to revive the spirit of the humble, and to revive the heart of the contrite ones" (Isa 57:15). Robert Jamieson, et.al. comments on this rightly, as follows:

> Paved ... tessselated, like mosaic pavement, with various acts and promises of love of Father, Son, and Holy Ghost (Zeph 3:17; 1 Jn 4:8,16), in contrast with the tables of stone in the "midst" of the ark, covered with writings of stern command.[96]

The only reason why the Lord condescended to manifest His presence over the Ark of the Covenant was that His commandments, engraved on tables of stone, were enshrined in the midst of it. This was typical of the New Covenant, according to which the Lord has promised to write His law in the hearts of believers by the Holy Spirit, as disclosed by Him through Jeremiah (Jer 31:31-33)

> Behold, the days come, saith the Lord, that I will make a new covenant with the house of Israel, and with the house of Judah: not according to the covenant that I made with their fathers in the day that I took them by the hand to bring them out of the land of Egypt.

---

[96] Robert Jamieson, et. al., *op. cit.*, p.496.

> ... But this shall be the covenant that I will make with the house of Israel; ... I will put my law in their inward parts, and write in their hearts.

In reality, Christ Himself was the Lawgiver as well as 'the end of the Law" (Rom 10:4). At the same time, He, the Love of the Father, is also "the fulfilling of the Law" (Rom 13:10). Over and above, the substance of all the commandments of God was, "Thou shalt love the Lord thy God with all thy heart, and with all thy soul, and with all thy mind," "and thou shalt love thy neighbour as thyself" (Matt 22:37, 39, 40). In essence, the new covenant that the Lord promised to make was the indwelling of Christ, the Love of the Father, by His Spirit, in the hearts of those who receive Him by faith. Seen in this light, the love with which the Lord paved the midst of the *appiryon* emerges to be a figurative description of the Lord, who is both the Law and Love of the Father, abiding in believers' hearts.

Go forth, O ye daughters of Zion, (11a).

The purposes for which the arrival of the King Solomon was heralded ahead of time to the daughters of Zion were three-fold.

(i). To make known that the Lord who appears by the received name of King Solomon in the Song was Christ, the Seed Par Excellence of the Abrahamic covenant.

(ii). To make known that the *appiryon* that the Lord made for Himself was typical of the heart of faith, and that His purpose in making it was to facilitate Him to ride to Zion, the temple mount, in order to abide among His people according to His covenant pledge.

(iii) To make known that His abiding among the people whom He had chosen for Himself is regarded in the Song typically as His wedding.

Behold king Solomon with the crown wherewith his mother crowned him in the day of his espousals, (11b).

As stated, the Lord who appears as "king Solomon" in the Song is Christ, the Seed Par Excellence of Abraham. His "mother" who had crowned Him with the crown for the day of His espousals was the Abrahamic covenant of promise. It was the very same covenant, which had crowned Him with the crown of thorns to redeem the true Israel of God, and wed her to be His eternal spouse.

And in the day of the gladness of his heart, (11c).

The greatest of all the gladness is the gladness of seeing millions and billions of souls being saved with eternal salvation accompanied with everlasting glory, as the reward of one's own sacrificial suffering and vicarious death. Cf. "What is our hope, or joy, or crown of rejoicing? Are not even ye in the presence of our Lord Jesus Christ at his coming?" (1 Thess 2:19).

The name "Solomon" means "Prince of Peace." Though the earthly king that bore that name succeeded David in his throne, the predestinated plan of God had been that the heavenly King, the real "Prince of Peace," must sit in David's throne and reign eternally (Isa 9:6).

2. *Israel, the Old Testament Church of the regenerated, Grows Up as the Body of Christ unto Half of the Measure of the Stature of the fullness of Christ, 4:1-5*

The section 4:1-7 is distinct from the rest of the sections of the former half of the Song, for the disclosure it makes of the growth and development of Israel, the Old Testament church of the regenerated, as the body of Christ, into half of the measure of the stature of the fullness of Christ that was destined for her, i.e. from head downwards to breasts.

As stated, from the time of her birth, Israel, the church of the regenerated, had been the body of the indwelling Christ. But that could not be made a subject of disclosure prior to this for the following reasons.

(1) The patriarchal church, the story of which is disclosed in the section, 1:2-17, was not a body of Christ large enough with numerous members to be given due prominence. For, it had consisted of only a puny band of seventy souls. In spite of this, according to 1:10, she had been possessed with bejeweled cheeks, which were, in fact, the twelve patriarchs, in their turn, and a neck adorned with golden chains, which was Joseph. Moreover, the patriarchal church speaks about her posterity, namely about Judah

and Israel in 1:13 as her breasts, (Cf. comment below, on v.4: 5).

(2). We do not know whether there were sufficient numbers of believers to constitute a church during the first two forty-year period of Moses' life, covered in the sections 2:1-6 and 2: 7- 3: 4, other than Moses himself and his parents. Even if there were a few more believers, such a small group of believers could not have become a body with considerable number of members. As for the third forty-year period of Moses' life, covered in vv. 3: 5-8, it was the period of the law, which was not of faith. Consequently, every one of them who received the Lord in the Sinai covenant had perished in the wilderness. No doubt, Moses, Joshua, and Caleb who had survived were stalwarts of faith in God, under the Abrahamic covenant of promise, but, as stated, just three persons could not have become the body of Christ, with considerable number of bodily members.

It becomes clear from the foregoing that Israel (the church), had become the body of Christ, with multitudes of active members, only during the period of time covered in section 4:1-7, of the near about four centuries of her redemptive history that began from the time Joshua and his men crossed over Jordan into Canaan by faith, to the end of the Solomonic epoch.

As the Song is the story of the love affair between Christ and the spiritual Israel, its focus throughout is on them and not on the national Israel and the historical facts pertaining to them. For the reason that Israel (the church) had been the heavenly bride/spouse of the Lord, she had also been His body. The body grew up commensurate with the addition of the souls of the soldiers of Israel who were saved by their action of faith, of taking possession of the Promised Land by possessing faith, during the course of the period, part by part, from time to time. Accordingly, as stated in the introductory section of this book, the Song portrays the faithful soldiers of Israel who took possession of the Promised land not as historical personalities, but as parts of the body of Christ, such as, seeing eyes, flowing hair, smiling teeth, confessing lips, praising mouth, contented cheeks, unbending neck, and youthful breasts. This accounts for the reason why we do not find direct references to the historical events, as such, in the Song. For the subject matter of the Song is the birth and growth of Israel, the heavenly bride "unto the measure of the stature of the fullness of Christ" (Eph 4:13), by means of being rooted and grounded in Him by implicit faith in His promise.

a. Joshua and his men: the seeing eyes of the body of Christ, 4:1a.

Behold, thou art fair, my love; behold, thou art fair; thou hast doves' eyes within thy locks (4:1a).

This verse is a facsimile of 1:15, with the words, "within thy locks," tagged to it. NRSV translates the verse correctly, "behind your veil."

The underlying idea of the statement is that of 2 Cor. 3:18:

> But we all, with open face beholding as in a glass the glory of the Lord, are changed into the same image from glory to glory, even as by the Spirit of the Lord.

It implies that the beloved's spiritual complexion had been changed from the blackness of her inborn sinful nature, to the fairness of the Lord's glorious image, by virtue of her beholding His glorious face, as in a glass, with the eyes of understanding that have been enlightened by the Holy Spirit, the heavenly Dove (cf. Eph 1:17-18). It is for accentuation that the words, "Behold, thou art fair" is repeated. (For details, see the exegetical comment on the v. 1:15, and the notes on, 'Metaphors in the song,' under the 'The Artful Use of Figures of Speech in the Song,' in the introductory Section of this book).

Behind your locks, (1c).

NIV, NRSV, " behind your veil."

When the metaphorical statement occurred for the first time in 1:15, it was plainly "Your eyes are doves" without the expression, "behind your veil." It means that the spiritual perception of the patriarchs to behold the glorious face of the Lord was unhindered, whereas, now, in Joshua's epoch a veil of obstruction remains before the eyes of understanding of the church to behold the Lord in the fullness of His glory. This is because the church belonged to the epoch of the Sinai covenant, despite the fact that Joshua and his men believed wholeheartedly the Lord in the promise that He made under the Abrahamic covenant. And as Paul makes it clear, "when Moses is read, the veil is upon their heart" (2 Cor 3:15).

b. The flock of God that rushed down the slopes of mount Gilead, poised to cross over Jordan into the Promised Land: the flowing graceful hair of the body of Christ, 4:1b.

4: 1.b Thy hair is as a flock of goats,
that appear from mount Gilead.

NRSV, "a flock of goats moving down the slopes of Gilead." JB, "a flock of goats frisking down the slopes of Gilead." NIV, "a flock of goats descending from Mount Gilead."

The viewer is the Lord Himself. He was watching from a vantage point by the side of Jericho, where He had arrived beforehand to Captain the host of the Lord (Josh 5:13-15). What appeared to His holy eyes, as a flock of black goats frisking down the steep slopes of mount Gilead, was actually the flock of God that had comprised of the young men of Israel, born and brought up in the wilderness. The flock was rushing down the slopes of mount Gilead, poised to cross over Jordan into the Promised Land, believing that the Lord who promised will enable it to possess the land. As none of the young men that constituted the flock were regenerated or circumcised at that point of time, they appeared to the Lord's holy eyes as though it were a flock of black goats frisking down the slopes of mount Gilead. In terms of the body of Christ that was in the making then, the men were performing the function of the graceful, downward flowing hair of the body.

To understand the full significance of the statement, one must contemplate on the actual historical event that is being described figuratively in this manner.

The army that comprised of the young men of Israel was descending down the steep slopes of mount Gilead, led by Joshua (the Heb. equivalent of the name Jesus), believing that the Lord Himself in some miraculous way will enable it to cross over the flooded Jordan and take possession of the land that He had promised to give them. Had they begun to reason with their brains, as did their fathers, the six hundred thousand valiant of the valiant men of Israel, their brains would either have crippled their legs or commanded them to stop moving forthwith.

The men were not descending down the slopes of mount Gilead by their own power, or for their own sake, but by the operation of the charismatic gifts of faith and power with which they were being endued by the indwelling pre-incarnate Christ, for the good of the whole body, the church. It means that they were performing the function of a part of the body of Christ. It is from this perspective that the Lord describes these soldiers of Israel, in the functions that they were performing, as being a newly added beautifying hair of His body.

The trans-Jordan plateau of Gilead is stated to be 4000 feet higher to a viewer who views from the vicinity of the city of Jericho, which is "800 feet below sea level."[97] It was natural, therefore, for the Lord who was looking up from that distant location to have felt that the long winding rows of black goats descending down the steep slopes of the towering mount Gilead were the downward flowing graceful hair of His body.

c. *The flock of sheep that came up from the ravines of the river Jordan and circumcised at Gilgal: the smiling teeth of the body of Christ, 4:2*

4: 2. Thy teeth are like a flock of sheep that are even shorn, which came up from the washing; whereof every one bear twins, and none is barren among them.

Thy teeth are like a flock of sheep, ...which came up from the washing, 2a.

We know from the book of Joshua that the flock of God which came up from the ravines of the river Jordan was the same flock of God that descended down the slopes of mount Gilead. The present imagery is of Israel, the 'flock of black goats,' which came down from the slopes of mount Gilead, encamping at Gilgal, after having been transmuted into a flock of snow-white ewes, in the course of its miraculous passage through the dry bed of the river,

---

[97] Joseph Gardner, *op. cit.*, p. 76.

and come up from the ravines of Jordan. The expression, "from the washing" refers spiritually to "the washing of water by the word" (Eph 5:26).

That are even shorn, 2a.

'That is, evenly circumcised.' After the flock of God came up from the ravines of Jordan and encamped at Gilgal, Joshua made for himself sharp knives and circumcised all the men of Israel, and said, "This day have I rolled away the reproach of Egypt from off you" (Josh 5:9).

Overjoyed by the phenomenal miracle of the waters of Jordan parting before their eyes and paving the way for them to enter into and take possession of the Promised Land, in fulfillment of their long cherished hope, the mouths of every one of the goat-turned ewes were filled with the laughter of spiritual liberty, and their tongues with singing (cf. Ps 126:2), showing out, in the act, the entire rows of their teeth.

Inasmuch as the men were performing this phenomenal act of faith by the operation of the charismatic gift of faith and power that was being imparted to them by the indwelling Christ, for the good of the whole church, the Lord describes them as being one more newly added part of His body, namely, the smiling teeth of spiritual liberty.

Whereof every one bear twins, and none is barren among them, (2d).

(Cf. comment on this clause, under, 'The 'Artful Use of Figures of Speech' in the introductory section of this book).

d. *Rahab, the harlot, who believed in the God of Israel, and confessed Him with her lips, and the men of Israel who took Jericho by the power of praise: the lips and mouth of the body of Christ, 4:3a,b*

4: 3.a,b Thy lips are like a thread of scarlet.
and thy speech is comely.

Thy lips are like a thread of scarlet, 3a.

The crucial role that "a thread of scarlet" played in the seizure of Jericho, the first and foremost of the well-fortified Canaanite bastions to fall to the invading army of Israel, after their advancement from their base camp at Gilgal, is well-known even to Sunday-school students. Rahab, the Canaanite harlot, along with the members of her household, were saved and added to the body of Christ by virtue of her confession of faith in the God of Israel (Josh 2:11), and her consequent action of faith, of binding "a line of scarlet thread" in her window for her and her family's salvation from annihilation.

Keeping the above in view, the Lord aptly describes Rahab as the scarlet thread colored lips of His body, saying, "your lips are like a thread of scarlet."

And thy speech is comely, 3b.

The Heb. word *midbar,* translated "speech" occurs parallel to the word "lips" of the preceding line. Therefore, the word should be understood as referring to the mouth, the organ of speech, rather than to speech itself. The Lexicons point out that the Heb. word translated "comely" is the very same word, which is used in Ps 33:1, for "Praise is comely for the upright." It was solely by the power of praise that the men of Israel brought down the mighty fortification walls of Jericho. Keeping this in view, the Lord describes the men who took the city of Jericho solely by the power of praise as the comely mouth of the beloved (church), which was His body, saying, "your mouth is comely."

e. *The contented generation of the Judges' period: temples of the body of Christ, 4:3c*

4: 3.c Thy temples are like a piece of a pomegranate within thy locks.

NRSV, "Your cheeks are like halves of a pomegranate behind your veil."

Interposed between the allusions to the conquest of Jericho, and the exploits of faith of David and his thousand mighty men of the succeeding verse, the present description of the cheeks of the Lord's beloved (church) can refer only to the complacent and contented generations of the Judges' period.

Temples are the seats of emotional expressions. As a cluster of grapes, pomegranates, and figs were the fruits that the spies cut down from the brook of Eschcol and brought down with them to Kadesh-barnea as proof of the fruitfulness of the Promised Land, the Song takes those fruits as symbols for the productivity of Israel, the church, that was planted in the Lord by faith (Cf. comment on 6:11; 7:12). The present statement, "your temples are like a piece of pomegranate," means that the church, the body of Christ, of the Judges' period has been content with "a piece" or "halves" of the promised inheritance.

This alludes to the lamentable state of affairs that had prevailed during the Judges' period. In the absence of the required faith and daring to oust the Canaanites from the pockets they were still occupying, the children of Israel lived in contentment among them. As a result, "they forsook the Lord God of their fathers" by and by, "and followed ... the gods of the people that were round about them" (Judg 2:12).

Within thy locks, (3b).

As was the case with 4:1a, the expression "within thy locks" should read as NRSV, "behind your veil." It was because her eyes of understanding were veiled from beholding the Lord in the fullness of His power and might that the church of the Judges' period lacked the power and vigor to oust the Canaanite remnants from the pockets they were occupying.

Significantly, in 4:13, the Lord describes the two cheeks of the consummated Old Testament church as "an orchard of pomegranates, with pleasant fruits," quite contrary to the present description, (cf. exegetical comment on 4:13).

f. ***David and his thousand mighty men: the sturdy neck of the body of Christ, 4:4.***

4: 4. Thy neck is like the tower of David
builded for an armoury,
whereon there hang a thousand bucklers,
all shields of mighty men.

Thy neck is like a tower of David, 4a.

All the achievements of Israel until David taken together were only a half, in comparison with the totality of the blessing, which was hers by promise. It was David and his mighty men of faith who finally took possession of the wholesome "pomegranate" of the promised blessing, through sheer courage, faith and daring, and handed it down to the earthly king Solomon. It is to signify this that the Spirit describes David and his thousand mighty men as the neck of the body of Christ, during the epoch to which they belonged.

Thy neck is like the tower of David builded for an armoury, (4a).

David writes frequently of the Lord as his "high tower" in 2 Sam 22:3, 51; Ps 18:2; 61:3; 144:2. He had started building up his faith in the Lord as his tower of refuge, strength and defense from the day he had to flee into the remote, inhospitable hiding places, on account of the threat to his life posed from king Saul. "There is no king saved by the multitude of an host: a mighty man is not delivered by much strength," he wrote (Ps 33:16) The context shows that the tower that David built for an armoury was the faith that he built on the Lord as his high tower and defense.

Whereon there hang a thousand bucklers (4b).

"Bucklers" are smaller shields. They are meant for defensive, not for offensive warfare. The "thousand bucklers" belonged to the thousand mighty men of David.

There are no swords or any other weapons of offensive warfare in the tower of David. The mighty men of David have hung up on the tower of David, even the small shields that they possessed, and are relaxing in quietness and confidence in the Lord, their defense. This signifies that they have put their whole trust in God as their defense. We know that "shields," "bucklers," and "tower" were the symbols used frequently by David to speak of his faith that the Lord was his defense (cf. Ps 3:3;18:2, 30, 35;28:7; 33:20;35:247:9;59:11;76:3;84:9,11;91:4;115:9;144:2).

The picture of David and his mighty men relaxing in quietness and confidence after hanging up their bucklers upon the tower of David, occurs in sharp contrast to the earlier depiction of 3:8, of the fear-gripped six hundred thousand valiant of the valiant men of Israel being held fast by their swords, as though the swords were saying that they would not let them free.

All shields of mighty men, (4c).

It does not mean that the men were physically mighty, but that they were "mighty through God to the pulling down of strong holds" (2 Cor 10:4).

g. *The unity and oneness of Judah and Israel: the two breasts of Israel, the body of Christ, 4:5*

4: 5. Thy two breasts are like two young roes
that are twins, which feed among the lilies.

The word "breasts" occurs in the Song as symbols for the seed. (Cf notes on 'the symbolic word "breasts," under the head, 'The Artful use of Figures of Speech in the Song,' in the introductory section of this book, and exegetical comment on vv. 8:8-10).

Thy two breasts are like two young roes that are twins, which feed among the lilies, (v.5)

The two breasts of Israel refer to Judah and Israel, the two warring factions that constituted the children of Israel. They had always been warring between themselves.

Perfect peace and harmony prevailed between them only during the Solomonic reign. Evidently, they broke off and formed into rival nations of Judah and Israel soon after the demise of Solomon.

The present picture of the two breasts of Israel, (the church), feeding together in perfect peace and harmony, unsuspicious of each other, as though they were twins of a timid gazelle feeding together undaunted by fears of any sort, occurs in perfect consonance with the description of 1 Kgs 4:25, "Judah and Israel dwelt safely, every man under his vine and under his fig tree, from Dan even to Beersheba, all the days of Solomon."

The young gazelles are brought into the picture here to reflect the unity and harmony that had prevailed between Judah and Israel during the Solomonic era, contrary to their characteristic mutual suspicion and fear.

"Lilies" occur as a symbol for the elect from among Israel. (See notes on, 'The symbolic word lily,' under 'The Artful Use of Figures of speech in the Song,' in the introductory Section of this book).

3. *The Lord declares His resolve to get Himself into the ritualistic Solomonic temple over Zion, the temple mount, 4:6*

4: 6. Until the day break, and the shadows flee away,
I will get me to the mountain of myrrh,
and to the hill of frankincense, (6).

As stated, the Lover's declaration of His resolve that He will get Himself to the mountain of myrrh, and to the hill of frankincense, occurs as a figurative description of the resolve made by the Lord that He will get Himself into the Solomonic temple on the auspicious occasion of its dedication. (For detailed notes on the verse, see under, 'The Identity of the Lover,' in the introductory Section of this book).

4. *The perfected bride, 4:7*

4: 7. Thou art all fair, my love;
there is no spot in thee.

The epithet, "my love" by which the Lord addresses His beloved church shows that she is as yet the bride and not the married wife. On the other hand, beginning from the succeeding unit He addresses her by the changed epithets "my sister, my spouse," denoting thereby that the wedding has taken place.

Thou art fair, my love, (7a).

This is the third time that the Lord appreciates the fairness of His beloved church. The first time that He appreciated her fairness was in 1:15, that is with regard to the fairness of the consummated patriarchal church. The second time that He appreciated her fairness was at the commencement of the present section, i.e., in 4:1b, with regard to the fairness of Joshua and the men of faith who were under his command. In both of these instances, the expression, "thou art fair," was supplemented by the words, "your eyes are doves, to indicate that their fairness owed to their eyes of understanding that were opened by the Holy Spirit to behold the Lord in the fullness of His glory. However, a veil of obstruction was stated to be remaining before the eyes of understanding of the spiritual vision of Joshua and his men of war to behold the Lord in the fullness of His glorious face.

In the present instance, however, neither the clause, "your eyes are doves," is added, nor the words "behind your veil." Instead, the word, "altogether" is added, showing thereby that the beloved church of the Solomonic epoch has attained the glory that was predestinated for her in the Old Testament dispensation.

The foregoing does not mean that the church of the Solomonic epoch had received the fullness of the light of the knowledge of God. It has already been made known by the statement of the preceding verse, "until the day break, and the shadows flee away," that the Solomonic epoch was a period of the night of spiritual ignorance.

As explained, during the period of over three centuries that had intervened between Joshua and Solomon, the beloved (church) had been growing as the body of Christ, commensurate with the addition from time to time of the faithful men of Israel who took possession of the promised inheritance solely by faith. Thus she grew up by now to half of the body of Christ, from the eyes and hair of her head, down to her breasts. She was not destined to grow any further in the Old Testament dispensation. The other half of the body was to constitute the Gentile converts to Christianity, and the Jewish Christians who would be instrumental in the Lord's hand to make the Gentiles partakers with the Jewish Christian church of the promised blessing of Abraham, in the New Testament dispensation (cf. comment on 7:1-9).

There is no spot in thee, (7b).

This refers to the spiritual perfection that was destined for her in the Old Testament dispensation, to some extent, in the sense in which Paul writes in his Epistle to the Ephesians concerning the perfected New Testament church, in his words, "that he might present it to himself a glorious church, not having spot, or wrinkle, or any such thing; but that it should be holy and without blemish" (Eph 5:27).

The statement can also be interpreted literally in the sense that all the regions coming within the parameters of the Promised Land had been possessed, and no spot was left un-possessed. However, this sense has no relevance here, in that the Song is the redemptive story of the heavenly Israel, and not of the earthly. That being the case, the Song is not concerned with earthly possessions as such, but with the faith by means of which the concerned earthly possessions were possessed.

VII. ISRAEL, THE MARRIED SPOUSE OF THE LORD, 4:8-15

This and the succeeding section, 4:16-5:1, are distinct from the rest of the sections of the Song, for the epithet "my spouse" (Heb. *kallah)* that the Lord uses to address His beloved (church).

1. *Israel, the Married Spouse of the Lord Takes Possession of the Last Vestiges of the Promised Land by the Power of the Indwelling Christ, 4:8*

4: 8. Come with me from Lebanon, my spouse,
with me from Lebanon: look from the top of Amana,
from the top of Shenir and Hermon, from the lions' dens,
from the mountains of the leopards.

Come with me from Lebanon, my spouse, with me from Lebanon, 8a.

The expression, "come with me from Lebanon, my spouse," shows that the Lord is leading Israel, His married spouse, back from the Antilebanon range, after enabling her to subdue the opposing forces, which dwelt over the mountain. Josephus describes the men who opposed the earthly Solomon at this point of time as "the Canaanites ... that dwelt in mount Lebanon, and as far as the city Hamath."[98] These were the last vestiges of the regions that came within the northern boundary of the Promised Land, which were yet to be taken possession of. On the way back, the Lord asks His beloved to have a panoramic view of the surrounding lands that He had subdued under her feet.

The change over to the epithet, "my spouse" (Heb. *kallah*) from "my love," by which the Lord had been addressing His beloved (church) until the preceding unit, is to signify that the wedding has taken place.

It may be objected that the Heb. word *kallah* means "bride," not "spouse." Taking for granted "bride" as the intended meaning

[98] Flavius Josephus, *op. cit.*, p. 180.

here, almost all the modern Versions translate the word *kallah* as "bride." However, according to BDB, the word can also refer to a bride "just before marriage," or to a bride "just after marriage = young wife," as in Hos 4:13, 14.[99] The context shows clearly that the word is used here in the sense of "young wife."

While interpreting this verse one must not forget that the beloved (church) consisted only of the regenerated heavenly seed of Abraham who were "like the stars of the heaven." Viewed from that perspective, the beloved (church) ought to have been seated with the Lord in the *heavenly places*, like the church, which was in Ephesus (cf. Eph 2:6). Evidently, the white snow capped Lebanon ranges occur in the Song as a symbol for *the heavenly places*. There can be no sense, other than this, for the Lord saying to His consummated spouse, "the smell of thy garments is like the smell of Lebanon," and that you are "a fountain of gardens, a well of living waters, and streams from Lebanon" (vv.4:11,15).

Look from the top of Amana, from the top of Shenir and Hermon, (8b).

Robert Young locates *Amana* at the northern tip of the Antilibanus range, *Shenir* at the middle and *Hermon* at the southern tip.[100] On His way back from the Antilebanon range, after enabling His beloved to subdue all the opposing forces under her feet, the Lord desires her to have a panoramic view from the vantage points over the pinnacles of the peaks of the range, namely, from the tops of *Amana, Shenir, and Hermon.*

The statement, "Come with me from Lebanon ... look from the top of *Amana,* from the top of *Shenir and Hermon*" suggests that the heavenly couple has traversed on foot over all of these last vestiges of the Promised Land in order to possess them, in accordance with the words of the promise made by the Lord to Abraham, saying, "Arise, walk through the land in the length of it and in the breadth of it; for I will give it unto thee" (Gen 13:17), and the words that He spoke to Joshua, saying, "Every place that the sole of your foot shall tread upon, that have I given unto you" (Josh 1:3).

---

[99] Brown, Driver, Briggs, *op. cit.*, p. 483.

[100] Robert Young, *Young's Analytical Concordance to the Holy Bible*, 8th ed., London: Lutterworth Press, 1975. p. 877.

From the lions' dens, from the mountains of the leopards, (8c).

Historically, the military expedition that the earthly Solomon led to Hamat-Zoba, far beyond the Lebanon ranges, is the only one of that type recorded in the Bible. Cf. 2 Chr 8:3, "Solomon went to Hamath-Zoba, and prevailed against it." However, according to Josephus, Solomon subdued also the "Canaanites ... that dwelt in mount Lebanon"[101] during this only military expedition that he led to Hamath-Zoba.

The "lions" and "leopards" allude probably to the combined forces of Hamath and Zoba. King Toi of Hamath was friendly with David. Hadadezar of Zoba, on the other hand, was a rebel. This is evident from the fact that David had to defeat Hadadezar on two occasions (cf. 2 Sam 8:3; 10:6-19). Unless Hadadezar had engineered yet another revolt against Solomon, the latter would not have had the need to venture against him. Hadadezar was an influential leader who was capable of mustering the support of other Aramaean states of the region.

In its spiritual perspective, the lions and leopards that the Lord brought under the feet of His spouse (the church) refer to the "principalities,... powers, ... rulers of the darkness of this world," and "spiritual wickedness in high places" (Eph 6:12).

2. *The Lord Eulogizes the Praiseworthy Aspects of His Consummated Spouse, 4:9-15*

This section, (4:9-15), consists of eulogies of the Lord over the praiseworthy spiritual characteristics and aspects of His spouse (the church). There exists a parallel between the portrayals of this section and those of the preceding section, 4:1-7. While studying the preceding section, we have shown demonstratively that the bodily parts attributed to the beloved there, such as, seeing eyes, flowing hair, smiling teeth, scarlet thread coloured lips, praising mouth, majestic neck, etc, were actually the living members of the church, in their acts of faith for the common good of the whole church, performed by the operation of divergent charismatic gifts.

Viewed from that perspective, the physical parts that are being attributed to the beloved (church) in the present section, 4:9-15,

[101] Flavius Josephus, *op. cit.*, p. 180.

such as, eyes and neck (v.9), lips and tongue (v.11), and two cheeks (v.13), also ought to be members of the church in the acts of faith that they were performing by the operation of the charismatic gifts for the common good of the whole church.

The present section is important for the introduction of the garden motif for the first time in the Song. Israel, the consummated spouse of the Lord is described here as a paradisiacal garden of the Lord (4:12-14). She, in turn, is described as a fountain of living waters from Lebanon that waters to life other gardens, namely, the Gentile nations of the earth (cf. 4:15).

The metaphorical descriptions of the church as the Lord's garden and individual believers as trees rooted and grounded by faith in Him occur both in the Old and New Testament books of the Bible. For instance, Paul writes to the Corinthian church, saying, "Ye are God's husbandry," and concerning individual believers, he writes, "I have planted, Apollos watered; but God gave the increase" (1 Cor 3: 6, 9). The garden motif, wherever it occurs in the Song, should be interpreted in the sense in which Paul describes the church of God by the metaphor of "God's husbandry."

All the fruit trees and aromatic plants mentioned in this section were actually "the planting of the Lord" (cf. Isa 61:3). "Rooted and grounded" (Eph 3:17) in His promises they thrived and bore fruits of the Spirit unto the Lord. The aromatic plants mentioned in the section refer to the believers who lived and made manifest the savour of the Lord's knowledge in every place, both by their life and word of testimony (cf. 2 Cor 2:14-16).

a. Of the efficacy of her faith, 4:9

> 4: 9. Thou hast ravished my heart, my sister, my spouse; thou hast ravished my heart with one of thine eyes, with one chain of thy neck.

Thou hast ravished my heart, my sister, my spouse; thou hast ravished my heart,(9a).

NIV "stolen my heart." BDB "encouraged me."[102] "Most translators and commentators have taken the verb in the privative

---

[102] Brown, Driver, Briggs, *op. cit.*, p. 525.

sense "take away, ravish, capture the heart."[103] The Heb. word *lebab*, translated "ravish," occurs only three more times in the Old Testament, of which two times it is translated "make cakes" (in the shape of heart), and one time "be wise" (in the sense of 'take heart,' 'be bold).'[104] The intended meaning appears to be 'won my heart' or 'stolen my heart.' Human beings cannot encourage God, or make His heart bold. We can win God's heart through the power of faith, prayer, love, and devotion.

As the intended meaning of the word is uncertain, the only option left is to find out the meaning from the context. In 6:5 the Lord tells His beloved, "Turn away thine eyes from me, for they have overcome me." There the statement occurs in the sense, 'turn your eyes away from me to the perishing world which is seeking after me.' The statement is reminiscent of the manner Peter, John and James wished to pitch tents and continue to remain beholding the glorious face of the transfigured Lord over the mount of transfiguration, unaware of the multitudes who were waiting for them at the foot of the mountain, with their sick and suffering.

No doubt, it is imperative for believers to wait on the Lord in prayer and meditation, and keep their spiritual eyes transfixed on His glorious face with unveiled face to be transformed into His very image and likeness. The heart of the Lord is sure to be moved by such ardent and incessant look of faith at His face. However, the purpose of doing so should not be just for self- gratification. We are saved to save. One who is possessed with the mind of Christ will naturally be gripped with His burden for the perishing world. It is from this perspective that the Lord admonishes His beloved in 6:5, saying, "Turn away thine eyes from me, for they have overcome me."

However, we must bear in mind that the occurrence of the statement of 6:5, "turn away thine eyes from me" to the perishing world of sinners is in the New Testament division of the Song. The present statement, 'you have won over or stolen my heart' occurs in the Old Testament division of the Song. Israel in the Old Testament dispensation possessed no such burden for the

[103] Marvin H. Pope, *op. cit.*, p. 479.
[104] James Strong, *op. cit.*, p. 68.

perishing world. Their concern primarily was to wait on the Lord and win over His heart for their own sake.

With one of thine eyes, 9b.

"The numeral is masculine, although eyes are normally feminine, as are other parts of the body occurring in pairs, with the notable exception of breasts. The usual expedient is to gloss over the difficulty by rendering *onr* as 'glance' or to supply a supposedly missing word."[105]

According to our line of interpretation, we do not face any difficulty with the expression, "with one of thine eyes." A Spirit-filled church is sure to have numerous eyes, to wit, members who are endued with the charismatic gift of enhanced spiritual vision to behold both the Lord and matters pertaining to His kingdom clearly. Here the Lord singles out one of the believers who has won over or ravished His heart. We are not given to know the identity of the person who is intended here. The earthly Solomon himself is known to have ravished the heart of the Lord by means of his spiritual vision when he preferred to choose spiritual wisdom to rule over God's own people rather than earthly riches and fame.

With one chain of thy neck, (9b).

NIV, "With one jewel of your necklace."

Spirit-filled believers who were sanctified by the Lord through fiery trials are described in 7:1 as "jewels, the work of the hands of a cunning workman." In 1:10 the twelve patriarchs were described as jewels adorning the cheeks of the patriarchal church, in their turn or according to their ranking. When the consummated primitive Jewish Christian church appeals to the Lord, her High Priest, in 8:6, to set her as a seal upon His heart and as a seal upon His arms, she is thinking of herself as the antitype of one of those jewels cut and engraved by Bezaleel, the cunning workman, with the names of the twelve tribes of Israel, like the engravings of a signet, and set upon the breastplate and ephod of the shoulders of the Aaronic high priests.

---

[105] Marvin Pope, *op. cit.*, p. 481.

Here the Lord singles out one of the persons of the Solomonic age whom He, "the cunning workman," has turned out into a precious jewel. He/she is one of the jewels belonging to the chain of jewels in the church's neck, who had ravished His heart. As for the person who is described as the neck of the church, Joseph was the one during the patriarchal epoch, and David and his thousand mighty men, during the pre-Solomonic epoch. We are not given to know the identity of the person who was the neck of the church during the Solomonic epoch.

b. *Of the mirth of her love, 4:10*

4: 10. How fair is thy love, my sister, my spouse!
How much better is thy love than wine!
And the smell of thy ointments than all spices.

The word *'shemen*, translated as "ointment," means simply oil or fat. However, the same word is used in Ps 133:2, for "the precious ointment upon the head, that ran down upon the beard, even Aaron's beard: that went down to the skirts of his garments." The word occurs in 1:3 and in Ps 133:2, in the sense of the anointing oil. This is discernible by the way divine love is being associated here with the anointing oil. Anointing oil typifies the Holy Spirit. One experiences the fullness of the love of God only when he or she is filled with the Spirit. Cf. "The love of God is shed abroad in our hearts by the Holy Ghost which is given unto us" (Rom 5:5). It emerges from the above that the Lord is admiring the church for being Spirit-filled.

How fair is thy love, my sister, my spouse! how much better is thy love than wine, (10a).

The analogy between the titillation of divine love and wine had occurred first in 1:2, 4, with reference to the Lord's love for His church. Here it occurs with reference to the church's love for the Lord. "We love him, because he loved us first," and poured out His love into our hearts. It is by the love that God pours out into our hearts that we love Him in return.

And the smell of thine ointments than all spices, (10b).

The beloved (church) adored her Lover's name in 1:3, saying, "thy name is as ointment poured forth," because she knew that she was adoring the name of the Messiah, the Anointed One who has poured out His life vicariously for her redemption. The beloved is also the 'anointed one' in the sense that she was anointed by the Holy Spirit. Here the Lord applauds His beloved (church) concerning the sweet savour of her Spirit-filled life, which is incomparable with the savour of all the literal spices of the world.

c. *Of the sweetness of her words, 4:11*

> 4: 11. Thy lips, O my spouse, drop as the honeycomb: honey and milk are under thy tongue; and the smell of thy garments is like the smell of Lebanon.

The Lord had promised that He would bring Israel "unto a land flowing with milk and honey" (Exod 3:17). The Song being the redemptive story of a female, namely, of Israel, the beloved (church), it has no concern with the land of Canaan and its characteristics, other than with the faith by which it was possessed. The beloved (church) appears in each of the successive units, if not in each of the verses of this section, 4:8-15, in the figure of divergent mystifying entities. In the section before us, for example, she appears in v. 8 in the figure of a mountain trekker, in vv. 9-10, in the figure of an attractive female lover, in v. 11, in the figure of the Promised Land personified, in v. 12, in the figure of a garden, a spring, and a fountain, in vv. 13-14,in the figure of an orchard of fruit trees and aromatic plants, and in v. 15, in the figure of a fountain of living waters and streams from Lebanon. The church's appearance in these manners, in the figures of variant mystifying entities, is not prone to confuse those who are equipped with prior knowledge of the book's theme and plot. Whatever problems may arise, they arise only for those who endeavor to interpret the Song in terms of a literal love Song. In the verse before us, the church is personified as the Promised Land.

Thy lips, O my spouse, drop as the honeycomb: honey and milk are under thy tongue, (11a).

Milk and honey flow from under the tongue of the beloved (church), instead of from the Promised Land. The ministers who preach the word of life are the tongue of the body of Christ. The sweet, edifying, winsome words of life that flows from their lips are metaphorically stated to be milk, honey and honeycomb.

And the smell of thy garments is like the smell of Lebanon, (11b).

The underlying idea is that of 2 Cor 2:15, "We are unto God a sweet savour of Christ." As stated, Lebanon occurs as a symbol for the *heavenly places*. Note the prominence given to Lebanon by its frequent use, in 3:9; 4:8, 15; 5:15; 7:4. The smell of the heavenly church's heavenly garments should consistently smell heaven.

d. *Of the chastity of her life, 4:12*

4: 12. A garden enclosed is my sister, my spouse;
A spring shut up, a fountain sealed.

Being separated unto the Lord as a "chaste virgin" (2 Cor 11:2) is the underlying thought of this verse. The natural Israel (not the church) was separated unto the Lord doctrinally from the rest of the nations of the earth.

A garden enclosed is my sister, my spouse, (12a).

The garden motif, which plays a very cardinal role in the remaining part of the Song, is being introduced here for the first time. Israel (the beloved church) is the paradisiacal garden (singular number) of the Lord here, in 4:16; 5:1 and 6:2. In the antithetical sense, the other nations of the earth are the gardens (plural number). (4:15; 6:2, 11; 8:13).

One and the same Heb. word *naal* is being translated in the present line as "enclosed" and in the succeeding line as "shut up." The literal meaning of the word is 'to nail,' 'to bolt,' 'to lock.'

A spring shut up, a fountain sealed, (12b).

The church, which was metaphorically described as a garden in the former clause is described here by the metaphor of a "spring" and of a "fountain." Even though different Heb. words are used here for "spring" and "fountain," the underlying idea is the same.

It was the Lord Himself who turned Israel (the church) into a spring and a fountainhead of "the spiritual blessings *in the heavenly places*." He had made her so, because He had called her in the Abrahamic covenant to become the promised blessing for all the families of the earth. The sealing and nailing up of the spring and fountainhead of the spiritual blessings for her alone was done by herself; not by the Lord; Israel, the church of the regenerated did so out of her own myopic religious bigotry.

e. Of the productivity of her life, 4:13, 14

> 4: 13. Thy plants are an orchard of pomegranates,
> with pleasant fruits; camphire, with spikenard,
> 14. Spikenard and saffron; calamus and cinnamon,
> with all trees of frankincense; myrrh and aloes,
> with all the chief spices:

The Heb. word *shelach* translated "plants" "has continued to be a stumbling block to translators and commentators," says Pope.[106] BDB gives three sets of meanings. (i). missile, weapons. (ii). sprout, shoot, and (iii). Figuratively, thy two cheeks.[107] NEB renders, "your two cheeks."

Pope writes, "some translators and interpreters ... have recognized that the reference is to a part of the lady's body."[108] In our line of interpretation, "thy two cheeks" suit the context better. Because, in 4:3b the beloved's cheeks were stated to have been like the halves of a pomegranate. In chronological sequence, that was in the Judges' period. It is quite consistent, therefore, for her cheeks to be "an orchard of pomegranates, with pleasant fruits," in the Solomonic epoch when she has consummated into her predestinated measure of a half of the stature of the fullness of the body of Christ. Not to be forgotten, what the Song portrays as parts of the body of Christ are the living members of the church of successive generations. Viewed from that perspective, the pomegranate and other fruit trees, as well as the aromatic plants that constitute to be the two cheeks of the church are figurative descriptions of divergent types of members of the church of the Solomonic epoch who bore different kinds of spiritual fruits, and emanated divergent types of sweet smelling savour unto the Lord.

The thought of the lives of the children of God becoming a sweet-smelling savour unto God and people was introduced first in 1:12, by way of the patriarchal church's statement, "while the

---

[106] *Ibid.*, p. 490.
[107] Brown, Driver, Briggs, *op. cit.*, p. 1019.
[108] *Ibid.*, p. 490.

king sitteth at his table, my spikenard sendeth forth the smell thereof." The same thought is introduced here by the description of the believers who have constituted to be the cheeks of Israel, the body of Christ, as divergent types of aromatic plants and trees emanating with divergent types of sweet-smelling savours.

To be an egoist is to be obnoxious and abhorrent to others. Such a person's life cannot be a sweet-smelling savour to God or to humanity. The continuing redemptive work that the Lord performs in a committed believer is leading him/her through the vehement fire of trials with a view to break and melt his/her ego. The Lord can mould the life of a believer according to the eternal purpose that He had purposed for him/her only after breaking and melting the person's ego.

The Heb. word *shelach* can also be interpreted in the sense of 'to send out' (a messenger, an arrow, shoots, etc.), (Carr).[109] In Ps 80:11 Israel is pictured as a spreading vine that "sent out her boughs unto the sea, and her branches unto the river." This refers to the spread of the kingdom of Israel as far as Lebanon and the Euphrates in the time of David and Solomon. In Isa 16:8, there is a metaphor of a vine whose shoots spread abroad. In Jer 17:8, one who trusteth in the Lord is compared to a tree that "spreadeth out her roots by the river." In the present context what Israel, the consummated church of the Solomonic epoch sends forth are not branches, but persons whose lives emanate the sweet savour of the knowledge of God. They are described figuratively as full-grown pomegranate and other pleasant fruit trees and pairs of aromatic plants, namely, "camphire, with spikenard, spikenard and saffron; calamus and cinnamon, with all trees of frankincense; myrrh and aloes, with all the chief spices." Coupled with this, she, the church, is "a fountain of gardens (i.e., to water to eternal life other nations), a well of living waters, and streams from (the heavenly) Lebanon" (bracketed portions mine). The pairing of aromatic trees and plants that the church sends out, as above, reminds us of the way our Lord sent out His disciples in pairs.

---

[109] G. Lloyd Carr, *op.cit.*, p 124.

f. Of her virtue as a life-giver, 4:15

4: 15. A fountain of gardens, a well of living waters,
and streams from Lebanon.

Obviously, the imagery is framed after the covetable characteristics of the Promised Land described in Deut 8:7:

> For the Lord thy God bringeth thee into a good land, a land of brooks of water, of fountains and depths that springs out of valleys and hills.

These covetable characteristics of the Promised Land are being transferred to the beloved (church), which is rooted and grounded in the Lord, by faith.

This is the first time the word "gardens" (plural) occurs in the Song. Gardens refer to the Gentile nations of the earth. In v.12, the beloved church was stated to be a "spring shut up, a fountain sealed." The shutting up and sealing was done for the time being, until she matures in wisdom and understanding to be free under the law of Christian liberty to mingle with the Gentiles and impart the knowledge of God to them. The ultimate call of Israel (the church), had been to be a "fountain" or "well of living waters," to water all the families of the earth with the covenanted blessing of Abraham. The imagery is reminiscent of the words of our Lord found in John 7:38, "He that believeth on me,... out of his belly shall flow rivers of living water."

VIII. THE WEDDING FEAST, 4:16-5:1

4: 16. Awake, O north wind; and come, thou south;
blow upon my garden, that the spices thereof may flow out.
Let my beloved come into his garden, and eat his pleasant fruits.

5: 1. I am come into my garden, my sister, my spouse:
I have gathered my myrrh with my spice;
I have eaten my honeycomb with my honey;
I have drunk my wine with my milk:
Eat, O friends; drink, yea, drink abundantly,
O beloved.

As explained under the head, 'The structure of the Song,' in the introductory section of this book, these two verses form the exact middle of the Song, leaving 111 lines before and after, denoting thereby the distinct identity and prominence given to the truths disclosed herein.

The words of the Lord,"I am come into my garden, I have gathered my myrrh with my spice" indicate that the section refers to harvesting the yields of His ripened garden. The concluding words, "I have eaten my honeycomb with my honey; I have drunk my wine with my milk: eat, O friends; drink, yea, drink abundantly, O beloved(s)," show that the verse pictures an ongoing wedding feast exclusively for the Lord's friends and beloved(s). Evidently, this is the first allusion to a historical event subsequent to that of the couple's trek back through the snow-clad peaks of the Anti-Lebanon Range, after annexing the last vestiges of the Promised Land, portrayed in 4:8. The verses 9-15 that occur thereafter consist purely of a series of eulogies that the Lord (the Lover) showers upon His beloved (church).

Awake, O north wind; and come, thou south; blow upon my garden, (16a).

The expression, "my garden," shows that the Lord is the speaker of these words. The beloved (church), who had been wary of being stirred up or awakened of her love affair thus far, now submits herself to be stirred and awakened by the mighty winds of opposition. She gives expression to this by her responsive words, "let my beloved come into His garden, and eat his pleasant fruits."

An absolute surrender to go through whatever way the Lord leads is the litmus test to know whether one is truly in Christ and His love. The beloved was, in fact, betraying herself to be not so, by the adjurations that she was making to the daughters of Jerusalem, by the timid roes and hinds of the field, saying, 'I adjure you ...not to stir, nor awaken my love affair with the Lord.' Touchiness is the characteristic of an immature believer who is not genuinely in Christ and His love. As Paul writes, genuine love "is not easily provoked ... beareth all things ... endureth all things" (1 Cor 13:5, 7). Paul himself was the best example of one who possessed such a genuine love of God. He writes:

> I am persuaded, that neither death, nor life, nor angels, nor principalities, nor powers, nor things present, nor things to come, nor height, nor depth, nor any other creature, shall be able to separate us from the love of God, which is in Christ Jesus our Lord. Rom 8:38-39.

The beloved (church) will grow in love to the degree of which Paul writes, only at the end, when she will confess, in similar words, saying,

> Love is strong as Death, jealousy relentless as Sheol. The flash of it is a flash of fire, a flame of Yahweh himself. Love no floods can quench, no torrents drown. Were a man to offer all the wealth of his house to buy love, contempt is all he would purchase. 8:6-7. JB

That the spices thereof may flow out, (16a).

The purpose of the Lord in commanding the strong winds of opposition to blow upon His garden and toss and stir it violently was that the self-preserved spices thereof may flow out for the benefit of His friends and beloveds, namely, His elect from among the surrounding nations. This, in fact, was the ultimate purpose for which He had so carefully planted and nurtured each of the fruit trees and aromatic plants of His garden.

Unlike the practice of human beings, the Lord does not extract and preserve His spices in costly alabaster boxes. Rather, He causes the sweet-smelling fragrance to ooze out within the persons whom He has chosen for Himself, by subjecting them to extreme pressures and unbearable stresses, and stores them within the persons themselves to be transported to pre-destined destinations in the form of living human packages.

Therefore, while interpreting these verses, the interpreter must forget all about the apparent literal garden he/ she is reading about, and interpret them with the crystal-clear understanding that he/ she is reading about Israel, the human garden that the Lord planted and nurtured to maturity and fruition. The spices that He caused to flow out of the garden through strong winds of opposition refer to the fragrant, sweet-smelling personalities, like Shadrach, Meshach, Abednego and Daniel, and the countless multitudes like them whom He scattered abroad among the Gentile nations of the world to spread the sweet savour of His knowledge among them.

Let my beloved come into his garden, and eat his pleasant fruits, (16b).

(As explained above)

I am come into my garden, my sister, my spouse, (5:1a).

One must bear in mind that it is the pre-incarnate Christ, the Spirit, who says this. He visits His church in manifold ways. Sometimes He visits her in the form of gentle breezes of spiritual revivals. At other times, He visits her through answered prayers. But there are also times when He visits her by way of the strong tossing and tearing winds of opposition. Nevertheless, it is during such times, when she is being horribly tossed and shaken that the Lord's presence becomes more palpable than ever, and His succor becomes sweeter and more consoling than ever. For, He is "a very present help in trouble" (Ps 46:1).

I have gathered my myrrh with my spice, (1b).

To be noted, the spices that the Lord gathered are those, which He has scattered or driven out by the tossing and tearing, strong winds of opposition. This is reminiscent of the words of Acts 11:19ff. "They which were scattered abroad upon the persecution that arose about Stephen traveled as far as Phenice, and Cypress, and Antioch, preaching the word.... And the hand of the Lord was with them: and a great number believed, and turned unto the Lord."

In fact, the hand of the Lord was both in the historical scattering and gathering of the Jews. According to His pre-destined plan, He had gathered together the Jews whom He had scattered abroad among the Gentile nations, in closely-knit religious communities, so that they would become a powerful agency to spread the sweet savour of His knowledge among them.

I have eaten my honeycomb with my honey; I have drunk my wine with my milk, (1c).

We know that the Lord does not consume earthly foodstuffs. The honeycomb that He ate was that which dripped from the lips of His beloved (the church), and the honey and milk that He took were those, which were under her tongue, namely, the sweet words of life concerning Himself and His glories that proceeded from the mouths of His witnesses, as was portrayed in v.11. To be recalled, wherever bodily parts of the church are mentioned in the Song, they refer to her living members who performed the function of that part of the body of Christ. Therefore, the lips of the church (the beloved), which dripped honeycomb, and her tongue, under which honey and milk remained, are figurative descriptions of the members of the body of Christ who ministered the sweet words of eternal life. Wine refers to the Love of God shed abroad in the hearts of the members of the church by the Holy Ghost.

Eat, O friends; drink, yea, drink abundantly, O beloved(s).

We have explained clearly, under the head, 'The Household of God,' in the Introductory Section of this book, that the "friends" and "beloved(s)" are not members of the household of God. They are the elect of God from among the Gentile nations of the earth. In the Heb. text, the word '*dodim*' translated "beloved" occurs in the plural number, 'beloveds.' This means that the Lord is motivating His elect from among the Gentile nations to cordially take in the words of life that flow from under the lips of His saints whom He had driven through strong winds of opposition to settle in their midst.

The disclosures of the redemptive story of the Old Testament Israel ends with that of this middle section of the Song, because by the Solomonic epoch of peace and plenty the Lord had performed and finished that part of the Abrahamic promise that pertained to the Old Testament dispensation.

The disclosure, which resumes from the succeeding verse, v. 5:2, pertains to the primitive Jewish Christian church of the first century AD. The duration of the time from the demise of Solomon to the beginning of the Christian era is being treated as a prolonged night of estrangement between the Lord and Israel, His '*kalla*,' i.e. bride after marriage.

PART FOUR

THE LATTER HALF OF THE SONG (FUTURISTIC PROPHECIES) 5:2 - 8: 14

TOPICAL INTRODUTION

IX. THE OBSCURE NINE CENTURIES BETWEEN SOLOMON AND CHRIST

(Considered as a prolonged night of estrangement between Israel and the Lord, the newly married couple).

The middle section of the Song had ended with the euphoric scene of 5:1, of the newly wedded couple being at the apogee of enjoying their marital bliss. Quite contrariwise, the succeeding section beginning from the next verse, v. 5:2, opens with the mystifying scene of a prolonged period of estrangement between the Lovers.

It begins with picturing the Lover as one who had been waiting patiently outside the closed door of His beloved's house throughout a prolonged misty night, knocking and calling upon her endearingly, saying, "Open to me, my sister, my love, my dove, my undefiled: for my head is filled with dew, and my locks with the drops of the night" (5:2). The beloved, who was half-awake, had been well aware of the fact that her newly married husband had been waiting outside throughout the night for her to open the door for Him. However, she had been engrossed within herself with finding out satisfactory answers for the arising, pestering religious questions, saying to herself, "I have put off my coat; how shall I put it on? I have washed my feet; how shall I defile them?"

One has only to go through the pages of the post-Solomonic books of the Old Testament to find out as to what this means. Soon after the demise of the earthly king Solomon, the theocracy broke up into two warring kingdoms. Led by the renegade general Jeroboam, the ten northern tribes dissented with Rehoboam, the son of Solomon, and formed themselves into the separate northern kingdom of Israel, leaving Judah, Benjamin and a half tribe Manasseh with Rehoboam to be the southern kingdom of Judah. As a subtle device to prevent his subjects from going to the Jerusalem temple to worship God during the yearly festivals, Jeroboam set up two golden bull calves; one at the ancient shrine-site at Bethel and the other at Dan, and told his subjects, It is too much for you to go up to Jerusalem: behold thy gods, O Israel, which brought thee up out of the land of Egypt. Thus the ten tribes of the northern kingdom became out and out idol worshippers just like the heathen nations around them. Neither was the southern kingdom of Judah free from idolatry. The people in general continued to worship Yahweh together with idols, which were introduced by none other than Solomon himself. As we all know, Israel never again reverted into the pure theocratic state that she had been in the early years of king Solomon's reign.

Wars and strife continued throughout the nine centuries between the time of Solomon's demise and that of the beginning of the Christian era. The first of the strong purposeful winds of opposition caused by the Lord to blow upon His garden was that which blew upon the northern kingdom of Israel in the form of the Assyrian onslaught that led to the carrying away of the very best of its population to other areas of the Assyrian empire. The next purposeful strong wind of opposition that He caused to blow upon Israel, His garden was that which blew upon the southern kingdom of Judah, about a century later, in the form of the Babylonian onslaught, which led to the carrying away of the choicest of its populace to Babylon. Exactly as the Lord discloses here, He gathered together the chosen ones of His garden whom He had scattered, into religious colonies and caused them to become the sweet-savour of His name among the Gentile populations of the regions.

As for the Song, it regards the entire period of the nine centuries between the day of Solomon's demise, and the day of Pentecost, as a prolonged period of cold, misty night of blurred vision. The beloved, who had been hesitant to open the door for the Lord despite knowing that He had been knocking at the door throughout the prolonged night and calling upon her to open for Him, was the "holy seed" (Isa 6:13). The door that the Lord had been calling upon her endearingly to open for Him was that of the decadent Judaism, which she describes in 8:2 as "my mother's house(hold)." He had been calling upon her to open the door, and follow after Him to witness Him to His elect from among the Gentiles, with words such as:

> Ye are my witnesses ... and my servant whom I have chosen. ... This people have I formed for myself; they shall shew forth my praise. Isa 43:10,21

and

> Awake, awake; put on thy strength, O Zion; put on thy beautiful garments, O Jerusalem, the holy city...shake thyself from the dust; arise, loose thyself from the bands of thy neck, O captive daughter of Zion. Isa 52:1-2

The reason for the beloved's hesitation to rise up and open the door for the Lord was not any lack of love towards Him. Rather, she had been, in the first place, engrossed with the question of the religious defilement that could possibly result thereby, and in the second place, counting the cost of opening the door of the decadent Judaism which was straightly closed by its rulers against the beloved bringing the Lord within. This is clearly evident from the manner the "watchmen" beat the beloved, and "the keepers of the walls" took away her veil from her, the moment she opened the door, and trespassed the walls (the Judaical laws), in search of the Lord who had withdrawn by then, as described in v.5:6-7.

THE PRIMITIVE JEWISH CHRISTIAN CHURCH PERIOD

Discernibly, the units constituting this latter division of the Song, 5:2-8:14, occur as prophetic disclosures of the happenings in the primitive Jewish Christian church period starting from the day of

Pentecost and ending with the day in which the apostles and elders of the church gathered at Jerusalem for the first Church Council and set the Gentile Christians free from observing the Jewish laws and traditional customs. Logically they cannot mean anything other than what we have interpreted them to be in the succeeding portions of this book.

THE MESSIANIC AGE

X. THE LORD AROUSES AND DRAWS AFTER HIM THE SLUMBERING REMNANT OF ISRAEL, AFTER NINE CENTURIES OF KNOCKNG AND CALLING, 5:2-7

5: 2. I sleep, but my heart waketh:
it is the voice of my beloved that knocketh, saying,
Open to me, my sister, my love, my dove, my undefiled:
for my head is filled with dew,
and my locks with the drops of the night.

3. I have put off my coat; how shall I put it on?
I have washed my feet; how shall I defile them?

4. My beloved put in his hand by the hole of the door,
And my bowels were moved for him.

5. I rose up to open to my beloved;
and my hands dropped with myrrh, and my fingers with sweet smelling myrrh, upon the handles of the door.

6. I opened to my beloved; but my beloved had withdrawn himself,
and was gone: my soul failed when he spake: I sought him,
but I could not find him; I called him, but he gave no answer.

7. The watchmen that went about the city found me,
they smote me, they wounded me;
the keepers of the walls took away my veil from me.

There are close similarities as well as marked differences between the poetic narratives of the 'seek/find' episodes of the cited verses, and that of the sections, 2: 8- 3:4. The narratives of the present section refers to the holy seed of Israel searching for and finding out the risen Lord after nine centuries of spiritual darkness that extended from the time of the demise of king

Solomon to the day of Pentecost. Whereas, the narratives of the former sections, 2:8-3:4, refer to the elect of Israel seeking and finding the missing Lord, after the four centuries of Egyptian captivity. A comparative study of the similarities and the differences between the poetic narratives of the sections is sure to throw much light on the overall theme of the Song.

SIMILARITIES

(i). Even as the four centuries of Israel's Egyptian captivity is portrayed in the former section as a cold rainy winter night that has passed (cf. comment on v. 1:13 with 2:11), the nine centuries between the Solomonic age and the Christian era is portrayed here as a prolonged, cold foggy night that is about to pass.

(ii). In both the cases, the beloved had been a prisoner. In the former, she had been within a prison house with latticed windows, which was located in a walled enclosure (cf. 2:9). In the present case, she had been within the closed door of her mother's house, opening which, and trespassing the boundary walls was a punishable offence.

(iii). In both the cases, the beloved had been half-awake throughout the long hours of the respective nights.

(iv). In both the cases, the Lord had called upon His beloved to rise up and come away. In the former, He called upon her endearingly, saying, "rise up, my love, my fair one, and come away" (2:10, 13). In the present, He had been calling upon her throughout the long night, saying, "Open to me, my sister, my love, my dove, my undefiled."

(v). In both the cases, the beloved's search for the Lord took place in a city; in the former, in the city of Ramses, in the present, in the city of Jerusalem.

(vi). In both the cases, the 'seek/find' motif occurs in three distinct stages:

a. *Nightlong, 3:1 with 5:2-3.*
b. An intermediate stage, which ends with the frustrated cry, "I sought him but found him not" (3:2 with 5:6).
c. That which starts with the words, "the watchmen … found me" (3:3 with 5:7).

DIFFERENCES

The following marked differences exist between the narratives of the former and the present cases:

(i). In the former case, the Lord came down from Horeb in the likeness of a roe or a young hart to visit the captive Israel, whereas, in the present, He had been waiting patiently throughout the long night knocking at the closed door of His apathetic beloved's mother's house, beseeching her to open for Him.

(ii). In the present case, the Lord withdrew Himself on account of His beloved's failure to open the door for Him on time, in spite of that He put in His hand through the keyhole in His bid to open the door by Himself, whereas in the former, the Lord tried to wriggle out of the encircling clutch of her hand, but she would not let Him go until she had brought Him by force into her mother's house and into the chamber of her that conceived her, (2:8-9; 3:4 with 5:2).

(iii). In both the cases, the watchmen found out the beloved as she was groping in the dark in search of her missing Lord. However, in the former case the watchmen were helpful guides, whereas in the present they were persecuting monsters. This is evident by the beloved's rueful bewail, saying, "The watchmen that went about the city found me, they smote me, they wounded me; the keepers of the walls took away my veil from me" (3:4 with 5:7).

(iv). While the watchmen were the ones who voluntarily showed the way for the beloved to find out the Lord, in the former case, here it is the daughters of Jerusalem, the ones whom the beloved had been severely charging and warning all the time not to stir up or awaken her love affair, who volunteer to join her in her search for her missing Lord.

I sleep, but my heart waketh, (2a).

She has not been fast asleep, but half-awake. In other words, she has been slumbering; not in the literal sense, but spiritually.

It is the voice of my beloved, 5b.

Being an invisible Spirit, the Lord does not appear anywhere in the Song in human form. His present appearance is only as a voice, "The voice of my beloved that knocketh." This is the second time that the beloved hears the voice of the Lord. The first time that she heard it was during the former episode, described in 2:8, "the voice of my beloved! behold, he cometh." These depictions occur antithetical to that of 8:13, wherein the beloved appeals to the Lord to cause her to hearken to His voice, implying that by then she had become hardened from hearkening His voice.

That knocketh, 5c.

The Lord did not knock at the door with His hand. Being a Spirit, as He always does, He 'knocked' by His voice. Cf. "it is the voice of my beloved that knocketh." It is not specified whether He had been knocking at the door of her house or at her heart's door. The beloved's statement in v. 7, that the watchmen beat and wounded her, and the keepers of the walls took away her veil from her, as soon as she opened the door and called upon her missing Lord who had withdrawn from the door by then and was gone, shows clearly that the closed door was that of the decadent Judaism, (which she terms as "my mother's house," in 3:4 and 8:2).

One should not misconceive that the Lord had been literally waiting outside the closed door of her heart or of her mother's house in the form of a human being and knocking throughout those nine centuries that are described figuratively as a prolonged night. His statement, "my head is filled with dew, and my locks with the drops of the night," is anthropomorphic.

The foregoing leads to the conclusion that the Lord had been communicating Himself with His beloved (people) throughout the past nine centuries of spiritual darkness and blurred vision, by way of knocking by His voice at the door of their individual hearts. The knocking must be understood in the sense that the Lord had been knocking at the door of her heart to open the door of her mother's house and follow after Him to witness Him to the non-Jews.

Taken in the sense that the Lord has been knocking at her heart's door, the emerging meaning could be as that of Rev 3:20:

> Behold, I stand at the door, and knock: if any man hear my voice, and open the door, I will come in to him, and will sup with him, and he with me.

Open to me, my sister, my love, my dove, my undefiled, (2b).

The Lord had been addressing His beloved (church) ever since the wedding, i.e., from 4:8-5:1, by the epithet, "my sister, my spouse." Now that the disclosures of the matters pertaining to the Old Testament Israel have come to an end in v. 5:1, and those pertaining to the primitive Jewish Christian church have begun from the present verse (v. 5:2), the Lord changes over the epithets by which He had been addressing her to, "my sister, my love, my dove, my undefiled." Significantly, the use of the term, "undefiled" is confined to the present verse and 6:9. Here it denotes that the body of the holy seed of Israel, whom the beloved represents, had kept herself undefiled by the sacrilegious practices of the nine centuries between Solomonic and the Christian eras.

For my head is filled with dew, and my locks with the drops of the night, (2b).

As stated, the statement is anthropomorphic. Its purpose is to indicate the prolonged period of time the Lord had been kept waiting. The "dew, and ... the drops of the night" by which the Lord's head and hairs are drenched, are those of the beloved's cold-hearted disposition towards the Lord and His entreaties.

I have put off my coat; how shall I put it on? I have washed my feet; how shall I defile them? (3).

"How?" The Heb. word *ekaka* occurs only here and in Esth 8:6 in the Old Testament. Esth 8:6 reads "How can I endure to see the evil that shall come unto my people? or how can I endure to see the destruction of my kindred." The intended sense is, 'how on earth can I?' It does not denote either the impossibility or the unwillingness, but the unperformability of the act, in view of its dreadful consequence.

The putting off of the "coat," Heb. *kethoneth* ("garment of man and woman, worn next to the person,")[110] appears to allude to Joshua's act of circumcising the men of Israel at Gilgal, which was described in 4:2, by the figure of shearing the flock of black goats of their coat of black hair. After circumcising the men, Joshua declared, "This day have I rolled away the reproach of Egypt from off you" (Josh 5:9). Likewise, 'washing feet' appears to refer to the crossing the river Jordan by Joshua's men, which was described by the figure of a flock of goats-turned-sheep that has come up from the washing, (4:2).

No doubt, despite the fact that she was beaten severely and excommunicated from her mother's household, as soon as she opened the door at long last, and crossed the walls (the Judaistic laws) in search of her Lord, her feet, which she had feared would be defiled, became exquisitely beautiful with shoes, like those of a prince's daughter (7:1), and in overall appearance, she became "the fairest among women" in the sight of the generality of the city of Jerusalem, described idiomatically as "the daughters of Jerusalem" (cf. comment on 5: 9; 6:1; 7:1).

My beloved put in his hand by the hole of the door, (4a)

This, clearly, is an anthropomorphic statement. Being a Spirit, the Lord does not possess hands. Hence the statement is not to be interpreted literally. The so-called "hole of the door" through which He thrust in His hand was that of the door of her heart, or else, of the door of her mother's house, namely, that of the decadent Judaism.

And my bowels were moved for him, (4b).

NIV, "My heart began to pound for him." NRSV, "My inmost being yearned for him." JB, "I trembled to the core of my being." NASB, "My feelings were aroused for him." Whatever may be the precise meaning of this statement, one thing is certain. It was this divine work, described in anthropomorphic terms, that ultimately shook up and emboldened the heart of the holy seed of Israel to rise up and open the door and go beyond the walls (Judaical laws),

---

[110] Brown, Driver, Briggs, *op. cit.*, p. 509.

in the face of severe beatings and humiliation; a very daring act, which she could never have done, during all through the past nine centuries.

We must take away our eyes from the figurative speech, and look straight at the history of Israel to find out the described momentous event that finally moved and emboldened the heart of the body of the holy seed of Israel to defy the perverted laws of the decadent Judaical rulers openly and, despite the consequent beatings and humiliations, follow the Lord. The outpouring of the Holy Spirit on the day of Pentecost and the subsequent events described in the Acts of the Apostles only fit to be the event described in this manner, figuratively. Perceived from the historical perspective, the outpouring of the Holy Spirit on the Day of Pentecost solely was that which ultimately emboldened the apostles to open the closed door of the decadent Judaism, and go beyond its laws (walls), in the face of stiff opposition, persecution and stripes to which they were subjected.

I rose to open to my beloved... I opened to my beloved, (5a, 6a).

She knew the dire consequence of opening the door of Judaism, which had been closed against the possibility of her bringing the Lord within, or following after Him. This accounts for the reluctance shown by the beloved to open the door forthwith.

My hand dropped with myrrh, and my fingers with sweet smelling myrrh, upon the handles of the lock, (5b).

That myrrh refers to the love of God is made clear from the metaphor of 1:13, "a bundle of myrrh is my well-beloved unto me; he shall lie all night betwixt my breasts." It is not by her own love that she resolved to keep the Lord in the embrace of faith close to her bosom all night long, but by the love of God that was shed abroad in her heart by the Holy Spirit. "We love him, because he first loved us" (1 Jn 4:19). Discernibly, liquid myrrh occurs here as a symbol for the love of God that was shed abroad in her heart by the Holy Spirit.

God pours out His love into our hearts to enable us to open the hearts of the sinful world for Him. Paul is the one who has set the best example for this. "Woe is unto me, if I preach not the gospel," he writes to the Corinthians (1 Cor 9: 16). However, the beloved was trembling with fear of the dangerous consequences of opening the door for the Lord and following after Him to witness Him openly, so much so that she spilled or wasted His love upon the handles of the door.

But my beloved had withdrawn himself, and was gone: ... I sought him, but I could not find him; I called him, but he gave me no answer, (6b).

"Seek ye the Lord while he may be found, call upon him while he is near" (Isa 55:6). All of us who live in constant communion with the Lord know that if we do not respond promptly when He calls, we lose the sensibility of His presence and of His knocking call. Instead, if we postpone, and call upon Him at our own convenient time, He would have been gone.

My soul failed when he spake.

Literally, 'my soul went forth when he spake.' The underlying idea appears to be that of love sickness. For she appeals to the daughters of Jerusalem in the succeeding verse (5:8), saying, "I charge you, O daughters of Jerusalem, if ye find my beloved, that ye tell him, that I am sick of love."

The watchmen that went about the city found me, (7a).

This is the second appearance of the watchmen over the historical arena. The first time that the watchmen appeared was in 3:3, in the persons of Moses and Aaron who had arrived at Ramses, and found out the body of the elect from among the captive Israel groping in the dark in search of her missing Lord. The watchmen who appear now in this New Testament division of the Song are those who sat in the seat of Moses and Aaron to rule over the decadent Judaism, according to the stipulations of the Mosaic Law, after the advent of the Holy Spirit, on the day of Pentecost. They found out the beloved (church) in the act of opening the closed door of their religious establishment and going beyond their walls (religious laws), in search of the risen Lord.

They smote me, they wounded me, (7b).

This occurs as a disclosure beforehand of the episode of the Jewish Council calling the apostles to appear before it, and, according to the advice of Gamaliel, beating and threatening them with dire consequences if they continue to speak in the name of Jesus. (cf. Acts 5:40)

The keepers of the walls took away my veil from me, (7c).

The Heb. word *shamar* translated "keepers" in the present line is the same word, which is translated as "watchmen," in the preceding line. Watchmen are appointed to watch from watchtowers over the city walls to see if anyone trespasses the walls. Cf. "I have set watchmen upon thy walls, O Jerusalem" (Isa 62:6). Here the intended sense appears to be as JB, "they who guard the ramparts," or walls. "Wall" is the Song's symbol for the Law. The first occurrence of the symbolic word was in 2:9, with reference to the harsh law, which the Pharaoh imposed upon the children of Israel. The word occurs again in 8:9 and 10, with reference to the Law of God, "If she be a wall," i.e., 'if she be a law unto herself,' and "I am a wall," i.e., 'I am a law unto myself.'

In the present case, the keepers of the laws (walls) of the decadent Judaism found out the beloved trespassing the walls (i.e. Judaical laws).

The Heb. word *redid* rendered "veil" refers to a "large veil," which is one of the items of women's finery listed in Isa. 3:23.[111] While beating an offender had legal sanction according to the Mosaic law, taking away the veil of a customarily veiled lady was illegal, and a gross violation of women's right. It is, therefore, an irony that the men who were appointed to maintain the sanctity of the law themselves were violating the law. One may raise eyebrows at this, but the fact remains that this is how the lawmakers and law-keepers of the world run it.

There is the possibility of the presence of a double meaning here; that the unlawful action of the rulers of the decadent Judaism of taking away the beloved's veil became an eye-opener (veil remover) to her.

---

[111] Brown, Driver, Briggs, *op. cit.*, p. 921.

XI. THE PRIMITIVE JEWISH CHRISTIAN CHURCH BEARS WITNESS TO THE GLORIES OF THE RISEN LORD TO THE CURIOUS CROWDS OF JERUSALEM, 5:8-6:3.

This section occurs as a prophetic disclosure of the curiosity that was aroused in the minds of the generality of the Jews of the city of Jerusalem upon the spread of the news of the Lord's crucifixion, resurrection, outpouring of the Holy Spirit, and of the opposition and persecution endured by the apostles thereafter for testifying Christ. The disclosure is being made here figuratively. The daughters of Jerusalem who represent the generality of the Jews of Jerusalem become considerate and sympathetic towards the beloved church all of a sudden, from their former attitude of meddling with her love affair, when they observed the watchmen beating and wounding her. They become impressed, particularly by the utmost patience with which the beloved endured the unjust and harsh treatments that were meted out to her by the watchmen and keepers of the walls, and consequently address her as "the fairest among women." Over and above, the daughters of Jerusalem appeal to the beloved for further enlightenment on the person and glories of her beloved Lord.

1. *Curiosity and interest arise in the hearts of the generality of the Jews of the city of Jerusalem to know more about the person and glories of the risen Christ, 5:8-9*

5: 8. I charge you, O daughters of Jerusalem,
if ye find my beloved, that ye tell him, that I am sick of love.
9. What is thy beloved more than another beloved,
O thou fairest among women?
What is thy beloved more than another beloved,
that thou dost so charge us?

I charge you, O daughters of Jerusalem, if ye find my beloved, (8a).

Discernibly, the authority with which Peter, standing with the eleven, preached Christ on the day of Pentecost is being prefigured in these words. Peter had actually charged the multitudes of Jews who thronged the upper room on the day of

Pentecost, saying,

> Therefore let all the house of Israel know assuredly, that God hath made that same
>
> Jesus, whom ye have crucified, both Lord and Christ.

"Now when they heard this, they were pricked in their heart, and said unto Peter and to the rest of the apostles, Men and brethren, what shall we do? Then said Peter unto them:

> Repent, and be baptized every one of you in the name of Jesus Christ for the remission of sins, and ye shall receive the gift of the Holy Ghost. Acts 2:36-38.

That ye tell him, that I am sick of love, (8b).

It does not mean that the apostles told this to the crowds verbally, but that they conveyed this by the love-sickness for the physically absent Lord that they really manifested on the day of Pentecost when they were filled with the love of Christ by the Holy Spirit sent from on high. Moreover, some from among the mob mocked at the disciples on seeing them behaving like drunken men, when they were overfull with the love of Christ, saying, "these men are full of new wine," But Peter corrected them, saying, "these are not drunken, as ye suppose,... but this is that which was spoken by the prophet Joel" (Acts 2:13-16).

This is the second time that reference to love sickness is made in the Song. The first reference to love sickness was in 2:5.

> What is thy beloved more than another beloved ... what is thy beloved more than another beloved?

JB, "What makes your beloved better than other lovers?" The repetition of the question is meant to highlight the intensity of the great curiosity to know more about the glories of the Lord that was roused in the hearts of the generality of the Jews of the city of Jerusalem, described here by the idiomatic appellative, "daughters of Jerusalem."

O thou fairest among women? (9b).

The emphasis throughout the latter half of the Song is on the church winning the world for the Lord by means of His beauty outshining in her corporeal life, rather than by preaching.

That thou dost so charge us? (9c).

Explained above, under v. 8.

2. *The apostles bear witness to the glories of Christ to the crowds of Jews of the city of Jerusalem who came running to the upper room, on the day of Pentecost, 5:10-16*

The apostles preached Christ wherever they went, not mere sermons (Acts 5:42; 8:35; 10:36). "Salvation is found in no one else," declared they, "for there is no other name under heaven given to men by which we must be saved" (Acts 4:12, NIV).

Inasmuch as this latter half of the Song consists of futuristic prophecies concerning the way in which Christ, the promised Seed of Abraham, came and made the primitive Jewish Christian church the promised blessing for all the families of the earth, the descriptions of the glories of the Lord that the beloved (Church) makes here should be interpreted as the actual revelation of the glory that our Lord obtained through His vicarious sufferings.

5: 10. My beloved is white and ruddy,
the chiefest among ten thousand.
11. His head is as the most fine gold,
His locks are bushy, and black as a raven.
12. His eyes are as the eyes of doves by the rivers of waters,
washed with milk, and fitly set.
13. His cheeks are as a bed of spices, as sweet flowers:
his lips like lilies, dropping sweet smelling myrrh.
14. His hands are as gold rings set with the beryl:
his belly is as bright ivory overlaid with sapphires.
15. His legs are as pillars of marble, set upon sockets of fine gold:
his countenance is as Lebanon, excellent as the cedars.
16. His mouth is most sweet: yea, he is altogether lovely.
This is my beloved, and this is my friend,
O daughters of Jerusalem.

These descriptions themselves are sufficient to show that the beloved is not describing the beauty of an earthly lover. For each of the figures of speech that she invokes are quite odd and bizarre to illustrate the likeness of the respective parts of the body of an earthly individual. What she describes here figuratively are the aspects and attributes of the divine-human glorified Christ.

My beloved is white and ruddy, (10a).

The Heb. word *tsach* means 'dazzling white.' The description suits the appearance of the glorified Christ, rather than that of any human being. As for the Heb. noun *adam* translated "ruddy," Carr says that 'man' "is a more likely source for the term here, in which case, her Lover is 'manly.'"[112] If this is the meaning intended here, the emerging sense is that her Lover is the glorified Man Christ Jesus.

The chiefest among ten thousand, (10b).

The Heb. word *dagal* rendered "chiefest" literally means 'banner or standard bearer.' It is sure that this is the meaning intended here, because in vv. 6:4 and 10, the church of Christ is pictured as marching ahead undauntedly, "terrible as an army with banners." The description implies that she was being marched ahead undauntedly against all odds, as described, by the glorified Christ, her banner-bearer. Moreover, the very same thought had occurred also in 2:4, where the beloved (there Moses) exults, saying, "He brought me to the banqueting house, and his banner over me was love."

The Heb. word *rebabah* translated "ten thousand" literally means 'myraid,' 'multitude,' millions,' or 'countless.' To say that the glorified Christ is the banner-bearer or Captain of a *rebabah* is as saying that He is the Commander-in-Chief of His church triumphant comprising of myriads or countless multitudes of His followers.

His head is as the most fine gold, (11a).

The "most fine gold" is the refined purest gold. "The head of Christ is God" (1 Cor 11:3). "Most fine gold" speaks of Sovereignty.

---

[112] G. Lloyd Carr, *op. cit.,* p. 120.

"I and my Father are one," said the Lord. It appears that the "most fine gold" occurs here as a symbol for the Lord's oneness with the Father, in His Sovereignty.

His locks are bushy, and black as raven, (11b).

According to Gesenius' Hebrew-Chaldee Lexicon, the Heb. word *taltalim* translated "bushy" means "pendulous branches of palms."[113] Taking this as the intended sense, JB translates, "His locks are palm fronds and black as raven."

We have asserted that the Spirit invoke only facts taken from the pre-Solomonic books of the Bible as figures of speech in the similes occurring in the Song, other than for a few exceptions. Further, we have demonstrated that the occurrence of black flowing or wavy hair in 4:1b was as the symbol for the flow of the natural lineage. Viewed from the foregoing perspectives, the flowing or wavy raven-black hair of the Lord, likened to palm (Heb. tamar) fronds must be occurring as a symbol for the flow or lineage of the Lord in His incarnation from Judah, in Tamar, the Canaanite woman, "in the likeness of sinful flesh, and for sin" (Rom 8:3). (Cf. comment on 6:5b; 7:5b,8).

His eyes are as the eyes of doves by the rivers of waters, washed with milk, (12).

NRSV, "His eyes are like doves beside springs of water, bathed in milk, fitly set." JB, "His eyes are doves at a pool of water, bathed in milk, at rest on a pool."

The metaphor, "eyes are doves" has occurred twice before; first in 1: 15, second in 4:1a. Its occurrence in both of these contexts has been to signify the acuity of spiritual vision granted by the Holy Spirit. Applied this to the present context, none ever had the perfect spiritual perception to behold the Father and matters pertaining to His kingdom, as our Lord did have by the Holy Spirit.

"Rivers of water" is also a well-known symbol for the Holy Spirit. However, as the symbol occurs here in association with eyes, it appears to refer to the tears shed by our Lord for the

---

[113] H. W. F. Gesenius, *op. cit.,* p.865.

salvation of the world, in the sense in which Jeremiah cries out in anguish, "*Oh that my head were waters, and mine eyes a fountain of tears*" (Jer 9:1). "Milk" is a symbol for the word of God (cf. 1 Pet 2:2). Taken together, the meaning comes to be that the Lord's eyes were like doves perched by the side of the flowing rivers of tears, and washed with the pure milk of the word of God.

His cheeks are as a bed of spices, as sweet flowers, (13a).

NASB, "His cheeks are like a bed of balsam." NRSV, "His cheeks are like beds of spices, yielding fragrance."

This description of the cheeks of the glorified Christ to be "a bed of spices," and as "sweet flowers" is made with reference to the following prophesies concerning the sweet saving fragrance that they were to emanate through the tortures to which He would submit them vicariously for the salvation of the world:

> "I gave my back to the smiters, and my cheeks to them that plucked off the hair: I hid not my face from shame and spitting." (Isa 50:6).
>
> "His visage was so marred more than any man, and His form more than the sons of men" (Isa 52:14). They shall smite the judge of Israel with a rod upon the cheek" (Mic 5:1b).

The sweet fragrance that has been emanating from the lacerated and tortured innocent cheeks of our Lord has led to the repentance and salvation of countless millions ever since He endured them.

The Heb. word *arugah* translated "bed" occurs only four times in the Old Testament; twice in the Song, (here and in 6:2), and twice in Ezekiel, (Ezek 17:7,10). The literal meaning of the word is 'furrows." In Ezekiel, the word is used for terraces or furrows in which vines were planted to facilitate watering them. The underlying idea appears to be of a garden plot as in 4:13-14 where the two cheeks of the beloved are depicted to be an orchard of pleasant fruits and all the chief spices. According to Strong's *Exhaustive Concordance*, the root word *arag* means 'to long for,' 'to cry,' 'to pant,' and refers figuratively 'to be raised by mental aspirations.'[114]

---

[114] James Strong, *op. cit.*, p. 110.

The Heb. expression, *migdelotmerquahim* translated "sweet flowers" is a combination of the words *migdol* and *merquahim.*

The word *migdol* means 'tower.' It occurs fifty one times in the Old Testament, out of which forty seven times it is translated "tower," one time "castle," and two times "pulpit."

The word, *merquahim,* occurs only here in the Old Testament. *Merquahim* means 'compounds,' ointments. Carr says that "the Hebrew *migdelot* is properly towers (cf.Song 4:4; 7:44; 8:10), here used in the sense of 'stronghold' or 'treasure-chamber."[115] Concerning the word *merquahim*, he says that the verb *raqah* used eight times ' (and other related nouns used about six times), describes the art of mixing ointments and perfumes."[116] Accordingly, for the compound word, *migdelotmerquahim* translated in the AV as "sweet flowers," there is a marginal reading, "towers of perfumes." Our Lord's cheeks that had endured unbearable torments for our salvation are truly our stronghold or a treasure chamber wherein all sorts of sweet-smelling heavenly perfumes are compounded and stored for the enjoyment of the elect of God who waits before Him in repentance and contrition.

His lips like lilies, dropping sweet smelling myrrh, (13b).

The word *abar* is translated "sweet smelling" here and in 5:5. The meaning of the word is 'to pass over,' 'to over pass.' 'Overflowing' appears to be the sense intended here. Overflowing myrrh refers to overflowing or boundless love. The present expression, "His lips dropping sweet smelling myrrh," means that the words that proceeded from His lips were words of unbounded love. The intended sense of the expression is better understood in the light of the words of our Lord found in Isa 50:4, "the Lord God hath given me the tongue of the learned, that I should know how to speak a word in season to him that is weary"(Isa 50:4).

Delitzsch comments:

She thinks of the lips as speaking. All that comes forth from them,

---

115 G. Lloyd Carr, *op. cit.*, pp. 141, 142.
116 *Ibid.*, p. 142.

> the breath in itself, and the breath formed into words, is ... most precious myrrh, viz. such as of itself wells forth from the bark of the balsamodendron.[117]

The symbolic word "lilies," refers to Israel, the chosen ones. (Cf. the notes on 'the symbolic word lily,'under the head, 'The Artful Use of Figures of speech in the Song,' in the introductory Section of this book).

His hands are as gold rings set with the beryl, (14a).

NRSV, "His arms are rounded gold, set with jewels."

"Burrows explains the rings as cylinders used as signets, such as are found in Nineveh" (JFB Commentary).[118] Taken in the literal sense of the AV rendering, "gold rings set with beryl," the reference appears to be to signet rings. "The Hebrew root *gll* ('to roll') suggests a circular form, perhaps a rod or cylinder.... 'Galilee', the 'circle of the Gentiles' (cf. Isa 9:1), is also derived from this root."[119] Whatever may be the exact meaning, the Father's authority with which our Lord "went about doing good, and healing all that were oppressed of the devil" (Acts 10:38) is the idea underscored here.

His belly is as bright ivory overlaid with sapphires, (14b).

Out of the thirty-two occurrences of the word *meah* in the Old Testament, twenty seven times it is translated "bowels," and only three times as "belly." In the present context the word should read "bowels," in the figurative sense of 'bowels of compassions' or as *Gesenius' Hebrew Chaldee Lexicon* suggests, "inmost soul."[120] Ivory is the teeth of elephants. However, the Hebrew word *'shen'* simply means 'teeth.' The word had occurred in the Song, in 4:2, "thy teeth are like a flock of sheep." The same expression recurs again in 6:6. In both of these verses, teeth occurred in the sense of smiling teeth of spiritual liberty. On the basis of the above, we conclude

---

117 Franz Delitzsch, *op. cit.*, p. 103.
118 Rev. Robert Jamieson, et. al., *op. cit.*, p. 499.
119 G. Lloyd Carr, *op. cit.*, p. 142.
120 H. W. F. Gesenius, *op. cit.*, p. 492.

the nearest meaning of the present description to be that the bowels of mercies of our Lord sprung from His "inmost soul," or from His heart of perfect spiritual liberty.

His legs are as pillars of marble, set upon sockets of fine gold, (15a).

NRSV, "His legs are alabaster columns, set upon bases of gold."

The word *shesh* translated "marble" in AV and "alabaster" in NRSV occurs only here and in 1 Chr 29:2 and Esth 1:6. Moses made sockets of silver as bases for the wooden boards of the tabernacle, to protect the wooden boards from touching the ground and getting decayed. But founding marble columns on sockets of fine gold, described here, is an unheard of thing. As marble is a far less inferior substance in comparison with fine gold, no one would ever think of setting up columns of marble on sockets of purified gold. However, the imagery becomes meaningful if taken as a figure of the risen Lord's stand of faith and solidarity with the Sovereign Father.

His countenance is as Lebanon, excellent as the cedars, (15b)

> Heb. Lebanon is derived from the root lbn, 'white.' The range owes this name to two factors: the white limestone of the high ridge of Lebanon, and especially the *glittering snows that cap its peaks for six months of the year.*[121]

The word *mareh* rendered "countenance" means 'appearance,' 'look,' 'aspect.' "Lebanon" had figured in 4:8, 11 and 15 as the symbol for *the heavenlies*. The word '*bachar*' rendered "excellent" means 'the chosen,' the preferred' or 'the approved' one. In the light of these meanings, the sense of the statement emerges to be that the countenance or aspect of the risen and glorified Lord is high and exalted above all, like the snow-clad Mount Lebanon that towers above all and like the tall cedar trees.

His mouth is most sweet, (16a).

Every child of God who lives by faith in the words that poured out of our Lord's mouth knows experientially that the words of His mouth were the sweetest.

---

[121] J. D. Douglas, et. al, *op. cit.*, p. 680.

He is altogether lovely. This is my beloved, and this is my friend, O daughters of Jerusalem, (16b).

By these succinct words the beloved, (church), sums up the testimony she was bearing of her Lover's aspects and attributes to the inquisitive crowds of the generality of the city of Jerusalem. This occurs clearly as a prophecy in sophisticated figures of speech of the challenging testimony that Peter, (standing up with the eleven), bore on the day of Pentecost, concerning the glories of the risen and glorified Christ, to the curious crowds of Jerusalem who came running to the upper room, on hearing the commotion.

3. "Pricked in their heart" by the church's challenging word of testimony, three thousand of the Jews out of those who came running to the upper room wish to know where the Lord has gone so that they may join her in her search for the risen Lord, 6:1

6: 1. Whither is thy beloved gone, O thou fairest among women?

Whither is thy beloved turned aside? that we may seek him with thee.

This obviously is a prophetic disclosure made beforehand of the positive change that came about in the attitude of the three thousand Jews out of the multitudes who came running to the upper room on the day of Pentecost, and heard the challenging testimony that Peter bore, proving from the Scriptures that Jesus whom they crucified was truly the Messiah and Lord. "Pricked in their hearts" they enquired of the apostles, "Men and brethren, what shall we do?" (Acts 2:37). Peter had answered them, saying,

> Repent, and be baptized every one of you in the name of Jesus Christ for the remission of sins, and ye shall receive the gift of the Holy Ghost. For the promise is unto you, and to your children, and to all that are afar off, even as many as the Lord our God shall call.

Whither is thy beloved gone, ... wither is thy beloved turned aside? (1a,c).

The Heb. word *panah,* means 'to turn the face.' The question therefore comes to be, 'whither has your beloved turned his face?' The Lord was not absent; He had only turned His face. In other words, He was invisible to them in that He had risen from the dead and was present as the Spirit that He had been.

O thou fairest among women, (1b)

As stated, the emphasis throughout the Song is on the church winning over the world by the beauty of the Lord outshining in her corporeal life, rather than by her profession and preaching.

Those three thousand souls who obeyed the Lord in water baptism and joined the church on the day of Pentecost did so because they saw the glory of the Lord outshining in the lives of the one hundred and twenty disciples who were filled with the Holy Spirit. This is signified by the way they epitomize the beloved (church), as "the fairest among women."

That we may seek him with thee, (1d).

Significantly, the word *baqash* rendered "seek" signifies to search out "in worship or prayer."[122]

4. *The beloved (Church) answers, 6:2-3*

> 6: 2. My beloved is gone down into his garden, to the beds of spices,
> to feed in the gardens, and to gather lilies.
>
> 3. I am my beloved's, and my beloved is mine:
> he feedeth among the lilies.

My beloved is gone down into his garden, (2a).

According to the Song's disclosure, this is the answer that the primitive Jewish Christian church furnished to the question that was raised by the three thousand Jews of the city of Jerusalem who accepted the Lord as the Messiah and Lord on the day of Pentecost. The first clause of their question, according to the figurative disclosure in the Song, was, 'whither has thy beloved turned his face that we may seek Him with thee in worship and prayer?' The church's answer to this was figuratively, "my beloved is gone down into his garden." As the beloved (church) herself is the Lord's garden, she has to be understood as saying that the

---

[122] James Strong, *op. cit.*, p. 22.

risen Lord, the invisible Spirit, has gone down into the hearts of her constituent members, in the sense in which the Lord had told them during His final discourse, saying,

> Yet a little while, and the world seeth me no more; but ye see me: because I live, ye shall live also. At that day (i.e. on the day the Spirit of truth will come) ye shall know that I am in my Father, and ye in me, and I in you. John 14:19- 20.

To the beds of spices, (2b).

In 4:13, the Lord had described the beloved church's cheeks to be "an orchard (or bed) of pomegranates, with pleasant fruits ... and ... all the chief spices." (Bracketed portion mine). Thereafter, in 5:13, the beloved church had described the glorified Christ's cheeks "as a bed of spices." In both the cases, the figure of "bed of spices" refers to the life of the Godly people from which the sweet-smelling fragrance of the nature and glory of God emanated as a result of the persecutions that they endured willingly for the glory of God.

Viewed from the foregoing perspectives, "the beds of spices" to which the Lord has gone should be either to the heart of those members of the body of Christ who were described as her cheeks; or to their dwelling place.

To feed in the gardens, (2c).

It may be recalled in this connection that "garden," in singular number, refers to Israel, the church, and "gardens," in plural number, to the rest of the nations of the earth. When the beloved (church) says that the glorified Christ has gone down to His garden (singular), to the beds of spices, she means that He has gone down into the hearts of her constituent members, whose lives had become sweet savour unto Him on account of the extreme fiery trials that they were enduring for His sake. However, when she adds that her beloved Lord has gone down also to feed in the gardens (plural), she means that the risen Lord has gone also to preach to, and teach in the neighbouring nations of the earth.

And to gather lilies, (2d)

We saw that the word "lilies" occurs as a symbol for the elect from among the Jewish people, in their myopic perception that the Lord feeds, i.e. shepherds, only among them. It is out of the same Jewish myopic misconception that the beloved (here the primitive Jewish Christian church) asserts that the Lord has gone to other nations, for the limited purpose of feeding, i.e., teaching, in those alien gardens and gathering lilies (i.e. gather His elect from among the Jewish Diaspora). Significantly, the beloved asserts this at a time when "they which were scattered abroad upon the persecution that arose about Stephen traveled as far as Phenice, and Cypress, and Antioch, preaching the word to none but unto the Jews only" (Ac. 11:19).

6: 3. I am my beloved's, and my beloved is mine:
he feedeth among the lilies.

This is a facsimile of v. 2:16, with the difference that the second clause "I am my beloved's," is now shifted to be the first clause. This is done to indicate the growing awareness that has come to the beloved (church) that she is the Lord's chosen one by virtue of the Lord's gracious choice rather than by that of her faith.

The purpose of interposing this pet slogan of Israel's religious bigotry at this juncture in the disclosure of her redemptive story is to show that the Jewish misconception that the Lord feeds i.e., shepherds, only among Israel, His lilies, still prevails in the collective heart of the church.

XII. THE CHURCH TRIUMPHANT NOW MARCHES INTO THE REGIONS OF SAMARIA AS AN ARMY WITH BANNERS, AND ASSIMILATES THE SAMARITANS WHO BELIEVED INTO THE BODY OF CHRIST, 6:4-9

The order in which the disciples reached out the world with the gospel of peace and reconciliation in Christ had been in the order, from Jerusalem to the whole of Judea, then to Samaria, and finally to the ends of the earth, exactly as the risen Lord had foretold them, saying,

> Ye shall receive power, after that the Holy Ghost is come upon you: and ye shall be witnesses unto me both in Jerusalem, and in all Judaea, and in Samaria, and unto the uttermost part of the earth. Acts 1:8.

The present section occurs as a prophetic disclosure of the triumphant march of the primitive Jewish Christian church into the regions of the ancient kingdom of Samaria and assimilating the Samaritan believers into the body of Christ, in the ministry of Philip, as recorded in Acts 8: 1-17.

1. *The Church's conquest of the Samaritans by the love of Christ likened to the conquest of Canaan by the army of Joshua and the Judges 6:4-7*

6: 4. Thou art beautiful, O my love, as Tirzah,
comely as Jerusalem, terrible as an army with banners.

5. Turn away thine eyes from me, for they have overcome me:
thy hair is as a flock of goats that appear from Gilead.

6. Thy teeth are as a flock of sheep which go up from the washing,
whereof every one beareth twins, and there is not one barren among them.

7. As a piece of a pomegranate are thy temples within thy locks.

As we have asserted earlier, that the figures which the Spirit invokes for illustration in the similes occurring in the Song are not imaginary, but actual facts taken from the redemptive history of Israel. Accordingly, all the three figures of speech that the Spirit invokes in the similes occurring in v. 6:4, cited above, namely, "as Tirzah," "as Jerusalem," and "as an army with banners," are not imaginary, but facts taken from Israel's redemptive history. The church, the body of Christ, is being described here by the similes, "beautiful ... as Tirzah, comely as Jerusalem," to show that, along with the Jewish converts to Christianity, the church, the body of Christ has now assimilated the Samaritan believers also as constituent part of the body. This shows also that the Jewish Christian church has changed the stance that she had expressed in the preceding verse that the Lord shepherds only among Israel, His white lilies. Accordingly, she has gone beyond the regions of Judaea, into Tirzah, which was the first capital city of the ancient kingdom of Samaria, preaching the gospel of Christ.

Likewise, the simile "terrible as an army with banners" that the Spirit invokes in the form of a figure of speech here to liken the church's advancement to the regions of the ancient kingdom of Samaria, is not imaginary. It refers to the terrible army of Joshua and his men whose advancement into the Promised Land solely by the power of faith had struck terror in the hearts of the Canaanite nations. It is to reaffirm this that the earlier figures of 4:1b-3, all pertaining to the conquest of the Promised Land by the triumphant army of Joshua, Judges and their men, are incorporated here almost verbatim. It implies also that the Great Commission given to the primitive Jewish Christian Church, by the Lord, of winning the world for Him by the conquering power of faith and love was equivalent to that which was assigned by Him to Joshua, Judges and their men of taking possession of the Promised Land solely by the power of faith. This depiction is reminiscent of the words of Paul who had stated concerning the conquering power of Christ's love with which the church of his time was endued, saying, "we are more than conquerors" (Rom 8:37).

Thou art beautiful, O my love, as Tirzah, comely as Jerusalem, (4a).

Tirzah had continued to be the capital city of the northern kingdom of Israel until Omri shifted the capital to Samaria. Evidently, Tirzah was going to be the capital of Samaria when the Spirit of Christ had sung the Song by the mouth of Solomon. It becomes clear from the present description that Tirzah was noted for its beauty during the Solomonic epoch. This accounts for the reason why the Spirit represents the regions of the ancient kingdom of Samaria by the city of Tirzah.

When Samaria finally fell to the Assyrians, the Assyrian king deported the upper layer of the Israelite population of the land to other parts of his empire and repopulated the land with non-Israelites brought from elsewhere. When the new settlers of the outlying districts of the land faced constant threats from lions, they resorted to seek protection from the God of the Israelites. Thus the population of the northern kingdom of Samaria became syncretistic in their religious beliefs and practices. Eventually, by the time of the primitive Jewish Christian church, the Samaritans had followed a corrupt form of the Pentateuch and worshipped the God of Israel on mount Gerizim, instead of in the Jerusalem temple. However, the Samaritans were favourably disposed towards our Lord and the gospel. This is evident from the episode of our Lord's encounter with the Samaritan woman at the well of Jacob, recorded in John. 4:1-42 and that of Philip's ministry in the city of Samaria, recorded in Acts 8:5-17, which is the topic of the prophetic disclosure of the present section.

Terrible as an army with banners, (4b).

The word "banners" occurs here as a symbol for the love of Christ. The meaning is divulged in 2:4, by the words, "his banner over me was love."

The picture presented here is that of the indwelling risen Christ, the banner-bearer of His church, marching her ahead undauntedly against all odds and conquering the Samaritans for Him, by the power of His conquering love.

The advancing primitive church of Christ also spread terror in the hearts of the Jewish religious leaders of their day, just as the advancing armies of Joshua and his men spread terror in the hearts of the Canaanite nations. This is the reason why the decadent Judaical rulers resorted to all sorts of persecutions to suppress the advancement and growth of the church of Christ.

Turn away thine eyes from me, for they have overcome me, (5a).

The modern Versions give different nuances to the word *rahab* translated "overcome." The NIV translates the word as "overwhelm," NEB,"dazzle," and JB, "hold captive." BDB suggests the meaning as, "alarm me."[123] JB's 'to hold captive,' or 'captivate' is the nuance suited to the present context. In 4:1a of the earlier section, the Lord had commended the beloved, saying, "Thou art fair, my love; behold, thou art fair." Evidently, the transformation that came about of her inner being into the fairness of the Lord was by the virtue of her beholding His glorious face, as in a glass with open face. On the other hand, here the Lord asks her to take away her eyes from Him and fix them on the multitudes of sinners

---

[123] Brown, Driver, Briggs, *op. cit*, p. 923.

seeking Him for salvation. That this is the intended sense is made clear from the figurative description, of the succeeding verse of the section, of sinners rushing down seeking salvation in Christ.

Thy hair is as a flock of goats that appear from Gilead, (5b).

This is a repetition of 4:1b, without the word "mount." It should be recalled here that the earlier occurrence of this statement in 4:1b was as a figurative description of the unregenerate and uncircumcised young men of Israel rushing down the slopes of mount Gilead poised to cross over Jordan to the Promised Land by faith. The very same flock of God was described as a flock of snow-white sheep, when it crossed over Jordan solely by faith and came up from the washing. Those symbolic expressions are incorporated here, in the New Testament division of the Song, to signify sinners rushing down to Christ to be transformed, washed in the water of baptism and become a part of the body of Christ.

It must be recalled, in this context, that black hair is the Song's symbol for natural lineage. The symbol derives its significance from the black goatskins with which Jacob covered himself to obtain his father's blessing fraudulently.

Thy teeth are as a flock of sheep which go up from the washing, (6a).

This is a rephrased version of 4:2a. The inapplicable words "that are even shorn," which had occurred as a figurative description of circumcision, is dropped. Likewise, the phrase, "that came up from the washing," is changed into, "which go up from the washing." The flock of black goats that 'came down' to the primitive Jewish Christian church, and the flock of snow-white sheep that 'goes up' from the washing occur here as figurative descriptions of the multitudes of Jews and Samaritans who had flowed down in steady streams to be saved, baptized and become parts of the body of Christ, during the period. Exactly as before, the sinners who flowed down to Christ in steady streams are described as being the downward flowing graceful (black) hair of the body of Christ, and the believers who go up from the washing are described as being the smiling teeth of liberty of the body of Christ.

Whereof every one beareth twins, and there is not one barren among them, (6b).

In the present context, bearing twins refers to bearing double number of spiritual seeds. One is saved to save. Paul writes to the Corinthians, "Woe is unto me, if I preach not the gospel" (1 Cor 9:16).

As a piece of a pomegranate are thy temples within thy locks, (7).

NIV, "Your temples behind your veil are like the halves of a pomegranate." NRSV, "Your cheeks are like halves of a pomegranate behind your veil."

As explained, a wholesome pomegranate stands for the fullness of the promised spiritual heritage. Cheeks are the index of expression. It shows that after winning over a group of Samaritans, the church remains content, unconcerned about the entire world of unreached Gentiles.

2. ***The constituent members of the household of Christ classified, 6:8-9***

6: 8. There are threescore queens, and fourscore concubines,
and virgins without number.

9. My dove, my undefiled is but one; she is the only one of her mother,
she is the choice one of her that bare her.
The daughters saw her, and blessed her; yea,
the queens and the concubines, and they praised her.

There are threescore queens, and fourscore concubines, and virgins without number (8).

The picture is that of a large household of God, consisting of the various categories of members. The idea of a large household of this type is, obviously, taken from the practice of ancient kings and men of means who maintained large households. Solomon himself had maintained exorbitant numbers of queens, concubines, and virgins.

The keys to identify the members of this figurative household of God, excepting that of the concubines, are given elsewhere in the Song.

The number threescore occurred earlier in 3:7 as the symbolic number of the six hundred thousand footmen of Israel who perished in the wilderness due to unbelief, and the consequent curse. They were the ones who had bound themselves to the Lord in the Sinai covenant to keep the Law. However, they perished for the reason that the Sinai covenant was not of faith. This, in turn, suggests that the threescore queens occur here as a figure of the law-keepers.

The keepers appear again in 8:11 as those to whom (the heavenly) Solomon let out His (figurative) vineyard. (For further details, see comment under 8:11).

The expression, "virgins without number," as explained under the head 'the Household of God," in the introductory Section of this book, refers to the natural seed of the covenant who were countless "as the sand which is upon the seashore."

My dove, my undefiled is but one, (9a).

The oneness of the body of Christ is underscored by this, exactly as Paul writes, "we, being many, are one body in Christ" (Rom 12:5). "There is one body, and one Spirit, even as ye are called in one hope of your calling; one Lord, one faith, one baptism, one God and Father of all" (Eph 4:4-6). There was "no schism in the body" of Christ that was born of God on the day of Pentecost; "The multitude of them that believed were of one heart and of one soul" (Acts 4:32). "And they, continuing daily with one accord" and "did eat their meat with gladness and singleness of heart" (Acts 2:46). These were the things that prompted the generality of the Jews of Jerusalem (the daughters of Jerusalem) to address the beloved (church) as "the fairest among women" (5:9; 6:1). The human-made doctrines divide, while the constraining love of God shed abroad in the hearts of the believers by the Spirit, unites the children of God (cf. Rom 5:5).

She is the only one of her mother, (9b).

The beloved's mother, as stated, was the Abrahamic covenant

of promise. The covenant was made by God to beget children unto Him through regeneration. Hence, the body of the regenerated ones, namely, the church, alone was the genuine daughter of the Abrahamic covenant.

She is the choice one of her that bare her, (9c).

The word *bar* rendered "choice" means, 'choice,' 'clean,' 'pure.'[124] The context favours the sense of the AV rendering, "the choice one." The church that appears as the Lord's beloved in the Song is the embodiment of the elect of God; the chosen ones.

The daughters saw her, and blessed her, (9d).

This, obviously, is a reworded version of Gen 30:13, wherein Leah is stated to have named Zilpah's second son as Asher (lit. happy), saying, "Happy am I, for the daughters will call me blessed."

Yea, the queens and the concubines, and they praised her, (9e).

The promise was, "thou shalt be a blessing: and I will bless them that bless thee" (Gen 12:2c, 3a). Here all the members of the household of God are stated to be blessing the beloved (church) and becoming blessed thereby.

XIII. THE DAY OF THE FULLNESS OF THE KNOWLEDGE OF HER CALLING DAWNS IN THE COLLECTIVE HEART OF ISRAEL, (THE CHURCH), AND SHE, IN TURN, DAWNS OVER THE HORIZON OF THE DARKENED GENTILE WORLD, 6:10

6: 10. Who is she that looketh forth as the morning,
fair as the moon, clear as the sun,
and terrible as an army with banners?

While commenting on the preceding section, 6:4-6, we have shown that the "terrible ... army with banners," that the Spirit invoked there in the form of a figure of speech, to liken the church's advancement to the regions of the ancient kingdom of Samaria,

---

124 James Strong, *op. cit.*, p. 22.

was actually the army of Joshua, Judges and their mighty men of faith whose advancement into the towns and cities of Canaan struck terror in the hearts of the Canaanites. The figure occurs in the Song only there and in the present context. The figure is invoked here to demonstrate the church's advancement into the regions of the Gentile world "terrible as" the army of Joshua, Judges and their men of faith. The uproarious welcome that is being accorded to the visiting beloved (church) by the so-called 'nut trees,' and the visiting church's words, "Or ever I was aware, my soul made me like the chariots of Amminadib," shows that the figurative descriptions are of the first ever trip of the primitive Jewish Christian church to Gentiles with the gospel of peace and reconciliation in Christ, in the episode of Peter's trip to the household of Cornelius.

However, as explained under the head, 'Methodology,' in the Introductory section of this book, the occurrence of the place-name, "*Mahanaim*" and the use of the over-enthusiastic words by which the so-called 'nut trees' welcome the beloved (church) back to their fold, shouting, "Return, return, ... return, return," prove beyond doubt that the present figurative description of Peter's trip to the household of Cornelius is based on the episode of the meeting between Jacob and Esau, which resulted in the undreamt-of peace and reconciliation between the two.

The peace and reconciliation that came about between Jacob and Esau took place when Jacob emerged from Peniel at dawn, after his nightlong wrestle with the Lord for power with God and with men, to overcome the approaching furious Esau and his four hundred men with genuine humility and divine love. In answer to Jacob's prayer, the meeting between the brothers resulted in the undreamt-of peace and reconciliation. Esau's burning anger dissipated, and he welcomed Jacob, back to Canaan and home, with open arms.

Who is she that looketh forth as the morning, fair as the moon, clear as the sun, (10).

NIV, "Who is this that appears like the dawn?" NRSV, "Who is this that looks forth like the dawn?"

The picture being drawn is bi-dimensional. The first dimension is that of the light of the knowledge of the purpose for which Israel, (the primitive Jewish Christian church), had been called dawning in her heart, and with that the darkness of religious bigotry, and the shadows of religious doubts and fears that had ruled her heart fleeing.

The second dimension is that of Israel, the beloved (the primitive Jewish Christian church), in her turn, dawning over the horizon of the darkened Gentile world, with the new light that has dawned in her heart, "fair as the moon, clear as the sun, and terrible as an army with banners."

The Heb. word *shaqaph* rendered "looketh forth" carry different nuances such as, 'to look out from above, "as a mountain looks over a plain or valley (Num 21:20,23:28; I Sam 13:18), and "as God looks down from heaven.[125] Delitzsch says that verb used signifies "to look toward something with head inclined" or bending "forward," and adds:

> The point of comparison is, the rising up from the background: Shulamite breaks through the shades of the garden-grove like ...the morning dawn; or, also: she comes nearer and nearer, as the morning-red rises behind the mountains, and then fills always the more widely the whole horizon.[126]

From the perspective of the episode of the meeting between Jacob and Esau, on which the present section is based, the beloved's action of anxiously "looking toward something with head inclined" alludes to the statement of Gen 33:1, "and Jacob lifted up his eyes, and looked, and, behold, Esau came, and with him four hundred men."

Terrible as an army with banners, (10b).

(See detailed comment above, under v.4).

---

[125] Marvin Pope, *op. cit.*, pp. 571, 572.
[126] Franz Delitzsch, *op. cit.*, p. 113.

1. *The Maiden Missionary trip of the church to the Gentiles, in the person of Peter, 6:11-13*

6: 11. I went down into the garden of nuts to see the fruits of the valley,
And to see whether the vine flourished, and the pomegranate budded.
12. Or ever I was aware, my soul made me like the chariots of Amminadib.
13. Return, return, O Shulamite; return, return, that we may look upon thee. What will ye see in the Shulamite? As it were the company of two armies.

I went down into the garden of nuts, (11a).

The word *egoz* rendered "nuts" occurs only here in the Old Testament. The context shows that the 'hard to crack' hardened people are the ones described figuratively as nuts.

To see whether the vine flourished, and the pomegranates budded, (11c).

Grapevines flourishing and pomegranates budding are the Song's symbols for sprouting forth of faith. (Cf. comment on 7:12). Here, this prefigures the inquisitive and quizzical frame of mind in which Peter went towards the house of Cornelius, and, in the episode of the undreamt-of peace and reconciliation that had come about between Esau and Jacob on which the New Testament story is based, the inquisitive and quizzical frame of mind in which Jacob went towards the approaching Esau and his men.

Unless the Lord prepares the hearts of people beforehand, the evangelists, pastors and teachers who preach the gospel preach in vain. "For it is God which worketh" in them "both to will and to do of his good pleasure" (Phil 2:13). Our Lord had also made this fact categorical when He said, "no man can come to me, except the Father which hath sent me draw him" (John 6:44).

Or ever I was aware, my soul made me like the chariots of Amminadib, (12).

NIV, "Before I realized it my desire set me among the royal chariots of my people." NRSV, "Before I was aware, my fancy set me in a chariot beside my prince." JB, "Before I knew … my desire had hurled me on the chariots of my people, as their prince." NASB, "Before I was aware, my soul set me over the chariots of my noble people."

"Commentators are unanimous that this verse is the most difficult in the Song and one of the most difficult in the Old Testament to make sense of," says Carr.[127] The difficulty arises only on account of unknowingness of what the section is all about. The statement occurs, as a figurative description of how Peter's soul, unaware to himself, so to say, hurled him onto the bandwagon of Cornelius and his household. And in the episode of the meeting between Jacob and Esau, on which the prophetical disclosure of the New Testament story is based, as to how Jacob's soul hurled him onto the bandwagon of Esau and his army of four hundred men. Needless to say, in both the cases, it was the love of God shed abroad in their hearts by the Holy Spirit that hurled the concerned party on to the bandwagon of the other.

"*Amminadib*" is a compound word combining *ammi*, which means, "my people," and *nadab*, which means, "liberal" or "willing." On combining the word meanings, the intended sense of *Amminadib* emerges to be, "my willing or liberal people."[128] According to Strong's *Exhaustive Concordance*, *nadib* carries a number of nuances such as, 'free,' 'liberal,' noble,' 'willing' (hearted)."[129] All of these meanings are apt to speak of how Peter's and Jacob's souls hurled them onto the bandwagon of the other, but the most appropriate among the suggested senses is 'one of the family of my willing people,' because in both of the cases, an otherwise unwilling people were made a willing people by God Himself. Consequently, on arrival at Cornelius' house, moved with divine love, Peter blurted out, saying, "Of a truth I perceive that God is no respecter of persons" (Acts 10:34).

As for the curious expression, "my soul" set or "hurled me on the chariots of my people," it appears to be an idiom for saying that the Spirit threw the speaker onto the bandwagon of the other

---

[127] G. Lloyd Carr, *op. cit.*, p. 151.
[128] Robert Young, *op. cit.*, pp. 32, 682.
[129] James Strong, *op. cit.*, p.91.

party, by the love of God, across the gulf of division that had existed between the two.

Return, return, O Shulamite; return, return, (13a).

"Shulamite,' (princess of peace), "is simply a feminine form of the name Solomon."[130] It is not a proper name, but a new name being given to the Church in recognition of the message of peace and reconciliation in Christ that she brought to the Gentiles.

In Jacob's case, he was returning home after about twenty years, unknowing whether Esau's burning anger against him has abated; whether he would be welcomed back. And, in Peter's case he was unsure of the purpose for which the Lord was directing him to go to the Gentiles from whom, he thought, the Lord Himself had separated his community.

What will you see in the Shulamite? As it were the company of two armies, (13c).

The Heb. expression, "*k/bimholat hammahanayim*, as/in the dance of the double camps has been variously rendered in both ancient and modern versions."[131] As for our line of interpretation, we need only to find out the intended meanings of the Heb. words, *meholah*, translated "company," and *hammahanayim*, translated "two armies" in the AV.

The word *meholah* translated company, in AV, actually means, "dancing, token of joyousness after victory" or "in worship, accompanied by timbrel."[132] *Mahanaim* was the name that Jacob gave to the place where the angels met him on his way back to Canaan, about twenty years after his flight to Haran for fear of Esau's burning anger. The word meaning of *Mahanaim* is two armies or camps. The exact location of the place is not known. The presence of the definite article in the text shows that the place known by the name is meant. "A number of modern translators and exegetes have assumed that the *Mahanayim* of the Canticles is none other than the place where the angels

---

[130] G. Lloyd Carr, *op. cit.*, p.154.

[131] Marvin Pope, *op. cit.*, p. 601.

[132] Brown, Driver, Briggs, *op. cit.*, p. 298.

confronted Jacob."[133] Pope says that, "*Mahanayim* is also the name of a town of Gilead, near the river Jabbok."[134] Going by the narrative of Gen 32, it appears that it was from *Mahanaim* that Jacob sent peace feelers to Esau, and it was from the same place that he crossed over Jabbok, and after dividing his wives and children into two camps, wrestled with God for power with God and with men to overcome the approaching Esau and his four hundred men. And possibly, it was at *Mahanaim* that the undreamt-of peace and reconciliation came about between the discordant brothers.

In the case of this episode of peace and reconciliation that came about between Jacob and Esau, on which the present imagery is based, the two dancing and rejoicing companies could have been Jacob and his company that constituted of his wives, concubines and their respective children, on one side, and Esau and the company of four hundred men who had accompanied him, on the other.

In the case of the peace and reconciliation that came about between the Jews and the Gentiles, in the episode of Peter's first ever missionary trip to the household of Cornelius, the Gentile, the two companies or armies that danced and sang together with accompaniment of timbrels, were Cornelius and his household on whom the Holy Spirit descended spontaneously, on the one side, and Peter and the Jewish Christians who had accompanied him, on the other.

XIV. THE CHURCH GROWS UP UNTO THE MEASURE OF THE STATURE OF THE FULNESS OF CHRIST, WITH THE INCORPORATION OF GENTILES INTO THE BODY OF CHRIST, 7:1-6

The church that was hid in the Father's redemptive scheme as a mystery from the foundation of the world had been "one new man" (Eph 2:15), comprising of both the Jewish and Gentile believers. The purpose for which the Lord called, saved and built

---

[133] Marvin Pope, *op. cit.*, p. 603.
[134] *Ibid.*, p. 603.

up Jacob and the elect from among his seed as His body was that she, in turn, should become the promised blessing of Abraham for the rest of the families of the earth and make them part "of the same body" (Eph 3:6). Israel, however, had misconceived that she was chosen, separated, and blessed for her own sake. Therefore, she had reckoned the Gentiles as an abomination to the Lord, and refused to share the blessings of God with them. As a result, the body of Christ had remained dwarfed to a half, from the eyes and hair of her head down to breasts, in the Old Testament dispensation.

Now that the day of the light of the knowledge of the purpose for which she was called had dawned in the heart of Israel, the church, as described figuratively in the preceding section, she had begun to evangelize the Gentile world, win souls and receive the souls won as members "of the same body." The present section shows the process of the Jewish Christian church winning over the Gentiles, and growing as the body of Christ "unto the measure of the stature of the fulness of Christ" (Eph 4:13), from feet upwards to the royal hair on the crown of her head.

7: 1. How beautiful are thy feet with shoes, O prince's daughter!
The joints of thy thighs are like jewels,
The work of the hands of a cunning workman.
2. Thy navel is like a round goblet, which wanteth not liquor:
Thy belly is like an heap of wheat set about with lilies.
3. Thy two breasts are like two young roes that are twins.
4. Thy neck is as a tower of ivory; thine eyes like the fish pools
in Heshbon, by the gate of Bath-rabbim: thy nose is as the tower of Lebanon which looketh toward Damascus.
5. Thine head upon thee is like Carmel, and the hair of thine head
like purple: the king is held in the galleries.
6. How fair and how pleasant art thou, O love, for delights!
7. This thy stature is like to a palm tree,
and thy breasts to clusters (of grapes).

The process of growth of the church as the body of Christ, assimilating the Gentile converts, unto the measure of the stature of the fullness of Christ is being described in this section in ascending order, from feet to the hair over head, whereas, in the former section, 4:1-7, it was described in descending order, from eyes down to breasts.

Another significant difference in the description of the growth of the church as the body of Christ being made in this section is the use of much more tangled and involved figures of speech, such as unidentifiable place-names and objects. For instance, "the fish pools in Heshbon by the gate of *Bath-rammim*," and "the tower of Lebanon which looketh toward Damascus."

1. *Evangelists: the beautiful, shod feet of the body of Christ, 7:1a*

How beautiful are thy feet with shoes, (1a).

The figure of the "beautiful feet with shoes" needs no explanation as it is a well-known symbolic expression for those "that publisheth peace; that bringeth good tidings of good, that publisheth salvation," namely, evangelists (cf. Isa 52:7, with Rom 10:15; Eph 6:15).

There was no evangelistic ministry to the Gentiles in the Old Testament dispensation, except the one undertaken by Jonah to Nineveh. The reason was the religious bigotry of the Jews. Consequently, the body of Christ did not possess "beautiful feet with shoes." Now that the day has dawned in the church's collective heart, of the light of the knowledge of the purpose for which she was called, a group of her members whom the Lord endued with the gift of evangelistic ministry have begun to walk up and down throughout the heathen lands preaching Christ to them. They are the ones described here as the church's "beautiful feet with shoes."

The described feet are predominantly those of Peter, Paul, Barnabas and their co-workers who were instrumental in preaching the gospel of God to the Gentiles, and making them partakers of the promised blessing in Christ.

It must be borne in mind here that the church's feet that have presently become exquisitely beautiful are the same feet, which she had feared would be defiled, if she opened the closed door of Judaism and ventured out in obedience to the Lord's call and witnessed Him to the non-Jews (cf. 5:2ff).

O prince's daughter, 1b.

It is in recognition of the fact that "as a prince," the beloved (church) had "power with God and with men, and hast prevailed" (Gen 32:28), to become a true daughter of Israel, the prince, that the Lord addresses her by the term "prince's daughter."

2. *The apostles who had walked throughout the length and breadth of the Jewish and Gentile lands: the rounded thighs of the body of Christ, 7:1b*

The joints of thy thighs are like jewels, the work of the hands of a cunning workman, (1b).

The thigh joints of the primitive Jewish Christian church were the apostles who performed the functions of the thigh joints of the church, which was the body of Christ, of walking up and down throughout the Jewish and Gentile lands "for the perfecting of the saints, for the work of the ministry, for the edifying of the body of Christ: till ...all come in the unity of the faith, and of the knowledge of the Son of God, unto a perfect man, unto the measure of the stature of the fullness of Christ" (Eph 4:12-13). In other words, the rounded thigh muscles of the church were the apostles who walked up and down throughout the length and breadth of the Jewish and Gentile lands, climbing up mountains and hills, and descending to the valleys, in order to keep the unity of the churches in doctrine, love, and growth. For the God-given burden of the care of all the churches was upon them.

The Heb. word *chammuq* translated "joints" means, 'round' or 'circuit.'[135] Interestingly, H.W.F.Gesenius, in *Gesenius' Hebrew-Chaldee Lexicon*, translates the present verse, "the circuit of thy

---

[135] H. W. F. Gesenius, *op. cit.*, p. 286.

thighs is like necklaces, that is, the knobs in the necklaces."[136] The context shows that the intended meaning is "jewels" as in AV, rather than "knobs." As the twelve patriarchs were described in 1:10 as "rows of jewels" adorning the cheeks of the patriarchal church "in their turn," the apostles of Christ, inclusive of Paul, Barnabas and others who had made most of the circuits for the propagation of the gospel ought to be the ones described as jewels here. The identity of the particular jewels meant here is being divulged by the qualifying expression, "the work of the hands of a cunning workman." Typically, "the cunning workman" was Bezaleel who cut and engraved jewels like the engravings of a signet with the names of the twelve patriarchs of Israel, and set them on the breastplate and ephod of the shoulders of Aaron, the high priest. Anti-typically, the cunning workman who made jewels of men in the furnace of fiery trials was our Lord Himself.

Evidently the "rounding" of the church's thighs, the rounding of Jacob's thighs, and the rounding of the "jewels," were all "the work of the hands of a cunning workman."

In fact, the present imagery refers to the rounding of the church's thighs, and alludes to the rounding of both Jacob's thighs and the rounding of the jewels. As for the 'rounding' of Jacob's thigh joints, it was performed by our Lord Himself (before incarnation). When He saw that he prevailed not against Jacob during the wrestling bout, "He touched the hollow of his thigh; and the hollow of Jacob's thigh was out of joint" (Gen 32:25). The very purpose of the Lord in wrestling with Jacob was to break his self-will and bring him under subjection. For Jacob had always been resisting to submit to the perfect will of God, and, instead, was doing his own thing.

In the case of Israel (the church), she too had been resisting the constraint of the love of God that was shed abroad in her heart by the Spirit, to share the love of God with the rest of the families of the earth. The Lord had, therefore, been wrestling with her by His Spirit to dispel the darkness of ignorance from her heart and cause the day of the light of the knowledge of the purpose for

---

[136] *Ibid.*, p. 286.

which He had called her dawn in her heart. This is evident from the earlier use of the expression, "until the day break, and the shadows flee away" in 2:17 and 4:6.

Now, with the dawning in her heart of the day of the light of the knowledge of the purpose for which she had been called, and her consequent walk throughout the length and breadth of the Jewish and Gentile lands, climbing hills and descending to the valleys, her thigh joints have rounded appealingly in the Lord's sight. Therefore, the Lord recalls her memory here to the long process by which He, "the cunning workman," did 'round' her thighs, as they are at present.

3. *The Spirit-filled members of the church: the navel of the body of Christ, like a large bowl that wanteth no liquor, 7:2a*

Thy navel is like a round goblet, which wanteth not liquor, (2a).

"Round goblet" refers to 'a large round bowl. Carr says, "the word is used of large two- or four-handled metal or clay bowls."[137] The word *mezeg*, translated "liquor," means, 'mixed; or spiced wine' of the Holy Spirit.'[138] In 1:2, 4, and 4:10 the intoxication of divine love by the Holy Spirit was stated to be better than that of literal wine. In 2:4 Moses had exulted, when the Lord brought him to "the banqueting house," i.e., 'to the house where wine is drunk.' that "his banner over me was love." The present imagery of the navel of the body of Christ being filled with liquor signifies that the whole church was Spirit-filled.

4. *A bumper harvest of Gentile souls: the belly of the body of Christ, like a heap of wheat set about with lilies, 7:2b*

Thy belly is like an heap of wheat set about with lilies, (2b).

"The Heb.word *beten*, means 'hollow and empty,' "used of the exterior belly ... or of the inside of the belly, both as the place filled with food ... and as the place where the foetus is conceived

---

[137] G. Lloyd Carr, *op. cit.*, p. 157.
[138] H. W. F. Gesenius, *op. cit.*, p. 461.

and formed."[139] "The seat of hunger." (BDB).[140] "A heap of wheat" signifies a bumper harvest. The imagery of the church's external or internal belly looking like a heap of wheat signifies that she has filled her belly with the souls harvested from the ripened Gentile fields, and has satisfied thereby her God-given hunger for souls.

Set about with lilies, (2c).

The Hebrew word *sug* translated, "set about" means, 'to fence.' This is the last time that the symbolic word "lilies" occurs in the Song. Compared to the bumper harvest of souls saved from the Gentile fields, the Israelites (the lilies) were proportionately only a few who shouldered the responsibility of watching over them.

5. *The unity and the oneness of the Jewish and Gentile believers: the two breasts of the body of Christ, like twin young roes,7:3a.*

Thy two breasts are like two young roes that are twins, (3a).

This is a repetition of the first clause of v.4: 5. The second clause, "that feed among the lilies" is sagaciously dropped, as it is irrelevant after the church has changed her former stance of religious bigotry, and has begun to make the Gentiles "fellow-heirs, and of the same body and partakers of his promise in Christ by the Gospel" (Eph 3:6).

In the Solomonic age of peace and plenty, the church's two breasts, which fed among the lilies, like two young roes that are twins, were Judah and Israel. But in the present New Testament dispensation, her two breasts described to be like twin young roes, are the Jewish and Gentile Christians.

6. *The body of believers in enjoyment of spiritual rest and liberty: the neck of the body of Christ, 7:4a*

Thy neck is as a tower of ivory, (4a).

To recall, during the patriarchal epoch, Joseph was the church's neck (1:10b), and during the epoch of faith that had extended from

---

[139] *Ibid.*, p. 113.

[140] Brown Driver Briggs, *op. cit.*, p. 105.

the time of Joshua, to the beginning of the Solomonic reign, David and his thousand mighty men of faith were her neck (4:4). However, in the present New Testament epoch of faith, courage and spiritual liberty, all the true members of the church were mighty through faith to the pulling down of strong holds (cf. 2 Cor 10:4). Collectively, the church was "terrible as an army with banners." From that perspective, all the believers of the primitive church had been, so to say, uplifted and fearless necks of the church.

In Hebrew, the word *shen* rendered "ivory" means 'tooth.' Out of fifty-eight occurrences of the word *shen* in the Old Testament, forty-four times it is translated 'tooth,' and ten times 'ivory.' In 4:2 and 6:6, the smiling snow-white teeth of the church were taken as the symbol for spiritual liberty of the regenerated souls. From this perspective, the imagery of the church's neck being as a tower built of snow-white teeth (of elephants) could possibly be a description of those members of the church who enjoyed the liberty of the Spirit and courage more than others.

7. *Tearful intercessors: eyes of the body of Christ, like the fishpools in Heshbon, by the gate of the daughter of multitudes, 7:4a.*

Thine eyes like the fishpools in Heshbon, by the gate of Bath-rabbim, (4b).

As we have pointed out earlier, the Spirit invokes only actual facts taken from the biblical record of the redemptive history of Israel for use in the form of figures of speech in the similes and metaphors occurring in the Song. But some of those used in this section appear to be a departure. Heshbon was a city situated "north of the lower part of Arnon. The ruins of Heshbon, twenty miles east of Jordan on the parallel of the north end of the Dead Sea mark the site."[141] "Remains of old pools and conduits may be seen in a branch of the present Wadi Hesban which flows by the city."[142] However, as the city does not exist in the form in which

---

[141] Robert Young, *op. cit.*, p. 478.
[142] J. D. Douglas, et. al., *op. cit.*, p. 472.

it had existed in Biblical times, we are unable to judge the exact point of comparison. Nor do we have any information left on the "gate of Bath-rabbim."

This appears, however, to be a case of play on words using the meanings of the Heb. words *berekah* (fishpools), *cheshbown* (Heshbon), and *bath-rabbim* (daughter of multitudes).

The word 'berekah' is from the root word *berek* which means 'to kneel' and is being used here for the idea of kneeling down before God to worship and praise Him. The words for blessing as well as for pools of water are derived from the same root. According to *Strong's Exhaustive Concordance*, "such reservoirs of water were the place where camels knelt as a resting place.[143]

The word *cheshbown*, (Heshbon), means, 'to device,' 'to account,' 'to reckon,' 'intelligence.'

The word *bath-rabbim* means, 'daughter of multitudes.' The word is used here in an idiomatic sense for the people of all the nations of the earth, Jew and Gentile, collectively, similar to those found in the prophetical books, such as, "the daughter of Egypt," "the daughter of Babylon," "the daughter of Philistia," and so on.

Arranging the meanings of these words in their proper order, the emerging meaning is that the church's eyes are like the worshippers kneeling in intercessory prayer in the place of reckoning, by the gate of the multitudes of all the nations of the earth. In substance, the church's eyes are her members who are engaged in praying and interceding incessantly in tears for the salvation of the multitudes of all the nations of the earth. The prayer burden described here are similar to that which Jeremiah gave vent, saying,

> O that my head were waters, and mine eyes a fountain of tears, that I might weep day and night for ... the daughter of my people.
>
> Jer 9:1

---

[143] James Strong, *op. cit.*, p. 23.

8. *Apostle Paul: the nose of the body of Christ, like the tower of Lebanon that looketh toward Damascus, 7:4c*

Thy nose is as the tower of Lebanon, which looketh toward Damascus, (4c).

The Heb. word *tsapha* translated "looketh" means "to lean forward, i.e., to peer into the distance; by implication, to observe."[144] Who could be this towering member of the primitive Jewish Christian church, who functioned as the church's nose by the operation of the corresponding charismatic gift; one who was firmly rooted and grounded on Christ up there in the heavenly Lebanon, and yet was leaning forward humbly in contrition to peer all the time into the distant Damascus valley?

As far as one could guess, the single person who towered above all the other members of the primitive Jewish Christian church; performed the function of the church's nose by the operation of the charismatic gift; stood firmly rooted and grounded in Christ up there on the heavenly Lebanon; yet humbly stooped forward in contrition and had his eyes set all the time on the gracious act of the Lord who had made him what he was then, was only Saul who became Paul.

The function of the church's nose is to smell and discern between the spiritual and the carnal; heavenly and earthly; and to judge whether the faith and practice of the church are according to the mind of Christ. *"The natural man receiveth not the things of the Spirit of God"* writes Paul,

> But he that is spiritual judgeth all things, yet he himself is judged of no man. For who hath known the mind of the Lord, that he may instruct him? But we have the mind of Christ. 1 Cor 2: 15-16

9. *Christ, the Head of the church: like mount Carmel, in majesty and excellency, 7:5a*

Thine head upon thee is like Carmel, (5a).

Heb. "Your head upon you like Carmel," (Carr)[145] Evidently,

---

[144] *Ibid*, p. 122.
[145] G. Lloyd Carr, *op. cit.*, p. 159.

the sentence is constructed designedly to give the head a distinct identity from the body. "Christ is the head of the church" (Eph 5:23). We do not have the required information to judge the point of comparison between Christ and Carmel. There is a reference to "the excellency of Carmel" in Isa 35:2. Possibly this can be the point of comparison here.

10. *The youthful vicarious death of Christ, the Head: the purple coloured hair of the Head of the church, like hanging threads of the weaver's loom after he has cut off the finished product, 7:5b*

And the hair of thine head like purple, (5b).

The 'hair of the head upon you' means the 'hair of Christ.' We have seen that hair is the Song's symbol for natural lineage. In 5:11, the hair of Christ's head was described as 'tamar fronds' "black as a raven." That was stated with regard to His natural lineage in His humanity, from Judah, in Tamar. The present description of His lineage (hair) being purple coloured refers to His royalty. Purple signifies royalty. This is the second time the word purple occurs in the Song. Its first occurrence was in 3:10, where the riding-seat of the *appiryon* was stated to be upholstered with purple coloured cloth, which, in turn, was paved with love for the daughters of Jerusalem. (Cf. comment on 1:5, 8, 4:1b, 5:11 and 6:b).

Interestingly, the word *dallah* translated "hair" in the present context is an altogether different word from those used for hair in all the other contexts in the Song. It refers to the threads hanging down in a loom after the weaver has cut off his finished product, and is used as a "simile for premature death."[146] Significantly, this occurs as a prophetic disclosure of our Lord's youthful vicarious death, occurring parallel to that of Isa 53:8b, "And who shall declare his generation? For he was cut off out of the land of the living." Our Lord did not leave an earthly lineage. The Father, who was the 'Weaver,' had cut Him off in His youth as His finished product, leaving His lineage in His descent from Abraham and

[146] Brown, Driver, Briggs, *op. cit.*, p. 195

Adam, respectively, hanging like the cut ends of the threads hanging in the loom (cf. our Lord's genealogy from Abraham and Adam, respectively, given in Matt 1:1-17 and Luke 3:23-38).

The king is held in the galleries, (5c).

The word *rahat* translated "galleries" means "tresses," or curls of the hair running in parallel lines. Each of the curls of the wavy hair running in parallel lines refers symbolically to the successive generations of the progenitors of Christ, the Head of the church, from Judah. "The king" who had been held in those curls was the promised Messiah. This statement occurs as a reference, in figure of speech, to Jacob's prophetic words concerning the coming Messiah, found in Gen 49:10, "the sceptre shall not depart from Judah, nor a law-giver from between his feet, until Shiloh comes; and unto him shall the gathering of the people be."

The reading, "the king is held captive," found in some of the modern Versions is interpretative. The Heb. word *acar* is used here in the sense of "held" as in the AV.

There is also the possibility here of the presence of an allusion to the superstitious method resorted to by Jacob of keeping peeled green rods of poplar, hazel and chestnut trees in the water troughs believing that the flocks that mate and conceive while drinking water from the troughs would bring forth ringstraked, speckled and spotted kids and lambs. If the device worked magic, that was only by the grace of the Lord who chose Jacob as the heir of promise, not because of his superstitious belief. Our thinking that the possibility of an allusion to this episode is present here is based on the fact that the Heb. word '*rahat*' translated "galleries" occurs only three more times in the Old Testament, out of which it is translated "gutters" in Gen 30: 38 and 41, in the narrative of the above stated episode and "trough" in Exod 2:16, in the narrative of the episode of other shepherds unjustly driving away the daughters of Jethro, the Midianite, preventing them from feeding their cattle with the water they themselves had drawn and filled the trough with.

11. *The consummated primitive Jewish-Gentile Christian church, 7:6*

How fair and how pleasant art thou, O love, for delights! (6).

This is the fourth time that the Lord makes approbatory remarks of this sort concerning the fairness of the beloved (church). It is noteworthy that approbatory remarks of this nature are being made at the consummation of each of the epochs of faith, excepting for the one that occurs in 4:1, which was made at the beginning of the epoch of faith, with regard to the spiritual vision of Joshua to behold the Lord in the fullness of His glorious person, and the change that had come about of his life thereby. The first time that the Lord made such a remark was in 1:15-17, at the consummation of the patriarchal church, and the third time that He made the remark was in 4:7, at the consummation of the age of the triumphant possessing faith that had extended from the time of Joshua to that of Solomon.

XV. THE LORD DECREES THAT THE GENTILES SHOULD BE "FELLOWHEIRS, AND OF THE SAME BODY, AND PARTAKERS OF HIS PROMISE, ... BY THE GOSPEL," 7:7-9

7: 7. This thy stature is like to a palm tree,
and thy breasts to clusters of grapes.
8. I said, I will go up to the palm tree,
I will take hold of the boughs thereof:
Now also thy breasts shall be as clusters of the vine,
And the smell of thy nose like apples.
9. And the roof of thy mouth like the best wine for my beloved,
that goeth down sweetly, causing the lips of those that are asleep to speak.

A mere glance over these verses is sufficient to show the presence of play on words using *palm* (Heb. *tamar), vine,* and *clusters* (Heb. *eschcol).*

"The vine" occurs as a symbol for Israel, as in Ps 80:8, "Thou hast brought a vine out of Egypt: thou has cast out the heathen, and planted it."

The (Heb. *tamar*), means palm tree. The name occurs here as a symbol for the Gentiles. The word *tamar* receives its symbolic significance from *Tamar,* the Canaanite daughter-in-law of Judah. As we have stressed earlier, the Spirit normally invokes only facts taken from the pre-Solomonic books of the Bible, as figures in the similes and metaphors occurring in the Song. In the Hebrew language, unlike in English, capital letters are not used for the first alphabet of proper nouns. Likewise, the word for tree does not occur in the Hebrew text. Therefore, the word *tamar* can mean either, the palm tree or the woman of that name).

Seeing that Judah was unwilling to give Shelah, his youngest son, to her in marriage, in keeping with the levirate law, Tamar entrapped Judah himself, posing herself to be a harlot, and got twins, Phares and Zerah. Phares ultimately became one of the predominant among the progenitors of David and of our Lord. There is the possibility of a play on the word, *tamar,* here using the dual meanings of the word.

This thy stature is like to a palm tree, (7a).

The Heb. word *qoma* "translated 'stature' technically means 'height' from the verb 'arise' or 'stand up', but includes the idea of 'bearing' or 'carriage.'"[147]

"AV and ASV correctly translate the demonstrative pronoun this" (Carr).[148] The pronoun refers to the overall stature of the church, the body of Christ that was described part by part, from her feet upwards to the hairs over her head, in the preceding verses, vv.7:1-6. 'This, thy stature,' says the Lord, 'is like to that of Tamar,' the Canaanite woman, who had ultimately become the mother of a multitude of mixed posterity in the patriarch Judah.

The comparison of the church with Tamar is most appropriate, because the church consisted, at this juncture of her redemptive story, of a mixed congregation of Jewish and Gentile believers. Moreover, Tamar, the Canaanite woman, and her mixed posterity in Judah had obtained the full right of citizenship in Israel. Over

---

[147] G. Lloyd Carr, *op. cit.,* p. 161.
[148] *ibid.,* p. 161.

and above, Tamar had emerged as one of the stateliest of the women in Israel. Having begun as the wife of Judah through immoral means, she had emerged ultimately, purely by the grace of God's choice in election, as the mother of the earthly lineage of King David, and of Christ, the Son of God. Christ came not only through Judah, but also through Tamar, Matt. 1:3; Heb. 7:14. Here is the introduction of foreign blood in the line at this early date."[149]

Taken as the tamar tree (date palm), it is "a tall, slender tree that typifies grace and elegance."[150]

And thy breasts to clusters (of vine), (7b).

AV's, "of vine," is in italics, indicating that this is the addition of the translators. Hence, the statement should read, *(And thy breasts to clusters).*

As the beloved (church) was a corporeal entity, she possessed no 'breasts.' Moreover, wherever parts of the body of Christ are mentioned in the Song, they refer to the members of the church, in the acts of faith that they were performing for the common good of the church, by the operation of the corresponding charismatic gift with which they were endued.

We have demonstrated under the head, 'the Symbolic Word 'Breasts,' in the introductory section of this book that the word "breasts" occur as a symbol for seed. The symbolic term "clusters" to which the church's "breasts," namely, 'spiritual seed,' is being likened here, refers possibly to the local churches, which were clustered together throughout Palestine and the surrounding Gentile nations of the civilized world of that day, rather than, as it appears, to fruit-clusters of the *tamar* (palm tree).

I said, I will go up to the palm tree, (8a).

A better translation would be, 'I said, I will go up to Tamar.' As stated, the possibility of the presence of play on words using the double meanings of *tamar* is discernible here.

---

[149] Miss. B. Van Vranken, *Pentateuch, Notes on Genesis,* Unpublished: Allahabad Bible Seminary, Allahabad, U.P., India, p. 27.

[150] *Ibid,* p.161.

The Heb. verb *alah* translated "go up to" does not necessarily mean 'to climb up a tree.' It simply means 'to go up to' any place located in a higher altitude, or a person living in such a locality. The same verb is used in Gen 38:13, "it was told Tamar, saying, Behold thy father in law goeth up (*alah*) to Timnath." The verb is used here in dual senses, to apply to 'going up to Tamar,' and to 'climbing up the tamar tree,' both being used as symbols for going up to the Gentiles.

I will take hold of the boughs thereof, (8c).

The word *sansinnim*, rendered "boughs," occurs only this once in the Old Testament. The *Gesenius' Hebrew-Chaldee Lexicon* suggests the intended meanings to be, "palm branches, pendulous boughs."[151] BDB, on the other hand, suggests, "fruit-stalk of date."[152] In *Gesenius' Hebrew-Chaldee Lexicon* the meaning of another Heb. word *taltalim* occurring in 5:11b is also translated as "pendulous branches of palm." [153]

The verb *achaz*, rendered "take hold of,"occurs here in the sense of 'taking possession of.' The divergent meanings given in Lexicons make it difficult to judge whether the Lord resolved to take possession of the pendulous boughs of the palm tree or its fruit-stalks. The renderings in the modern Versions also are equally confusing. NRSV renders, "branches." JB, "clusters of dates." NASB, "fruit stalks," and NIV, "fruits." However, going by the statement of v. 7, "This thy stature is like to Tamar (AV's, "to a palm tree" is interpretative), and thy breasts to clusters," it becomes clear that the breasts are the object of the Lord's grasping. "Most commentators identify her breasts as the object of his grasping" (Carr).[154]

Now also thy breasts shall be as clusters of the vine (8c).

But what perplexes one with regard to the cited statement is this. After declaring, 'I said, I will go up to tamar, I will take hold

---

[151] H. W. F. Gesenius, *op. cit.*, p. 591.
[152] Brown, Driver, Briggs, *op. cit.*, p. 703.
[153] H. W. F. Gesenius, *op. cit.*, p. 865.
[154] G. Lloyd Carr, *op. cit*, p. 162.

of the *sansinnim* thereof' (whatever the word *sansinnim* means), the Lord decrees, 'let your breasts be as clusters of the vine,' instead of decreeing, 'let your breasts be as clusters of *tamar*' (of Tamar, the Gentile woman or of the palm tree). One who goes up *tamar* (palm tree) should seek for clusters of *tamar* i.e., of the palm tree, not clusters of the vine. There is room here for ambiguity, because "breasts" belong to the women, not to the tree; and clusters belong to the tree or plant, not to the women.

In fact, the entire imagery is contrived purposefully to bring to this conclusion. That is, the Lord decrees that when He goes up to tamar, (that is to say, to the Gentiles), and takes hold of her breasts/seed clusters thereof, the breasts/seed clusters of *tamar* (the Gentiles), that He takes hold of should be treated as the breasts/seed clusters of Israel, the vine.

The New Authorized Version (NAV) omits the expression, "now also" and changes the statement into the form of a decree, "Let now your breasts be like clusters of the vine." In reality, the jussive form of the verb translated "let" occurs as in Gen 1:3, "And God said, "let there be light." The use of the selfsame verb here conveys the sense that the Lord wills that the "breasts" or seed of the symbolic *tamar* (of the Gentiles) that He takes hold of should be treated as the breasts/seed clusters of the vine (of the Jewish Christian church). In other words, the Lord wills, saying, 'Let the Gentile Christians be "fellow-heirs, and of the same body and partakers in his promise in Christ by the gospel," (Eph 3:6), with the Jewish Christians.

And the smell of thy nose like apples, (8d).

"Apples" are the fruits of the Apple tree of 2:3, which occurs there as a symbol for the Lord Almighty. Sitting under His shadow, and relishing His fruit, the beloved had exulted, saying, "His fruit was sweet to my taste," lit. 'to my palate.' Later, in 2:5, having come under the intoxication of the wine of divine love, she had cried out to the Lord, saying, "comfort me with apples" (2:5). Towards the end of the Song, in 8:5b, the Lord recalls His beloved's (church's) memory to the event of His act of bringing her forth in the covenant, saying, "I raised thee up under the apple tree: there thy mother brought thee forth: there she brought thee forth that bare thee." It means that the beloved's (church's) mother (the covenant) conceived and brought her forth under the Lord's own shadow, and brought her up on apples, i.e., on His own promises. It is clear from the above that 'apples' occurs in the Song as a symbol for the promises of God. The same word *tappuach* is translated both as "apples" and as "apple tree."

We have adjudged that the nose of the church, described in 7:4c "as the tower of Lebanon which looketh toward Damascus" was Paul. Paul should, then, be the nose of the church that emanates the smell of apples, namely, of the promises of God.

And the roof of thy mouth like the best wine for my beloved, that goeth down sweetly, causing the lips of those that are asleep to speak (9a).

Like the other parts of the body of Christ described in the preceding verses, the roof of the mouth of the body of Christ has to be referring to the members of the church who witnessed Christ to those people who were asleep in trespasses and sins.

The Heb. word *chek* translated "roof of thy mouth" literally means 'palate.' The same word is translated "taste" in 2:3, and "mouth" in 5:16. The word is used in Job 31:30 and in Hos. 8:1 with reference to the internal part of the mouth, and in Prov 5:3; 8:7 with reference to mouth as the organ of speech. In the present context, the roof of the mouth or palate occurs in the sense of mouth, the organ of speech.

The figure of "best wine" occurs as the symbol for the love of God shed abroad in the hearts of believers by the Holy Spirit throughout the Song. In 4:11 the lips of the beloved (church) were stated to be dripping honeycomb, and honey. Honey and milk were stated to be under her tongue. In 5:13, the lips of the Lord were stated to be dropping sweet smelling myrrh, and in 5:16, His mouth was stated to be most sweet. The same analogy must be followed in interpreting the present imagery of the roof of the beloved church's mouth being like the best wine. It speaks about the words of divine love that proceeded from the mouth of those members of the church who performed the function of the mouth of the body of Christ, by the operation of the relevant charismatic gift.

The clause, "that goeth down sweetly, causing the lips of those that are asleep to speak," has been posing serious problem both for translators and commentators on account of an abrupt shift to the masculine from the feminine endings of the preceding clause. RSV and NEB emend the masculine form to solve the problem. JB, NIV and NAV retain the masculine form and attribute the words to the Lover.

However, the gender shift makes no difference in understanding the intended sense of the verse. Whoever may be the speaker, what matters here is the substance of what the person speaks about, namely, that the best wine of the divine love and life that proceeds from the mouth of those members of the church, who perform the function of the church's mouth, flow down sweetly (Heb. *meyshar* means with perfect agreement and concord, or straightly) without any resistance, to those who are asleep in trespasses and sins, and quickens them to move their lips to confess Christ and to witness Him, in their turn.

With regard to the expression, "for my beloved," it appears that it occurs in the sense that witnessing Christ and His love is done for Him; i.e., on His behalf and for His glory.

XVI. THE CHURCH SETS HER MIND ON WINNING THE GENTILES FOR CHRIST, ON THE JEWS' REFUSAL TO ACCEPT THE MESSIAHSHIP OF JESUS OF NAZARETH, 7:10-13

7: 10. I am my beloved's, and his desire is toward me.

11. Come, my beloved, let us go forth into the field;
let us lodge in the villages.

12. Let us get up early to the vineyards;
let us see if the vine flourish, whether the tender grape appear,
and the pomegranate bud forth: there will I give thee my love.

13. The mandrakes give a smell,
and at our gates are all manner of pleasant fruits, new and old,
which I have laid up for thee, O my beloved.

When the Jews of Corinth rejected Paul's teaching that Jesus of Nazareth is the Christ, (the Messiah), Paul shook his raiment and said, "Your blood be upon your own heads; I am clean: from henceforth I will go unto the Gentiles" (Acts 18:6). Discernibly, this section occurs as a prophetic disclosure beforehand of this historic turning point in the church's outreach ministry. The mandrakes are mentioned only once more in the Bible, that is, in the episode of Leah hiring Jacob from Rachel with the mandrakes that her son Reuben brought from the field, to lodge with her for a night, in a cottage in the field. The occurrence of mandrakes here shows that the imagery is framed after the narrative of that episode found in Gen 30:14-18.

I am my beloved's, and his desire is toward me, (10).

This is the third in the series of this form of confessional statement that the Spirit puts in the mouth of the beloved (church). The first time that He put the confessional statement in her mouth was in 2:16, "My beloved is mine, and I am his: he feedeth among the lilies." The purpose of the Spirit in putting the statement in her mouth at that historical juncture in her redemptive story was to expose her conceited belief that the Lord belongs to her more by virtue of her faith in Him, rather than by that of His election and choice, and that He feeds His flock only among Israel (2:16), the lilies. The second time that the Spirit put the confessional statement in her mouth was in 6:3, "I am my beloved's, and my beloved is mine: he feedeth among the lilies." There, the Spirit gave pre-eminence to the clause, "I am my beloved's" by positioning it as the first clause of the confessional statement. This was done to show that she has begun to realize that she belongs to the Lord, more by virtue of His grace of choosing her, than by that of her faith. Now, at this third and final time, the Spirit makes a thorough change in the confessional statement that He puts in her mouth, by dropping the clause, "my beloved is mine," and substituting it with the clause, "and his desire is toward me." The change is being made at this final stage of her redemptive story to show that she has grown in the realization that she belongs to the Lord solely by virtue of the desire that the Lord had set on her from eternity, and that she has no work to do for her salvation other than casting herself and all that concerns her on Him by faith, and enjoying the ultimate blessedness of spiritual rest and liberty.

Significantly, the Heb. word *teshuqah* rendered "desire" is a rare word, which occurs only on two more occasions in the Old Testament; first, in Gen 3:16, "thy desire shall be to thy husband," and second, in Gen 4:7, "if thou doest not well, sin lieth at the door. And unto thee shall be his desire." The word connotes the sense of "craving impulse."[155]

Come, my beloved, let us go forth into the field; let us lodge in the villages, (11).

As stated, this occurs as a prophetic disclosure of the church's final resolve to take the gospel to the Gentiles on the Jews' refusal to accept the Lord as the Messiah and Lord. Significantly, the Heb. word *luwn* rendered "lodge" is used here in the sense of 'lodge all night' or pass the night. The Heb. word *kopher* rendered, "villages" has diverse nuances, such as village, henna flowers, pitch, bribe, ransom, satisfaction, atonement, etc. It is used here in the sense of an "un-walled village" as against Jerusalem, the walled city, and also in the sense of henna bushes as against Israel, the lilies. The word had occurred in 1:14 and 4:13, where it is translated "camphire" in the sense of henna-plant from which is "the copper coloured cosmetic dye extracted."[156] (Cf. comment on 1:4).

Let us get up early to the vineyards, (12a).

The idiomatic expression, "get up early to" refers properly to starting early on a journey having loaded the personal belongings on the back of a man or an animal.[157] In the present context vineyard refers to Israel's missionary field among the Gentile nations.

In Jeremiah, the expression, "rising up early and speaking" is used often to mean 'earnestly' or 'urgently' (cf. Jer 7:13,25; 11:7; 25:3,4; 26:5; 29:19; 32:33; 35:14,15; 44:4).

---

[155] William. L. Holladay, *op. cit.*, p. 369.
[156] G. Lloyd Carr, *op. cit.*, p.165.
[157] James Strong, *op. cit.*, p. 141.

Let us see if the vine flourish, whether the tender grape appear, and the pomegranates bud forth, (12b).

(See comment on 2:11-13 and 6:11).

The mandrakes give a smell, (13a).

Leah was waiting on the way of Jacob's return, with part of the mandrakes that Reuben, her son had brought from the field, to entice him with them to spend the night with her in a cottage in the field. "The *mandrake* or 'love apple' is a pungently fragrant plant that has long been considered an aphrodisiac" (Carr).[158]

And at our gates are all manner of pleasant fruits, new and old, which I have laid up for thee, O my beloved" (13b).

The word '*ab*' translated "fruits" connotes the idea of freshness and greenness. The origin of the word is from Abib, the first month of the Heb. calendar. Hence,'early and first fruits.' The word *meged* used here as adjective means 'most precious' or 'distinguished.'

The verb *tsapan* rendered "laid up" means 'to hide', 'conceal.'[159] The thought of keeping the most precious from among the first fruits of the field for the head of the family, out of the reach of others, somewhere near the entrance of the cottage, appears to be borrowed from Leah's story. The underlying thought of the imagery is that of Jas 5:7, "Behold, the husbandman waiteth for the precious fruit of the earth." The church labours in the Lord's field to produce precious fruits and lay them up safely, at her gate, ready for the Lord to come and take them away at any time.

The expression, "new and old" refers to the New Testament and Old Testament saints.

---

[158] G; Lloyd Carr, *op. cit.*, p. 165.
[159] H. W. F. Gesenius, *op. cit.*, p. 716.

XVII. HAVING BEEN EXCOMMUNICATED FROM JUDAISM, THE BELOVED (CHURCH) EXPRESSES HER ANGUISH OVER HER INABILTY TO BRING THE LORD TO HER BRETHREN ACCODING TO THE FLESH WITHIN JUDAISM, 8:1-4

8: 1. O that thou wert as my brother, that sucked the breasts of my mother! when I should find thee without,
I would kiss thee, yea, I should not be despised.
2. I would lead thee, and bring thee into my mother's house,
who would instruct me: I would cause thee to drink of spiced wine of the juice of my pomegranate.
3. His left hand should be under my head,
and his right hand should embrace me.
4. I charge you, O daughters of Jerusalem,
that ye stir not up, nor awake my love, until he please.

To be noted, vv. 1-3 of this section occurs as nostalgic versions of the former vv. 3:4 and 2:6. In 3:4 the beloved had described how her mother's household received the Lord in the Sinai covenant, when she found Him without, kissed, led and brought Him by force into her mother's household. On the other hand, at present her mother's household has closed the door against her bringing the Lord within and be taught by Him. Moreover, even if she did find Him without the household at present and kissed Him, as before, she would be despised. In the given constraining situation, she longs for the former experience, and cries out nostalgically, saying, "O that thou wert as my brother ... when I should find thee without, I would kiss thee, yea, I should not be despised. I would lead thee, and bring thee into my mother's house(hold)." Likewise, v.3 is a nostalgic version of v.2:6, wherein the beloved (there Moses) had described how the Lord supported her from falling down out of the imbalance brought about by the inebriation with divine love and laid her down in His lap and caressed her. Here she (the primitive Jewish Christian church) nostalgically longs for that experience of the past. It must be borne in mind here that both of these experiences of the past that the beloved (the primitive Jewish Christian church) nostalgically longs for, pertains to the Mosaic epoch.

O that thou wert as my brother, (1a).

Factually, the Lord was her brother in that both were seeds of the Abrahamic covenant of promise. The beloved has particularly the Messianic prophecy of Deut 18:18 in mind when she cries out in anguish, "O that thou wert as my brother." In Deut 18:18, the Lord had promised to Moses, saying, "I will raise them up a Prophet from among their brethren, like unto thee." At this juncture, the beloved church comprises only of those who were born of God by believing that Jesus of Nazareth was Christ, the Prophet like unto Moses, whom God had raised up from among her brethren, (cf. 1 Jn 5:1). Her frustration and anguish arise from the fact that her mother's household, namely, her brethren according to the flesh that constituted the decadent Judaism of that time, refused to accept the risen Lord as the Prophet like unto Moses who was to incarnate as the Messiah, for the sheer fact that He was not at all "like unto" Moses in faith and practice. Had He been precisely "like unto" Moses in faith and practice, her mother's household would certainly have received Him gladly as they had received Him before, as described in 3:4. Hence her anguished nostalgic cry, saying,

> O that thou wert as (like unto) my brother (Moses), that sucked the breasts of my mother! when I should find thee without, I would kiss thee; (as before), yea, I should not be despised. I would lead thee and bring thee into my mother's house (paraphrase mine).

That sucked the breasts of my mother, (1b).

All the modern Versions render, "who nursed at my mother's breasts." In the case of the former episode, narrated in 3:4, the beloved had brought the Lord forcibly into her mother's house and into the chamber of her that conceived her. Needless to say, the breasts that she had sucked were the breasts of her mother who had conceived her, namely, of the Abrahamic covenant of promise. Both her brother Moses, and the Lord, her Lover, who had incarnated as the Prophet "like unto" her brother Moses, had also sucked the very same breasts of the Abrahamic covenant of promise, by faith. But her brethren according to the flesh mistook that Moses, the Mediator of the Sinai covenant of the law (cf. Gal 3:19 with Exo 20:19), had sucked the breasts of the Sinai covenant.

It was for this reason that they had excommunicated the beloved (church), and closed the door of Judaism, (described as the beloved's mother's household), against the beloved (church) bringing the Lord within and letting Him teach her brethren according to the flesh (who constituted the Judaism of the day).

Reference to "mother's breasts" occurs this once only in the Song. The milk of the covenant of promise was the promises of God. One can imbibe the promises of God only by faith. Moses was one of the predominant persons from among the Old Testament saints who had lived on the "sincere milk" (1 Pet 2:2) of all the promises given by God to Abraham. Even though the Sinai Covenant of the law was added later because of Israel's transgression, Moses had continued to trust God at His promise, rather than depending on the dead works and rituals of the Sinai covenant for justification. Unless Moses was a man of faith, "the Lord could not have spoken unto him "face to face, as a man speaketh unto his friend" (Exod 33:11).

As for our Lord Jesus Christ, He had placed the whole emphasis of His teaching on believing the Father whole heartedly and receiving Him (the Son) as the Promised Messiah whom the Father has sent, rather than on keeping the law. Viewed from this perspective, there was no difference between our Lord and Moses, in the matter of faith and trust. In the eyes of the natural Israel, however, Moses was a man of the law, rather than of faith. All the vehement opposition of the Jews towards our Lord and His teachings were mainly on the ground that He did not keep the Mosaic law.

The anguish that the beloved (church) expresses here over her inability to lead the Lord to her mother's household, namely, to her brethren according to the flesh that constituted the decadent Judaism of the day, occurs as a prophetic disclosure of the anguish that Paul was to express in Rom 9:1-3, saying,

> I lie not, my conscience also bearing me witness in the Holy Ghost, that I have great heaviness and continual sorrow in my heart. For I could wish that myself were accursed from Christ for my brethren, my kinsmen according to the flesh.

When I should find thee without, I would kiss thee; yea, I should not be despised, I would lead thee and bring thee into my mother's house, (1c, 2a).

By these nostalgic words, the beloved longs for her former experience described in 3:4, of how she had found out "him whom my soul loveth" without her mother's household, after she had passed a little from Moses and Aaron, the watchmen sent by the Lord, and how she kissed Him and holding Him within the encircling clutch of her arms" (Carr),[160] brought him forcibly into her mother's household. At that time no one had despised her for kissing him without the household. Kissing and bringing the lost one home is the Song's symbol for acceptance.

Who would instruct me, (2b).

On account of an existing ambiguity in the grammatical construction, translators of the different Versions of the Bible render the statement differently. NIV renders, "she who has taught me." NRSV omits the statement altogether. JB, on the other hand, taking the lover to be the teacher, renders, "You would teach me." According to our line of interpretation, JB's rendering is the correct one. The Lord, the Lover is the teacher. The covenant is the mother, but she does not teach. Moreover, the focal point of the entire imagery of this unit is on the anguish of the beloved (church) over her inability to bring the Lord to her brethren according to the flesh within the household, so that He would teach within the household for the benefit of her "kinsmen according to the flesh."

I would cause thee to drink of spiced wine of the juice of my pomegranate, (2c).

As stated, the Lord being a Spirit, He does not consume earthly foods and drinks. That being the case, the longing desire that the beloved (church) expresses here to have caused the Lord to drink of the spiced wine of the juice of her pomegranate has no relevance literally. It appears to refer to the church's longing desire to make the heart of the Lord rejoice with exceeding joy and gladness by means of her deep devotion and Spirit-filled worship, within her mother's household, namely, within the Jewish religious

---

160 G. Lloyd Carr, *op. cit.*, p. 110.

establishment of the day. Our Lord had said, "The hour cometh, and now is, when the true worshippers shall worship the Father in spirit and in truth" (John 4:23). But there was no room for such worship in the decadent Jewish religious establishment of the day, nor is there room for it in the majority of the nominal Christian religious establishments of our day. Truly, the Lord's heart longs for the day when all Christians worship the Lord in the fullness of the Spirit, with the manifestation of all the Spiritual gifts, within the existing religious establishments, as the one hundred and twenty disciples worshipped Him on the day of Pentecost and the whole of the primitive Christian church worshipped and served Him thereafter. How much do our hearts long for such a Spirit-filled and single-hearted worship of the Lord of the kind we read in the first four chapters of the Acts of the Apostles! Our hearts long to worship the Lord, just as the newborn church continued to worship Him "daily with one accord in the temple ... with gladness and singleness of heart" (Acts 2:46).

Genuine Spirit-filled believers do not favour schism. The love of God shed abroad in their hearts by His Spirit would naturally constrain them to continue to remain within the respective established religious systems and make the rest of the congregation partakers of the same blessing. It is only when the unbelieving members of the establishment obstruct freedom to worship the Lord in the full liberty of the Spirit and rejoice in Him spontaneously within, that division and strife develop. In fact, the primitive Jewish Christian church did not separate herself from the Judaism of the day; rather she was debarred by the Judaical rulers from preaching Christ and worshiping Him spontaneously within it.

'Wine' has occurred before as a symbol for divine love in 1:2, 3; 2:4; 4:10; 5:1 and in 7:9. 'Pomegranate' occurs in the Song as the symbol for the fullness of the promised blessing (cf. 4:3b, 13; 6:7). The expression, "spiced wine of the juice of my pomegranate," simply means the essence of the fullness of the promised blessing, which is the gift of the Spirit. When one imbibes the spiced wine of the essence of the promised Holy Spirit, he/she is sure to be intoxicated with the same divine love, as the disciples experienced on the day of Pentecost.

His left hand should be under my head, and his right hand should embrace me, (3).

The addition here of this nostalgic version of the wine-house experience of the beloved described in the former v. 2:6, makes it unambiguous that she is recalling her own experience of the banqueting house, of being drunk by the love of God therein, when she says nostalgically that she would have brought the Lord to her mother's house, and caused Him to drink of the spiced wine of the juice of her pomegranate. At that time the Lord had brought her to the wine house of divine love and had caused her to drink His love so much so that she had to call upon Him to support her from falling down out of the imbalance brought about by inebriation with divine love and lay her down within His embracing and supporting arms.

I charge you, O daughters of Jerusalem, that ye stir not up, nor awake my love, until he please, (4).

This is the third time that this adjuration occurs (cf. 2:7; 3:5). However, its present occurrence is with certain alterations. The expression, "by the roes, and by the hinds of the field," that reflects timidity, has been omitted, as the church is now courageous and daring "as an army with banners." In chronological sequence, the beloved (church) makes this adjuration at the time when the natural seed was persecuting her more than at any other time in her redemptive history. In spite of this, the beloved church's attitude towards the natural seed (described idiomatically as the daughters of Jerusalem) is milder and more tolerant than ever. This is evident from the manner she tones down the words by which she charges them from the stern, "I charge you, O ye daughters of Jerusalem, that ye stir not up and awake my love (affair)," to 'why should you stir up or awaken my love affair.' "The substitution of the Hebrew *mah* for the earlier *im* used in oath-formulas is consistent," says Carr, "the form *mah* is generally considered to be negative in this context ... but the more normal meaning is 'what' or 'why'."[161]

---

[161] *Ibid.*, p. 168.

XVIII. THE ENDS OF THE TANGLED STORYLINE, 8:5-7

8: 5. Who is this that cometh up from the wilderness, leaning upon her beloved? I raised thee up under the apple tree: there thy mother brought thee forth: there she brought thee forth that bare thee.

6. Set me as a seal upon thine heart, as a seal upon thine arm:
for love is strong as death; jealousy is cruel as the grave:
the coals thereof are coals of fire, which hath a most vehement flame.

7. Many waters cannot quench love, neither can the floods drown it:
if a man would give all the substance of his house for love,
it would utterly be contemned.

The much-sought-after ends of the tangled storyline are being divulged by way of this section. Verse 5a shows the consummated beloved (the primitive Christian church) leaning on the bosom of the gracious Lord in absolute surrender, as she comes up from the wilderness of this world, at the end of her earthly pilgrimage. In v. 5b, the Lord reminds His beloved (church), which is leaning upon His gracious bosom, as to how He had quickened her into existence under the *tappuach* (apple tree). Verses 6-7 refer to the beloved church's eternal hope and destiny.

Who is this that cometh up from the wilderness, leaning upon her beloved, (5a).

By these words, the Spirit draws an accurate picture of the consummated primitive Christian church coming up from the wilderness of this world leaning in absolute surrender and dependence upon the gracious bosom of the Lord, after having run her race and finished her course. Both the mystery of faith and of the Christian perfection is implied in the portrayal.

To grasp the intended significance of the portrayal, one needs to be equipped with the prior knowledge of the basic principles of Christian faith, righteousness and perfection.

Human beings are sinners by nature. The depravity brought about by the Fall has deprived humanity of its ability to live up to the demand of God's standard of righteousness. Apostle Paul, having tried in vain to perform the works of the law and obtain the righteousness that comes thereby, finally cries out in anguish, saying, "In me (that is, in my flesh) dwelleth no good thing: for to will is present with me; but how to perform that which is good I find not. ... O wretched man that I am! Who shall deliver me from the body of this death" (Rom 7:18, 24). This testimony of no less a person than Paul rules out the claim of any person, whosoever he/she may be, of being or becoming righteous in the sight of God by the works of the law (cf. Rom 3:20). It is from this perspective that the scripture asks hypothetical questions, such as, "Can the Ethiopian change his skin, or the leopard his spots? then may ye also do good" (Jer 13:23). "How can he be clean that is born of a woman? " (Job 25:4). "There is none righteous, no, not one," asserts Paul, "all have sinned, and come short of the glory of God" (Rom 3:10, 23).

The foregoing passages lead to the conclusion that the hope of humanity of being righteous lies only in God Himself. Recognizing that the law is "weak through the flesh," God Himself had done and finished, on behalf of humanity, "what the law could not do" by "sending his own Son in the likeness of sinful flesh, and for sin," and condemning "sin in the flesh" (Rom 8:3). This means that God does not demand of humanity obedience to His moral Law, by own effort, any more, but to trust Him on the ground of the gracious work of salvation that He has performed and finished for humankind once and for all. This is the spiritual significance of leaning on the Lord.

The foregoing, however, is easier said than done. For we, human beings are egoistic by nature. Hence, we are uninclined to concede, in the first place, that we are sinners who stand in need of a Saviour and salvation. In the second, we are naturally self-confident and are prone to keep trying to perform the works of the law by ourselves and win God's favour thereby.

This trait is not only a part of the 'natural man,' but also of all the initial and immature believers. The work of salvation that the

Lord begins and finishes in the believers is mainly breaking and melting their ego to bring them to the place wherein they would trust God and God only for each and everything of their life.

The unprecedented severe trials and persecutions through which the Lord led the primitive Christian church were aimed at bringing her to such a state of leaning absolutely on Him alone by faith.

The more one leans on to the Lord by faith and trust, so much the more he/she will be filled with the fullness of God. The mystery of Christian perfection is to be filled with all the fullness of God. Unless one is totally emptied of self, God cannot fill him/her with Himself wholly. To be filled wholly with Christ, "the hope of glory" (Col 1:27), is the ultimate mark of the high calling towards which every true child of God presses on. Paul is the best Biblical example of one who had to a great extent arrived at the mark of that high calling, who writes in Gal 2:20

I am crucified with Christ: nevertheless I live; yet not I, but Christ liveth in me: and the life I now live in the flesh I live by the faith of the Son of God, who loved me, and gave himself for me.

The late Pastor Paul, Founder of the Ceylon Pentecostal Mission, was one such, in my knowledge who had learned to trust the Lord absolutely. In the last message that he gave before his death, he said in substance, 'When I began my Christian life, I learned to trust the Lord for one fourth of my life and needs. That one fourth the Lord faithfully took care of, but the remaining three fourth I had to do myself. As the days went by, I learned to trust the Lord for half of my life and needs. That half the lord faithfully took care of, but the other half I had to do myself. Still later, I learned to trust my Lord for three fourths of my life and needs. That three fourths the Lord faithfully took care of, but the remaining one fourth I had to do myself. But now I have learned to trust the Lord for my entire life and needs. The Lord faithfully takes care of everything, and I have nothing to do whatsoever. I enjoy His perfect peace and rest in my soul.'

The present picture of the consummated primitive Christian church coming up from the wilderness leaning upon her beloved should be understood in this light.

I raised thee up under the apple tree: there thy mother brought thee forth: there she brought thee forth that bare thee, (5b).

This alludes to the promise made by the Lord to Abraham and Sarah, while they were dwelling under the oak (Heb. *terebinth*) of Mamre, saying that the ninety years old barren Sarah will conceive and bring forth the promised seed, within a year's time.

Though Sarah was the mother who conceived and brought forth Isaac, the promised seed under the *terebinth* of Mamre, the Song regards that God's covenant of promise made with Abraham was the mother, and that the child that she conceived was Israel, the church of the regenerated. For the ultimate purpose of God in making the covenant with Abraham was generating a church comprising of the countless multitudes of seed that He was to regenerate from among the natural seed of Abraham through faith. The Heb word translated "raised" means 'to rouse from sleep.' Its use here is in the sense of quickening from the sleep of spiritual death in trespasses and sins (cf. Eph 2:1).

It may be argued, on the basis of the masculine suffixes appearing in the Masoretic Text, that the love, and not the lover, is the speaker of the words of v. 8:5b. But, as most commentators do, we follow the Old Syriac Version, which has the correct feminine endings. Delitzsch writes with regard to this, that "we must then here altogether change the punctuation of the text and throughout restore the fem. suffix forms as originally used ... in which we follow the example of the Syr."[162] And he continues, "if the masculine suffix is changed into fem., we have a conversation perfectly corresponding to the situation."[163]

"Virtually all interpretations go against the MT vocalization of the object suffixes of this verse which are all masculine."[164] "Most commentators and many translations (e.g. JB, NEB) recommend changing these to feminine forms" (Carr).[165] After all, the expressions of v.5, "I raised thee up under the apple tree

162 Franz Delitzsch, *op. cit.*, p. 142.
163 *Ibid*, p., 143.
164 Marvin Pope, op. cit., p.663.
165 G. Lloyd Carr, *op. cit.*, p. 169.

... there she brought thee forth that bare thee," are fitter to proceed from the mouth of the male than from the mouth of the female. Moreover, as the Apple tree stood for the Lord in 2:3, it cannot be otherwise here.

Set me as a seal upon thine heart, as a seal upon thine arm: for love is strong as death, (6a).

To understand the content of this ardent appeal, one must identify:

(i). The persons who constituted the church that makes this ardent appeal to the Lord.

(ii). The historical juncture in which she makes the appeal.

(iii). The identity of the seal, of which the beloved (church) craves to be the antitype, and to be set upon the heart and upon the arm of the Lord.

(iv). The rationale for the beloved basing her appeal on the Lord's love, which is "stronger than death?"

The answers to the above are as follow:

(i). It is Israel, the consummated primitive Jewish Christian church that had comprised of Paul, Peter, John, and the host of saints of the time who had co-labored and had hazarded their lives for the propagation of the gospel that makes the appeal.

(ii). The historical juncture of her redemptive story in which she makes the appeal is just before the Jerusalem Council, (see comment on vv. 8-10 below). This means that the risen and ascended Lord to whom she appeals is seated on the right hand of the Father in performance of His High Priestly office.

(iii). The seals, of which the consummated primitive Jewish Christian Church craves to be the antitype, and to be set upon the heart and upon the arm of the Lord, refer to those jewels which were cut and engraved by Bezaleel, the cunning workman, with the names of the tribes of Israel, like the engravings of a signet, and set upon the breastplate and ephod of the shoulders of the Aaronic high priests of Israel.

Those seals were, in fact, typical of the church that had comprised of the Jewels of 'men' whom Christ, "the cunning workman," the heavenly High Priest was to cut, engrave and to set by the bond of His inseparable dying love, upon His heart and upon His arm (shoulders), as His trophy, when He enters the Father's presence to atone for their sins. Evidently, the very same Heb. word *chotham* is translated "seal" in the present context, and "signet" in Exod 28:11, 21. It is worth mentioning, in this context, that the Heb. word *zerowa* translated "arm" can also refer to shoulder.[166]

(iv). The reason why the church bases her appeal to the Lord, her High Priest, to set her upon His heart, and upon His arm, as the antitype of those signet seals, on the ground of His love which is "strong as death," is that the Lord had purchased her by giving His life as a ransom for her soul. This is cogent, because the very purpose for which high priests entered the presence of God within the holy of holies was to atone for the sins of his own people. Furthermore, without the blood of atonement, the high priest was debarred from entering the presence of God within the holy of holies.

In fact, the Lord had set the church as the antitype of those seals upon His heart, and upon His shoulders, from the moment she accepted Him as her substitute and Lord. And, now, when she makes the appeal, the beloved (church) knows for sure that her eternal place of rest is there in the heart and shoulders of the Lord, her High Priest who was seated on the right hand of the Father.

Jealousy is cruel as the grave, (6b)

The Heb. word *quinah* rendered "jealousy" refers to 'envy' or 'jealousy.'[167] Here it refers to the jealousy of the carnal seed against the spiritual. The Heb. word *sheol* rendered "grave" literally refers to the underworld. Out of the sixty-five occurrences of the word

---

[166] James Strong, *op. cit.*, p.39.
[167] *Ibid.*, p.126.

in the Old Testament, thirty-one times it is translated "grave," thirty-one times as "hell," and three times as "pit."

For AV's "cruel" NASB has "severe" and JB "relentless." The intended meaning is 'hard,' 'obstinate,' 'inflexible.' The cruelty or obstinacy of religious jealousy of the carnal seed against the spiritual, which is equivalent to hell-fire, is being stated here primarily with reference to the unjust judgment and cruel treatments that were meted out to our Lord by the Jewish religious hierarchy. However, it is being stated also as a general rule, in the sense of 2 Tim 3:12, "Yea and all that will live godly in Christ Jesus shall suffer persecution." The history of the first century church, and that of the reformation period has demonstrated to us clearly how much ruthless, devilish and hellish the religious jealousy of the carnal rulers of the nominal church against the spiritual can turn out to be.

The coals thereof are coals of fire, which hath a most vehement flame, (6c).

JB, "The flash of it is a flash of fire, a flame of Yahweh himself." NASB, "Its flashes are flashes of fire, the very flame of the Lord."

The Heb. word *Yah* translated "vehement" is equivalent to *Jah,* which is the short form of the divine name Yahweh. The Masoretic Text has, "flame of fire from *Yah.*" The intended meaning is that the fire of the jealousies of carnal men, which often flare up like flashes of fire against the elect of God are, in fact, the fire of Yahweh Himself. The underlying thought is that of Isa 53:10, "it pleased the Lord to bruise him; he hath put him to grief: when thou shalt make his soul an offering for sin, he shall see his seed."

The idea of the Lord being a cunning workman who makes jewels of 'men' in the hellish fire of the jealousies of carnal 'men' runs like a silver lining throughout the Song.

Many waters cannot quench love, neither can the floods drown it, (7a).

Love refers here primarily to the love of Christ, the Son of God who gave Himself as a ransom for the redemption of His church. Secondly, to the love of Christ that He shed abroad in the hearts of believers by the Holy Ghost. The thought is the same as in Rom 8:35, "Who shall separate us from the love of Christ?" shall tribulation, or distress, or persecution, or famine, or nakedness, or peril, or sword? The expression, "many waters" occurs parallel to "floods" of the succeeding clause, and refers to the multitudes of people who rose up against our Lord in particular, and against the children of God, in general.

If a man would give all the substance of his house for love, it would utterly be contemned, (7b).

The word *ish* translated here as "man," is translated elsewhere as 'any" (twenty-six times) and as "one" (seventy times). In 2 Kgs 18:33 and Isa 36:18, the same word is translated "any" in "any of the gods of the nations." It was the devil who had offered all the substance of his house to our Lord, in return for falling down and worshipping him. The devil did so to dissuade the Lord from offering His life as a ransom for the world of sinful humanity (cf. Matt 4:9). The Lord put him to rout by sternly rebuking him with the words, "Get thee hence, Satan: for it is written, Thou shalt worship the Lord thy God, and him only shalt thou serve" (Matt 4:10).

XIX. A FIGURATIVE DESCRIPTION OF THE ONGOING DELIBERATIONS IN THE JERUSALEM CHURCH COUNCIL ON WHETHER OR NOT TO IMPOSE THE JEWISH LAW UPON THE GENTILE CONVERTS, 8:8-10

8: 8. We have a little sister, and she hath no breasts:
What shall we do for our sister in the day
when she shall be spoken for?
9. If she be a wall, we will build upon her a palace of silver:
and if she be a door, we will enclose her with boards of cedar.
10. I am a wall, and my breasts like towers:
then was I in his eyes as one that found favour.

This unit occurs in the form of a rehearsal of the ongoing deliberations that took place in the Jerusalem Church Council on whether or not to impose the Jewish religious laws and traditional customs upon the Gentile converts. The imagery is framed after the episode of the life-long rivalry that took place between Rachel and Leah to bear larger number of children unto Jacob and win his favour thereby.

When Paul and Barnabas were staying for a long time at Antioch, after their return from their first missionary journey, "certain men which came down from Judaea taught the brethren, and said, Except ye be circumcised after the manner of Moses, ye cannot be saved." When the matter became a subject of great dissension and disputation, the church determined "that Paul and Barnabas, and certain other of them, should go up to Jerusalem unto the apostles and elders about this question" (Acts 15: 1-2). The present section prefigures the discussions that took place in the Council of the apostles and elders at Jerusalem. According to the Song's imagery of the event, the matter that came up for discussion centered on their immature "little sister," namely, the growing Gentile church," as to what they should do when she matures and be "spoken for" (the Lord.)

We have a little sister, she hath no breasts, (8a).

The "little sister" alludes to Rachel. But, in the ongoing disclosure of Israel's redemptive story, "the little sister" refers to the growing Gentile church. The statement, "she hath no breasts" occurs in dual senses, first, that she is spiritually immature, and second, that she has no spiritual seed of her own. (Breasts occurs in the Song as a symbol for seed, cf. notes on 'the symbolic word breasts' under the head, 'the Artful use of Figures of speech in the Song' in the introductory section of this book).

What shall we do for our sister in the day when she shall be spoken for, (8b)

The key to the entire mystery of the Song lies in this question. We saw that the Lord had wedded Israel symbolically when He entered into the Solomonic temple on the auspicious occasion of its dedication, declaring, "until the day break, and the shadows flee away, I will get me to the mountain of myrrh, and to the hill of frankincense," (v.4:6). The question arises therefore, as to 'how, then, can the little sister be "spoken for" marriage to the Lord, as and when she matures?' 'Does it not bring about the problem of attributing polygamy to the Lord?'

The answer to these questions is this. We have asserted from the outset that the Song occurs as a disclosure of the way in which the Lord fulfilled the promise that He made to Abraham, saying, "In thee shall all the families of the earth be blessed." The disclosure is now about to conclude with the picture of the Lord dwelling with the newly wedded Gentile church, after having deprived the Jewish Christian church of the favored status that was bestowed to her.

If she be a wall, we will build upon her a palace of silver, (9a).

Silver is the symbol for redemption in the Bible, in general, and in the Song, in particular. The Heb. word *tieah* rendered "palace" occurs only eight times in the Old Testament, out of which three times it is translated 'castle,' one time 'goodly castle,' two times 'palace,' one time 'habitation,' and one time 'row.' The BDB suggest the meanings, such as, 'encampment,' 'battlement,' 'habitation,' etc.[168]

The presence of play on words is discernible here using the dual meanings of the Heb. word *'bana'* rendered "build." In addition to its normal meaning, 'to build up,' the word has also the meanings 'to have children' or 'to obtain children and build up a house' thereby. These latter meaning is used in Gen 16:2, where Sarah prays to Abraham to go unto Hagar that "I may be builded by her," and in Gen 30:3, where Rachel says to Jacob, "Behold, my maid Bilhah, go in unto her that I may "be built by her" (cf. AV margin).

The palace of silver that the Council desires to build on the little sister, namely, the growing Gentile church, as and when she is spoken for the Lord is one to be built up of her spiritual seed. The imagery, as stated, is framed after the episode of the life-long vying that went on between Rachel, the younger sister, and Leah, the older sister, to bear larger numbers of children unto Jacob and build a larger house for him thereby. Here the vying of the sisters

---

[168] Brown, Driver, Briggs, op. cit, p. 377.

between themselves to bear larger number of children and win Jacob's favour is being transferred to the Jewish and Gentile churches.

The issue at stake before the Council was spiritual maturity. The desired palace of silver, namely, a church of the regenerated seed can be built upon the little sister only if she be "a wall," i.e., a law unto herself. "Wall" is the Song's symbol for the law. (cf. comment on 5:7b).

And if she be a door, we will enclose her with boards of cedar, (9b).

"A door" occurs here in the sense of an open door, i.e., lawless. The Heb. word *tsur* translated "enclose" means, 'to fortify.' A different Heb. word, namely, *naal,* meaning, 'to nail up,' is translated in 4:12, as "enclose." Even though the different Heb. word *tsur* is used here, the thought of 4:12, of nailing up is implied here in that cedar boards can be fixed only by nailing up. Nailing up a woman who is an open door within the Mosaic laws and Jewish customs could have been, at best, a temporary measure of restraint until she becomes a "wall," to wit, a law unto herself. That is why the Council finally decided not to impose the Mosaic laws, and the traditional custom of circumcision upon the Gentile Christians. They were directed only to restrain themselves from fornication and eating blood.

I am a wall, and my breasts like towers: then was I in his eyes as one that found favour (10)

Leah bore more children than Rachel and built up the twin symmetrical towers of Judah and Israel unto Jacob. Then was she, the formerly un-favored wife, become in Jacob's eyes "as one that found favor." Likewise, Israel, the older sister had thus far been the favoured wife of the Lord, in that she bore innumerable spiritual seed, and built up of them twin (silver) towers of the regenerated of Judah and Israel unto Him. For this reason, she had remained in His eyes as one that found favor. Now the situation is about to change when the growing Gentile church, (the little sister), matures spiritually, and is wedded to the Lord. She will begin to bear far more spiritual children unto the Lord from the entire Gentile world and build up a grandiose silver tower for an eternal habitation of the Lord. Israel, the former wife, on the other hand, will be dispossessed of her favoured status that she possesses at present of being the Lord's beloved spouse. The Song is heading towards this paradoxical resolution after the next unit comprising of vv.11-12.

XX. HEIRS OF THE LORD'S VINEYARD OF FAITH VERSUS KEEPERS OF HIS VINEYARD OF THE LAW, 8:11-12

8: 11. Solomon had a vineyard at Baal-hamon:
he let out the vineyard unto keepers; every one for the fruit thereof
was to bring a thousand pieces of silver.
12. My vineyard, which is mine, is before me:
thou, O Solomon, must have a thousand,
and those that keep the fruit thereof two hundred.

These parables of the two types of vineyards belonging to the Lord (the Solomon of the Song), refer to the two covenants of the Lord, namely, the vineyard of the covenant of His promises and the vineyard of the covenant of His law.

In the case of the vineyard of the covenant of His promise, the Lord Himself was its keeper. He kept His promises faithfully and truthfully, to the very letter and spirit, on behalf of His beloved (church), which was rooted and grounded in Him by unquestioning faith in His promises. As a result, she produced the required thousand-fold fruits of righteousness. Fruition, in this case, involved no work, labour, or any sort of effort on her part; she flourished and bore fruits of righteousness, spontaneously. The Lord and His spouse (the church) were joint heirs of the vineyard and its fruits, by virtue of their birth unto the Father in the same covenant of promise, and by that of their marital relationship. That is the reason why Israel, the beloved church says, "My vineyard, which is mine, is before me: thou, O Solomon, must have a thousand."

His vineyard of the covenant of His law, on the other hand, was situated at a place called, *Baal-hamon,* meaning, "the Lord of the multitude." The Lord of the multitude let out the vineyard of His moral law to keepers to keep the law and bring Him the stipulated thousand-fold fruits of righteousness. This demand of the Lord was not only from those who had received His law in the Sinai covenant, but also of all humanity, as He had written His moral law in the conscience of every human being whom He has created in His own image and likeness (cf. Rom 2:11-16).

The keepers of the covenant of law of whom He demanded a thousand-fold fruits of righteousness were aliens. The thousand pieces of silver that every one of the keepers owed to the Lord of the multitude were the price of the thousand-fold fruits of righteousness that they were required to produce by keeping His vineyard of the law. The paradox of the demand was that the Lord of the multitude made it knowing fully well that it was beyond the ability of the keepers to meet. The question arises, then, as to why He bound the keepers under the covenant of His law knowing fully well that they would certainly violate it and come under self-condemnation? The answer is, to bring them down to their knees before Him, out of self-condemnation, and thereby to lead them to Godly sorrow and grace, if they will.

Solomon had a vineyard at Baal-hamon, (11a).

The Heb. word *kerem*, translated "vineyard" means 'an enclosed place' or "a field set with plants of noble quality cultivated as a garden or orchard."[169] According to Young's Analytical Concordance, *Baal-hamon* was a place near Samaria.[170] But Carr refutes the suggestion. As for our line of interpretation, it is immaterial whether or not a literal place called Baal-hamon existed. It is the meaning of the place-name, namely, "the Lord of the multitude," that is relevant to the parable.

He let out the vineyard unto keepers; every one for the fruit thereof was to bring a thousand pieces of silver, (11b).

The vineyard that the Lord of the multitude, who appears as Solomon in the Song, let out to keepers refers to the covenant of the law, as stated. Every one of the keepers was required to keep the vineyard of the law, and produce a thousand-fold fruit of

---

[169] H. W. F. Gesenius, *op. cit.*, p. 414.
[170] Robert Young, *op. cit.*, p. 65.

righteousness. It refers to the demand of the conscience of every human soul, irrespective of whether one has received the stipulations of the moral Law under the Sinai covenant or not; for the Law is written in everyone's conscience (Rom 2:14-16). The thousand pieces of silver that He demanded of each of the keepers were the price of the thousand-fold fruits of righteousness in terms of redemption money.

My vineyard, which is mine, is before me: thou, O Solomon, must have a thousand (12a).

At the beginning of the Song, i.e., in 1:6, the beloved (there Jacob) had ruefully lamented, saying, "mine own vineyard have I not kept." At that point of time she was immature to be cognizant of the fact that she belongs to the Lord's vineyard of the covenant of promise and that the Lord Himself was its keeper. But, now, by this final stage of her redemptive story, she has come to the full realization that the Lord who had made the promise is also the keeper of the vineyard of His covenanted promises, and hence her saying, "My vineyard, which is mine, is before me: thou, O Solomon must have a thousand." This occurs parallel to the description of Rev 4:10-11, of the four and twenty elders casting down their crowns before the throne of the Lamb, saying, "Thou art worthy, O Lord, to receive glory and honour and power."

And those that keep the fruit thereof two hundred, (12c).

The text does not say 'those that keep the vineyard,' but "those that keep the fruit thereof." The fruits of the Spirit, such as "love, joy, peace, longsuffering, gentleness, goodness, faith, meekness, temperance" (Gal 5:22-23), etc., are sure to sprout forth in the lives of those who are rooted and grounded in the Lord by faith in His promises. The individual believer, in particular, and the church, in general, must keep afresh the fruits of the Spirit that manifest spontaneously in them by maintaining the unity of the Spirit and standing firmly rooted and grounded in the Lord by faith in His promises. Any laxity on the part of the believer and the church to keep the precious fruits of the Spirit afresh and aglow can lead to ruin ultimately. There is a reward for keeping the given fruits of the Spirit fresh and aglow. But, comparatively, it is just a fifth of the reward that goes to the Fruit-giver.

XXI. THE TRANSFERRAL OF THE KINGDOM OF GOD TO THE GENTILES, 8:13-14

8: 13. Thou that dwellest in the gardens,
the companions hearken to thy voice:
cause me to hear it.

14. Make haste, my beloved, and be thou like to a roe
or to a young hart
upon the mountains of spices.

To be recalled, the Song is a prophetic disclosure of the way in which the Lord fulfilled the promise that He made to Abraham, saying, "I will bless thee, ... thou shalt be a blessing, ... and in thee all the families of the earth be blessed." Accordingly, the book concludes with this section showing the Lord abiding among the Gentile churches in marital relationship, while Israel, the beloved, who has been dispossessed of her favoured status pleading to Him from without to restore her spiritual faculty to hearken to His voice.

Unfortunately, as Pope points out, "versions are not in agreement as to the Gender and number of the participle. MT *hayyosebet* is feminine singular with the article functioning as the vocative. LXX *ho katemenos* offers the masculine singular.... Syriac reads the masculine plural collective."[171] The context, however, makes it unambiguous that the masculine singular as found in the LXX is the correct rendering from the original.

The conclusion of the Song as it does, with the words of the present section, signifies the following facts:

i. That the Lord has made the primitive Jewish Christian church the promised blessing for all the families of the earth, in accordance with the promise He made to Abraham.

ii. That Israel, the church of the regenerated has made the Gentiles partakers of the blessing of the Abrahamic covenant, fulfilling thereby the vocation for which she had been called.

---

[171] Marvin Pope, *op. cit.*, p. 693.

iii. That the "little sister," namely, the growing Gentile church, of v.8, has been "spoken for," and consequently the Lord has wedded her and is presently abiding with her in accordance with His covenant pledge.

iv. That the time allotted to Israel in the covenant has come to its end, and the time allotted to the Gentiles has begun.

v. That "blindness in part is happened to Israel, until the fulness of the Gentiles be come in" Rom 11:25).

vi. That when the fullness of the Gentiles has come in, Israel shall ultimately turn to the Lord.

Thou that dwellest in the gardens, 13a.

As we have explained earlier, "garden" (singular number) is the Song's symbol for Israel, and "gardens" (plural number) for the Gentiles. Likewise, the depiction of the Lord (the Lover) dwelling among His elect in covenant relationship is the Song's symbol for wedding (cf. comment on 4:6). From the above perspectives, the present depiction of the Lord dwelling in the gardens (plural number) signify that "the little sister," namely, the growing Gentile church, of v.8 has by now matured, has been spoken for the Lord, and consequently, He has wedded her, and is presently, dwelling with her.

The companions hearken to thy voice, 13b.

The term, "companions" was put in the lad Joseph's mouth in 1:7 for the first time to speak of the Gentiles as the Lord's companions. The introduction of the term there was designedly, to be used in the present context.

Christ is "the Voice," "the Word," or the expression of the Father. It is as the "Voice" that He had appeared to His beloved in 2:8 and 5:2. The thought of hearkening to the voice of the Lord occurs here in the literal sense.

It was at a time when none of the nations of the earth was hearkening to His voice that the Lord appeared to Abraham in the covenant pledge. Abraham hearkened to the voice of the Lord, and it was counted to him for righteousness. The Heb. word *qashab* translated "hearken" means, 'to prick up the ears, i.e., to hearken: - attend, (cause to) hear(-ken), give heed, incline, mark (well), regard.[172] These nuances of the word '*qashab*' that is used here shows that that companions were not simply hearing the Lord's voice, but believing and giving heed to it heartily, as Abraham did.

Cause me to hear it, 13c.

The ability to hearken to the Lord's voice, when none of the other families of the earth were hearkening to it, was granted to Israel as a special gift of grace, to enable her to fulfill the vocation of bringing the blessing of Abraham upon the Gentiles for which she was called. Now that she has fulfilled the vocation for which she was called, the special grace that was granted to her for the purpose of hearkening to the voice of the Lord is withdrawn.

It is the hope that ultimately all Israel will be saved that prompts Israel, the beloved (church) to cry to the Lord from without, saying, "cause me to hear it."

Make haste, my beloved, and be thou like to a roe or to a young hart upon the mountains of spices, 14a.

Superficially, this statement has the appearance of 2:17, which occurs in the form of the words by which Moses bade farewell to the Lord on the eve of his departure from Horeb, "the mountain of God," to bring the light of the knowledge of the God of their fathers to Israel, in Egypt, saying, "turn, my beloved, and be thou like a roe or a young hart upon the mountains of Bether." Even so, both the statements present more contrasting views than parallel, as detailed below:

Song 2:17	Song 8:14
Turn, my beloved, and be thou like a roe or a young hart upon the mountains of *Bether,* 2:17	*Make haste,* my beloved, and be thou like to a roe or to a young hart upon the mountains of
Speaker of the statement of this verse *is Moses*	*Speaker* of the statement of this verse *is the hardened Israel*

[172] James Strong, *op. cit.*, p. 126.

Song 2:17	Song 8:14
The statement is addressed to *the preincarnate Christ*	The statement is addressed to *the risen glorified Christ.*
The statement is being made *by Moses in the vicinity of Horeb, i.e. Sinai*	The statement is being made *by the hardened Israel from the place of her banishment.*
Ocassion: *On the eve of his departure for Egypt, before* making the Sinai Conenant.	*After the expiry of the time allotted to Israel,* in the Father's redemptive scheme.
Appeal: i. *Turn, i.e., return.*	i. *Make haste.*
ii. Be like a roe or young hart, i.e., concealed and	ii. Be like a roe or young hart, i.e., concealed and unseen *upon the mountains of spices.*

ANALYSIS:

Though the usual meaning of the Heb. word *barah* translated "make haste" is "flee away," in the present context BDB gives the meaning "come quickly." [173]

"The mountain of spices" refers to Zion, the temple mount, which was described as "the mountain of myrrh and the hill of frankincense," in 4:6.

The present depiction occurs in the context of Rom. 11: 25-26:

> For I would not, brethren, that ye should be ignorant of this mystery, lest ye should be wise in your own conceits; that blindness in part is happened to Israel, until the fulness of the Gentiles be come in. And so all Israel shall be saved: as it is written, There shall come out of Sion the Deliverer, and shall turn away ungodliness from Jacob

The words of Zachariah (Zac 12:10ff.), agree with this.

> And I will pour upon the house of David, and upon the inhabitants of Jerusalem, the spirit of grace and of supplications: and they shall look upon me whom they have pierced, and they shall mourn for him, as one mourneth for his only son, and shall be in bitterness for him, as one that is in bitterness for his firstborn.

---

[173] Brown, Driver, Briggs, *op. cit.*, pp.137-138.

Taken in this light, the prayer of the hardened Israel emerges to be, 'Hasten or come quickly, my beloved, to restore my spiritual faculty to hearken to your voice, and until that time, be thou concealed and unseen as always upon Zion, the temple mount, where we worship you outwardly and ostentatiously, under the stipulations of the Mosaic law.'

This is reminiscent of the words spoken by our Lord to the Samaritan woman, saying,

> Ye worship ye know not what: we know what we worship: ... But the hour cometh, and now is, when the true worshippers shall worship the Father in spirit and in truth.
>
> *John 4: 22-23.*

BIBLIOGRAPHY

Brown, F., Driver, S. and Briggs, C. *The Brown-Driver-Briggs Hebrew and English Lexicon* (coded with Strong's Concordance Numbers), (eighth printing): Massachusetts: Hendrickson Publishers, 2004.

Cameron, W.J. *The New Bible Commentary*. London: The Inter-Varsity Press, 1967

Carr, G. Llyod. *The Song of Solomon, An Introduction and Commentary*. Leicester: The Inter-Varsity Press, 1984.

Delitzsch, Franz. *Commentary on the Song of Songs and Ecclesiastes*, (trans. M.G. Easton). Edinburgh: D.D. Grand, 1985.

Douglas, J.D., and others. *The New Bible Dictionary* (fifth ed.), London: The Inter-Varsity Fellowship, 1967.

Flavius, Josephus. (trans. Whiston, William). *Josephus' Complete Works*. (9th ed). Michigan: Kregel Publications, 1971.

Gardner, L. Joseph. *Atlas of the Bible*. New York: The Readers' Digest Association, 1981.

Gesenius, H.W.F. *Gesenius' Hebrew-Chaldee Lexicon to the Old Testament* (trans. Samuel Prideaux Tregelles, LL.D.), Michigan: Baker Books, 1979.

Gordis, Robert. *Poets, Prophets and Sages*. London: Indiana University Press, 1971.

Holladay, William. L. *A Concise Hebrew and Aramaic Lexicon of the Old Testament*. Michigan: William B. Erdmans Publishing Co., 1980.

Illson, Roberts and others. *Great Illustrated Dictionary*. New York: Readers' Digest Association, 1985.

Jamieson, Robert and others. *Commentary, Practical and Explanatory, on the Whole Bible*. Michigan: Zondervan Publishing House, 1978.

Pope, Marvin H. *Song of Songs, A New Translation with Introduction and Commentary.* New York: Doubleday and Company, Inc., 1977.

Smith, William. *A Dictionary of the Bible.* Iowa: Riverside Book and Bible House, 1979.

Strong, James, LL. D., S.T.D. *The New Strong's Exhaustive Concordance of the Bible* (Large Print ed.), Nashville: Thomas Nelson Publishers, 1995.

Young, Robert. *Analytical Concordance to the Bible. (8th ed).* London: Lutterworth Press, 1975.

APPENDIX

1. THE FALLACY OF PURSUING SPECULATIVE METHODS TO INTERPRET THE INSPIRED WORD OF GOD.

A navigator navigating in an open sea should direct his vessel accurately towards the port he is destined for, using his chart, compass and computerized equipments, lest he drifts away in a different direction, or runs aground and gets stuck up in quick sand. The case is no different with a commentator who endeavors to write a commentary of the Song of Songs on speculative ground, without knowing its theme and plot. Unless the interpreter interprets the book correctly on the lines of its known theme and plot, he/she is sure to drift away from its subject matter and produce a commentary, which contains anything but what the book is all about. Ruefully, none of the commentators have been observing this fundamental guiding principle heretofore. One has only to skim through the pages of the existing commentaries on the Song to be alarmed and taken aback by the extent to which their authors have missed the mark and arrived at totally absurd, nonsensical, and even immodest, shameful conclusions.

"Let God be true, but every man a liar," writes Paul, to expose the fallacy of the unbelievers of his day who were treating the word of God with contempt. The Bible is God's book; the channel He devised to communicate Himself with humankind. Each word in the Bible bears the stamp of His ownership and the seal of authenticity (unintended copyists' errors discounted). This had been the faith of our Lord Jesus Christ who had stated categorically, "one jot or one tittle shall in no wise pass from the law, till all be fulfilled" (Matt 5:18). It was by the power of this unquestioning, absolute faith in His Father on the ground of the veracity and plenary verbal inspiration of His word that our Lord brought heaven down to earth, and put to rout the devil and the demons. It was by the same faith in the Father, on the ground of the veracity and immutability of His word, that He healed the sick, and performed unheard-of miracles. "Where is the wise? Where is the scribe? Where is the disputer of this world? hath not God made foolish the wisdom of this world?" (1 Cor 1:20).

One who endeavors to interpret the Song of Songs or any other prophetic books of the Holy Bible must bear the foregoing in mind. "For the prophecy came not in old time by the will of man: but holy men of God spake as they were moved by the Holy Ghost" (2 Pet 1:21). And "no prophecy of the scripture is of any private interpretation" (2 Pet 1:20).

This is not to deny that the Song is the most arduous and knotty for interpretation among the books of the Old Testament. However, that is no reason for anyone to bring out speculative commentaries on it out of one's own imaginative ingenuity. Instead, he/ she must wait prayerfully and patiently on the Lord for enlightenment, with an open, unbiased heart and mind that are emptied of all preconceived notions.

The so-called modernistic and post-modernistic learned brethren of our day may not take kindly to these assertions. These may rather sound amusing to their rationalistic minds. But, in spite of all their intellectual ingenuity and learning, the brethren woefully fail to realize that they are on a futile pursuit when they rely upon their reason to know God. For God is an intangible Spirit who exists in the timeless, space-less, spiritual world, which is not governed by the laws and principles governing the world of this material universe.

On the other hand, we, being part and parcel of the material universe wherein we exist, can think and reason only in terms of the laws and principles governing the world of matter. Scientific studies and achievements over which we pride so much are based on the observation of the working principles governing the world of the material universe. Even the little that we know of the unimaginably colossal material universe in which we exist is based on the things that we are given to know through the extremely limited God-given senses and the relatively puny brain that we possess. We have no way whatsoever to think and reason in terms of immateriality, infinity and eternity.

In view of the above, we, the human beings, can know God only to the extent to which He has been pleased to reveal Himself to us, as found written down in the canonical books of the Holy Bible. Those who believe verbatim the things about God and the way of His salvation that are written down in the inspired books of the Bible with an unquestioning heart and soul are sure to know Him experientially. Experiential knowledge of God is the only true knowledge of God, even as David wisely writes, "O taste and see that the Lord is good"(Ps 34:8).

It is with these facts in mind that Paul writes to the Corinthians, saying,

> The things of God knoweth no man, but the Spirit of God. Now we have received, not the spirit of the world, but the Spirit which is of God; that we might know the things that are freely given to us of God. 1 Cor 2:11, 12.

One who has little or no experiential knowledge of God and the ways of His operation should therefore desist from "intruding into" the things of divine inspiration "vainly puffed up by his fleshy mind" (Col 2:18). Only those who are "in the Spirit" are qualified to understand and interpret the things about God and the ways of His operation written down by the holy men of God under the inspiration of the indwelling Holy Spirit.

One may be well versed in all the languages and literatures of the ancient cultures of the pagan world, but that alone is no credential to regard him/her as a competent Biblical interpreter, capable to rightly divide the inspired word of truth. What one painfully observes in the so-called liberal scholastic world of our day is an absolute disbelief in the verbal inspiration of the written word. This has been another reason why the Song has continued to remain enigmatic heretofore. For every word in the Song is irrefutably an inspired word of God, impregnated with profound spiritual meanings.

www.ingramcontent.com/pod-product-compliance
Ingram Content Group UK Ltd.
Pitfield, Milton Keynes, MK11 3LW, UK
UKHW041842190726
13854UKWH00002B/670